The Royal Parks of London

By the same author

The Age of Agony: the Art of Healing *c* 1700–1800

Caroline of Ansbach, wife of George II – a lady
with a genius for laying out royal parks

Guy Williams

The Royal Parks of London

Academy
Chicago
Publishers

Published in 1985 by

Academy Chicago Publishers
425 N. Michigan Ave.
Chicago, IL 60611

Library of Congress Cataloging in Publication Data

Williams, Guy R.
    The royal parks of London.

    Bibliography: p.
    Includes index.
    1.   London (England) —Parks.   I.   Title.
DA689.P2W68   1985   942.1   85-1405
ISBN 0-89733-146-X
ISBN 0-89733-145-1 (pbk.)

Contents

Illustrations

Acknowledgements

I offer my dutiful thanks to Her Majesty the Queen for her gracious permission to consult and quote from the papers in the Royal Archives.

I am deeply grateful, too, to Sir Robin Mackworth-Young, K.C.V.O., Her Majesty's Librarian, and to Miss Jane Langton, Registrar of the Royal Archives, who has given me every assistance in her power. Miss Langton's helpers, during the time I have been working in the Royal Archives, have also been most memorably kind.

Many other people have helped with the preparation of this book. I am especially grateful to Mr Benjamin Glazebrook, who first agreed that this might be an interesting field of research. My thanks are due, too, to Mr Bernard Nurse, M.A. (Oxon), A.L.A., of the Tower Hamlets Local History Library and to Mr David Webb, F.L.A., Librarian of the Bishopsgate Institute, for their invaluable advice and assistance; to Mr Raymond Alwin-Hill, for much help with the preliminary research; to the staffs of the Local History Libraries at Chiswick, Greenwich, Richmond and Twickenham; to the staff of the East Sheen branch of the Richmond Libraries, who have kindly obtained books for me, some of them rare, and have assisted in many other ways; and to the Superintendents of the Royal Parks of London, and the members of their staffs, to whom I am deeply obliged. I am particularly grateful to Mr Michael Baxter-Brown, Superintendent of Richmond Park; Mr G. W. Cooke, Superintendent of Hampton Court Gardens;

Mr R. W. Legge, Superintendent of Regent's Park; Mr J. M. Murray, Superintendent of Greenwich Park; and Mr R. A. Stephenson, Superintendent of Hyde Park, Kensington Gardens and St James's Park. Mr J. A. Bagley, Assistant Keeper of the National Aeronautical Collection, had kindly provided me with much extraordinary information about the early balloonists who ascended from, or passed over in some exciting fashion, the Royal Parks of London.

Introduction

London is the third biggest city in the world (only Tokyo and Chicago are larger). Despite its formidable size – the built-up area of the British capital sprawls from Hillingdon in the west to Great Warley in the east, a distance of thirty-five miles – London still remains one of the pleasantest of the world's great cities to visit, and there are thousands of people who, even if they had the chance, would live nowhere else.

Many people believe that London owes its unique charm, not so much to its historical associations or its extraordinary variety of buildings as to its parks. But other great cities have parks. What is there that is so very special about London's green open spaces?

The answer to that question is implied by those adjectives: they are so very green and they are so very open. One only has to see the grass in, say, Hyde Park burned to a uniform light-brown in an exceptionally hot summer to realize how extraordinarily verdant London's parks are under more normal British conditions. To the same almost miraculous degree, they are open.

And London's parks are situated, by a series of historical accidents, with an apparently careless yet inevitable perfection. Anyone who is not a complete stranger to London is bound to feel sure – even if only subconsciously – that, within easy distance of Westminster, the City, or the suburbs, there is a pleasant and countrified retreat.

In its original state a park is, by definition, a very private place. According to one well-known dictionary, it is a 'tract of land, enclosed by a high wall or fence, and intended for keeping beasts of the chase in conditions in which they can be easily found and then fairly and enjoyably hunted'. The high wall or fence will properly be intended, clearly, for keeping out intruders, such as possible poachers, as well as for confining the beasts.

For several centuries, though, the reigning sovereigns of Britain have allowed members of the general public to enter their parks and to enjoy themselves there and on certain occasions, when some of their less benevolent or more officious subjects have wished to take it away, they have taken steps to see that this privilege should be preserved. This book deals, then, only with the parks that are in or near the London area and are still, nominally at least, the property of the Sovereign.

Originally, each of the royal parks of London was closely associated with a royal home and would serve, in fact, as one of its principal amenities. In some cases, the royal home has actually survived, and in two instances at the time of writing – St James's Palace by St James's Park, and Kensington Palace near Kensington Gardens – it is still lived in by a member or members of the Royal Family. It may have been the urge for greater privacy that led Queen Caroline, wife of King George II, to ask the Prime Minister, Sir Robert Walpole, what it would cost to restrict the use of St James's Park to members of the Royal Family. Walpole's famous reply – 'Only three crowns, Madam'[1] was sufficiently intimidating to deter the Queen from her purpose.

As the population of London increased during the eighteenth and nineteenth centuries, it became more and more difficult for the officials of the Crown to preserve the amenities of the royal parks in and near the capital, and to control the behaviour of the citizens admitted to them. So, in 1851, the duties and powers of management of the parks were transferred by the Crown, through Parliament, to the Office of Works and Public Buildings, the expenses incurred as a result of this change being met from public funds voted by Parliament. Today, as a result of further legislation, the royal parks of London are in the responsible keeping of the Ministry of the Environment, the detailed management of each park being in the hands of a Superintendent. But that does not mean to say that the Sovereign is no longer interested. Far from it. One of the Park Superintendents has told me recently that he is still liable to find a sharpish Memorandum on his desk if he makes a change of which the Sovereign does not approve.

Chapter 1

Greenwich Park – the beginning

On its way down to the sea from the Cities of Westminster and London, the River Thames passes several ancient hamlets that have had very romantic histories but are now somewhat sombre and depressed – Ratcliffe and Wapping on the north bank, for instance, and on the south bank Rotherhithe and Deptford. Greenwich, a mile or so to the east of Deptford, is the most attractive of all these old Thames-side villages because it is, with its gently curved Georgian terraces, its centuries-old almshouses, its historical riverside taverns, and its charming little alleyways, at once the most elegant and the best preserved.

There was a human settlement of some kind at Greenwich at least two thousand years ago. (There are tumuli in Greenwich Park that were probably dug in the Bronze Age. Remains of a substantial Roman villa or temple have also been found here, and have been dispersed. The site is now railed round and was, when I last looked at it, sad and unappreciated.)

From the settlement by the river – which was principally inhabited, in all likelihood, by fishermen and their families, for the unpolluted Thames teemed, in those days, with fish – a road led up the steep hillside to the south, and that road still exists. It was called, originally, 'crom' or 'crum', meaning 'crooked'. It is known now as 'Crooms Hill Road' and it is possibly the oldest human thoroughfare in the Greater London area that is still in use.

In 1012 the little settlement at Greenwich suddenly became nationally important when the Danes, who had invaded Britain

and were encamped there, raided Canterbury and carried off
Alphege, the revered Archbishop. Holding the Archbishop prisoner
at Greenwich, the Danes then demanded a substantial sum for his
release. Alphege, seeing clearly that the kidnapping of distinguished
persons for financial gain might, if his captors succeeded in their
aims, become fashionable (as it has so markedly done in the second
half of the twentieth century) refused to allow his friends to contribute a single penny towards his release from captivity. Instead,
he stood up valiantly and suffered his Danish captors to stone him
to death. For his noble act, Alphege was later promoted by the
authorities of the Holy Roman Church to the hallowed rank of
sainthood, and some very fine churches have since been successively
erected on the plot of ground on which he is believed to have
undergone his martyrdom. (The building to which Samuel Pepys
travelled by coach for 'a good sermon' and 'a great company of
handsome women' was largely destroyed in the historic storm of
1710, but the baroque church designed by Nicholas Hawksmoor
with which it was replaced is still one of the chief glories of Greenwich.)

By the river near St Alphege's Church, and approximately
where Sir Christopher Wren's 'Greenwich Hospital' (or 'The
Royal Naval College') stands now, there stood, in the early Middle
Ages, when the slopes to the north of the Thames at Greenwich
were largely covered with forest, a house named the 'Old Court'.
This house belonged, with the Manor of Greenwich, to the Abbots
of Ghent. In 1414, however, King Henry V introduced a bill that
disallowed the possessions of alien monasteries, and the Manor of
Greenwich reverted to English hands. It must have been a very
desirable property.

Eight years after that, King Henry died of dysentery, leaving as
his heir a son who was less than twelve months old. Parliament was
compelled to appoint somebody who would act as Regent for the
new Sovereign. The obvious choice was John Plantagenet, Duke of
Bedford, the late King's brother, but he would be fully occupied
with the war that was being waged against France. In his place,
another of Henry's brothers, Humphrey, was given the responsibility.

Humphrey had been made Duke of Gloucester by his elder brother, the King, in 1414. Then, from 1415 to 1420, he had served in a number of campaigns over in France. But by nature Humphrey was a scholar rather than a soldier – he was one of the first Englishmen of any note to appreciate classical Greek and Roman literature – and he must have welcomed the chance to settle by the riverside at Greenwich with his growing collection of books.

Not satisfied with the austere and old-fashioned building that had belonged until quite recently to the Abbots of Ghent, Duke Humphrey decided to have it pulled down. In its place, he put up a mansion, 'crennelled and embattled', that would be worthier of such a lovely site. The riverside house, which the Duke called 'Bella Vista', became a celebrated centre of learning.

By 1425, Duke Humphrey had become embroiled with his uncle Henry Beaufort, Chancellor and chief minister of the realm, in a bitter struggle for power. The feud continued until the mid-1430s, but before it was over Duke Humphrey and his wife Eleanor managed to obtain from the King, with the assent of his Lords Spiritual and Temporal and of the Commons, a licence to enclose 'two hundred acres of their land, pasture, wood, heath, virses and gorses' that ran down the hill to Greenwich from Black Heath. As the western boundary of his new enclosure – it was cut off at first from the surrounding countryside with a wooden fence – Duke Humphrey took the ancient Crooms Hill Road. The first of the present Royal Parks of London had been given its shape.

On top of the hill that sloped down towards his house from the rough and wild expanses of Black Heath, Duke Humphrey built a tower. This tower was intended to serve, primarily, as a look-out post, since the approaches to London by way of the Thames and across the Heath were at that time of great strategic importance. Duke Humphrey's tower has disappeared, but as its place was taken by the original Royal Observatory it is easy to see where it stood.

In 1437, the young King Henry VI was declared 'of age', and the Beauforts, who had won almost complete ascendancy over him, were virtually the rulers of England. Two years later, Duke

Humphrey gave Oxford a present of 129 books which was said to be 'a more splendid donation than any Prince or King had given since the foundation of the University'. The Duke's luck, however, was running out.

It was the young King's betrothal to the Princess Margaret of Anjou that brought Duke Humphrey finally to his knees. The Duke advised against the marriage. The members of the Beaufort faction were all for it. The Beauforts won the argument. As a result, Duke Humphrey earned the undying hostility of the self-willed fifteen-year-old bride, and his days at Greenwich were numbered.

On the tenth day of February 1447, a Parliament was invited to meet at Bury St Edmunds, and Duke Humphrey was ordered by William de la Pole, Earl of Suffolk, who had succeeded Henry Beaufort as First Minister, to attend. On his arrival at Bury, the father of the 'New Learning' in England was taken into custody. Next morning, he was found paralysed in his cell – almost certainly, he had been violently assaulted – and, clearly, he was dangerously ill. On the twenty-third day of that month he died. Next day, Parliament heard Margaret's plans to take over all Duke Humphrey's manors – she had particularly fancied Greenwich, with its secluded and attractive Park, and by Easter she was in possession of it. One of her first actions on entering her new property was to change the name of the riverside mansion to 'The Pleasaunce'.

The Wars of the Roses rumbled on for years after that, the English crown at the time seeming to us now like a political football that was being kicked backwards and forwards between two power-hungry teams whose mercenaries were financed largely from sources abroad. Eventually, however, on the twenty-second day of August 1485, the Lancastrian Henry Tudor, Earl of Richmond, seized the crown at the Battle of Bosworth, leaving the Yorkist King Richard III dead on the field. Soon after, Henry took over the Manor of Greenwich, and made The Pleasaunce, enlarged and renamed 'Placentia', one of his principal homes.

In this rambling palace, plentifully supplied with towers and gables, armouries and banqueting halls, and as inconvenient as any medieval castle in Wales, four of England's future sovereigns were born: Henry, the infant who was to be King Henry VIII, and, successively, in the next generation, Henry's children, the future King Edward VI and the future Queens Mary and Elizabeth I. All four of these young royals spent much of their childhood at the riverside Palace of Placentia, enjoying, in its adjoining parkland, an almost endless round of hunts, tournaments, May revels, troop reviews, and other royal entertainments typical of the time. Thus all of them would have regarded a private, enclosed and well-tree'd deer park such as the one at Greenwich an absolutely necessary amenity for a royal home – as essential, in its way, as a bathroom in a modern suburban villa.

King Henry VIII, the first of these Greenwich-born sovereigns, inherited his father's business acumen and his acquisitiveness, and he had an abnormal amount of animal energy of his own. It is hardly surprising therefore that, almost as soon as he was in a position to do so, the second Tudor monarch started to enclose more under-valued land, in other places than Greenwich, to make more Royal Parks for his own and his family's exclusive use. Fortunately for us, today, Henry 'thought big', and he did not hesitate to set about his acts of enclosure on a truly massive scale. Fortunately for us, too, he did not fail to do one of his most spectacular enclosure acts at a distance that was not too far from the prevailing Seat of Government, which happened then to be at Westminster.

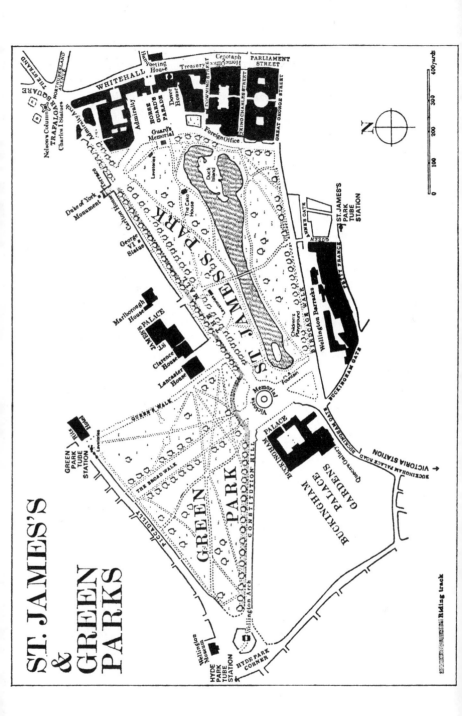

Chapter 2

St James's Park

St James's Park is, of all the Royal Parks of London, the most supremely royal. It is surrounded by palaces, by royal residences and one-time royal residences, such as Buckingham Palace, Clarence House, Marlborough House, and the venerable palace that gives it its name. On the south stretches Whitehall, the site of one of the most romantic palaces of all, and parts of its other sides are bounded by a long terrace that commemorates Carlton House, the Prince Regent's palatial London residence, and by the barracks of the Brigade of Guards, the reigning sovereign's own personal body-guard.[1]

Some quarter of a mile to the west of Charing Cross there stood, in very early times, a hospital. It was right out in the midst of the fields, it was well shaded by trees, and like all the hospitals of the time it was a religious foundation, being dedicated to a St James, possibly the first Bishop of Jerusalem. The hospital was intended for female patients only – maidens suffering from the foul disease of leprosy. According to John Stow, the house was founded by the citizens of London 'before the time of man's memory', and it had appended to it 'two hides of land, with the usual appurtenances, in the parish of St Margaret's Westminster', as well as a variety of other endowments. There were eight 'brethren' attached to the house, to solemnize religious services, and to discharge the 'cure of souls'.

King Edward I confirmed the gifts that had been made to the lepers' hospital, and he gave the inmates, too, the privilege and profits of a fair 'to be kept on the eve of St James', the day, and the morrow, and the four days following' – the origin, this, of the once famous 'May Fair' which was held in the fields near Piccadilly.

In the year of his marriage to Anne Boleyn, King Henry VIII took a keen look at this old hospital, in its relative isolation, and seeing that it was 'fair to view' and that it would make a good, private country home – not too far from the Palace of Whitehall, where he could continue to hold his Courts – he threw out the occupants, had the building pulled down, and, in Stow's words, 'a goodly manor' put up on the site. The gatehouse of King Henry's 'goodly manor' still stands, at the lower (south) end of St James's Street.

Once he was established at St James's, King Henry lost no time in surrounding himself with all the contemporary aids to amusement. There was already a tilt-yard in front of the Palace of Whitehall – nearly on the site of the present Horse Guards Parade – and Henry added to this a pit for cock-fighting which is said to have survived, at least in part, until the year 1816. But these were relatively small-scale improvements. Having spent so much of his early life at Greenwich, which had a deer park as one of its most cherished amenities, King Henry had to provide one for his new home. He therefore took in the marshy fields that had surrounded the old hospital and enclosed them as the private demesne of his new palace, partially drained them, and set up in them a nursery for deer. The shape of another of London's present-day Royal Parks had been determined.

St James's Park remained after that, for another hundred years, a suitable place for royal enjoyment and for military reviews. At its north-east corner there was a rural garden – used, by those who could afford to go there, for refreshment and relaxation. The garden contained a pleasant yard, a pond for bathing, and some butts where shooting might be practised. The garden's proper name, the Spring Garden – the name survives there to this day – was derived from a novel fountain or spring introduced during the reign of Queen Elizabeth I, which would be set in motion every time a passer-by trod on a secret mechanical device.

By 1626, part of the Spring Garden had evidently been turned into some kind of royal menagerie, for a document preserved among the State Papers (31 January 1626) directed that £75 5s. 10d. a year should be paid for life to Philip, Earl of Montgomery, 'for keeping the Spring Gardens, and the beasts and fowls there'. Then, in 1630, King Charles I made the garden by royal patent a 'bowling green', though this patent was revoked four years later after the patrons were accused of 'continual bibbing and drinking wine all day under the trees' and of quarrelling, two or three times in every week. (When Lord Digby was reprimanded for fighting in the King's garden, he retorted that he had taken it for a common bowling place, where all who had paid for admission had a right to quarrel or fight duels.) The Spring Garden was re-opened shortly after, but it was closed again by Oliver Cromwell and his serious-minded associates, after which the Mulberry Garden, sited where Buckingham Palace stands now, was, said Evelyn, 'the only place of refreshment about the towne for persons of the best quality to be exceedingly cheated at'.

On the morning on which King Charles I was due to meet his executioner on a scaffold outside the Banqueting House in Whitehall, he took his last walk across St James's Park, dressed in a black cloak, preceded and followed by detachments of soldiers with banners flying and drums rolling. He had spent the previous night in St James's Palace, sleeping for more than four hours, with his attendant, Herbert, resting on a pallet by the royal bed. Before daybreak the King had aroused Herbert, saying that 'he had a great work to do that day'. Prayers, Holy Communion, and a 'glass of claret and a morsel of bread' had followed, lest any faintness should be felt on the scaffold and be misinterpreted. At the corner of the Park nearest to the Spring Garden the King turned to take a last look at a tree that had been planted there, in happier times, by his brother Prince Henry.

Though both James I and Charles I had carried out a number of small 'improvements' in the park at St James's, it was King Charles II who, on his return from exile abroad, remade the place to look rather more nearly as we know it now – for which his memory should be for ever revered by all Londoners.

While Charles, then a cast-out Prince, had been on his enforced

travels in Europe, he had been suitably impressed by the magnificently civilized landscapes with which the ruling families over the
Channel surrounded their homes, and he had grown to regard the
grandeurs of the grounds of Versailles and various other extremely
stately homes as everyday and normal.

When he returned to London, and the gentlemen of his body-
guard set up their camp on the level field that has now become the
Horse Guards Parade, the new King of England must have noticed
the unkempt and badly drained ground that lay immediately to the
south of St James's Palace, and he cannot have thought much of it.
(Most of the mature and dignified trees that he would have remembered had been cut down, during the Commonwealth, to provide
fuel for the impoverished citizens.)

Charles therefore gave orders at once that the rough ground that
separated his principal London homes should be laid out with
pleasant walks and flower beds, like the environs of the palaces he
had seen on his journeys abroad. He sent for advice from the great
French garden architect André Le Nôtre, intending, no doubt,
that Le Nôtre should produce a plan that might even rival Versailles;
but the Frenchman, to his everlasting credit, 'was of the opinion
that the natural simplicity of this Park, its rural and in some places
wild character, had something more grand than he could impart
to it, and persuaded the King not to touch it'.[2]

The King, however, pressed on, though on a more modest scale.
He saw that by joining most of the small and unattractive ponds
with which the old Leper Hospital grounds were dotted, an artificial
canal could be made, 100 feet broad and 2,800 feet long and quite
straight, on which he could feed his ducks and beside which he
could exercise his favourite spaniels. (This 'Dutch Canal' was later
to be converted into the less formal lake that is so much admired
today, but in its magnitude and its situation this great sheet of
water is an asset that we owe to none other than King Charles II.)

One pond only was left out of King Charles's scheme – Rosamond's Pond, in the south-west corner of the park. This little pool
was allowed to remain more or less as it had been, and in the heady
days of the last Stuart Kings it became a favourite meeting place
for society ladies 'on the loose' and their clandestine lovers. Later,

it was given the nickname of 'Suicide Pond', on account of the number of desperate maidens who, disappointed in love – or, perhaps, by lovers who failed to keep their appointments – plunged into it and drowned themselves.

Charles II was fond of exotic animals and birds as his father and grandfather had been before him, and this possibly inherited propensity of the newly restored Sovereign is still commemorated by the name given to the road that runs along the south margin of the park – 'Birdcage Walk' – for it was roughly here that the King had a long range of aviaries set up. The entrance to the park known now as 'Storey's Gate' was so named after one Edward Storey, 'Keeper of the King's Birds', whose house is believed to have stood on this spot. (Those who doubt this derivation can be shown an entry in the registers of the Knightsbridge Chapel recording the marriage of one Thomas Fenwick 'of St Margaret's, servant to Storey, at ye Park Gate'.) The carriage road between Storey's Gate and the Buckingham Gate was until 1828 open only to members of the Royal Family and to the Hereditary Grand Falconer, the Duke of St Albans.

Among the more curious birds collected by King Charles II were two pelicans given him by the Russian ambassador. These were the forerunners of the pelicans that can normally be seen today on the lawns and rocks at the Horse Guards Parade end of the lake. (In Stuart times, the King's pelicans lived, among a wide variety of waterfowl, on a small island at the western end. This resort, which came to be known as 'Duck Island', was made by cutting channels parallel to the main canal, with some other inter-connecting channels at right angles to them.)

As well as being fond of walking in gardens that were well stocked with birds, King Charles II was keen on 'Pall Mall'. This was a game that had originated in Italy in the Middle Ages – a Florentine carnival song printed about 1500 refers to a 'Giocator di Palla a Maglio' (a player of 'Ball to Mallet') – and under the name 'Paille Maile' had become the fashionable craze in France. So the King's newly improved park at St James's had to contain a royal Pall Mall alley.

According to a work, *Nouveaux Règles pour le Jeu de Mail*,

published by Lautier in 1717, there were four different forms of Pall Mall – *au rouet* (or 'singles'); *au partie* (with two or more players on each side); *aux grands coups* (a competition to see which player could drive a ball furthest); and *à la chicane* (the game played in open country, with all its hazards). The first three variants were played on a smooth, prepared surface in an alley that was several hundred yards long and walled in with moderately thick planks of oak. The purpose of this barrier – the *tambour* – was to contain the ball. If any player's ball went over the *tambour*, he would suffer a penalty of two strokes.

The fixtures in the game were either an iron peg at each end of the alley, or a hoop (or sometimes a ring on the end of a spike) at each end and an iron peg in the middle. The ball had to be played from one peg to hit the other, or through the further hoop and back to the central peg, in both cases in fewer strokes than one's opponent. (In the long driving contests, accuracy was not called for: one had merely to hit the ball as far as possible, 405 paces being described as a good drive.)

The balls were made of boxwood, and their size was not fixed by the rules. (In fact, the players were recommended to use small balls when the ground was wet and sticky, and larger, heavier ones when the ground was dry and fast.) Much depended on the skill of the ball-maker. One ball became so celebrated that it was even given a name: 'La Bernarde'. It could always be driven further than any other. The striking faces of the mallets were hooped with iron and set back at a slight angle to give the ball the necessary 'lift'.

The site chosen for the new royal alley was just inside the northern wall of the park. On the other side of the wall ran an ancient highway – it was a continuation, in fact, of the Strand, and it went on past St James's Palace towards the west. On the north side of the road, again, there was a long avenue of trees along which Pall Mall may also have been played. Much trouble was taken to see that the new alley should be worthy of the royal sportsman who was to use it, and it was fitted out with little regard to expense. As Samuel Pepys noted in his *Diary*:

... I walked in the park, discoursing with the Keeper of the Pell Mell, who was sweeping of it, who told me of what the earth is mixed that do make the floor of the Mall, and that overall there is cockleshells, powdered and spread to keep it fast; which however in dry weather turns to dust and deadens the ball. . . .

On this surface, kept carefully watered by the man known officially as 'The King's Cockle Strewer', the game was played with a proper respect for appearances (the ruling in *Jeu de Mail* was: 'It is not pleasant to see persons of quality playing in public without a jacket or waistcoat, or without a wig') In spite of these sartorial handicaps, the King seems to have been a reasonably good player, earning this tribute from Edmund Waller, a notable sycophant:

Here a well-polished Mall gives us the joy
To see our Prince his matchless force imploy;
No sooner has he toucht the flying ball,
But 'tis already more than half the mall,
And such a fury from his arm has got
As from a smoking Culverin 'twere shot.
May that ill fate my enemies befall
To stand before his anger or his ball.

Angry, the King seems often to have been, for the clouds of dust that were stirred up by the carriages on the old highway just over the park wall tended to blow over into the alley and to prove troublesome to the players. At last, in July 1661, Charles decided to take drastic action to abate this nuisance: he would fence off the old highway, which had been used by the public at least since the year 1200, and he would have a new road made along the old tree-lined avenue that ran parallel to it, and a little to the north, in St James's Fields. This road was at first called 'Catherine Street', as a compliment to the King's shy Portuguese girl bride, but most Londoners were not very impressed by her or her abnormally short legs, and the name soon fell into disuse, 'Pall Mall' being preferred – the name it bears today.

Into the garden that his workmen were creating between his

Pall Mall alley and his bird cages, King Charles welcomed as many of his citizens as cared to enter, and they were not slow to make use of this new amenity. On 15 July 1666, for instance, Samuel Pepys, finding it 'mighty hot and himself weary', there 'lay down upon the grass by the canalle and slept awhile', as so many of his successors in the Civil Service have done since. The King strolled among his subjects with apparent ease, doing so on some occasions entirely unattended – a proceeding, the informality of which could never be understood by foreigners. On other occasions, he would have company with him, as when Mr Pepys saw him with the Queen and Lady Castlemaine and Mrs Stuart and others walking about:

> . . . All the ladies walked, talking and fiddling with their hats and feathers, and changing and trying one another's heads, and laughing. But it was the finest sight to see, considering their great beauties and dress, that ever I did see in all my life. . . .

On the whole, the citizens behaved well, though harsh penalties had to be decreed for any gentlemen who should be so rash as to draw their swords in the park, and any pickpockets carrying on their trade there, if detected, would invariably be punished by being thrown into the canal. It may have been an unscrupulous visitor who ran off with one of the King's little pets, causing His Majesty to issue this advertisement:

> . . . Lost four or five days since in St James's Park, a Dogg of his Majestie's; full of blew spots, with a white cross on his forehead, and about the bigness of a Tumbler. . . .

In hard winters, the canal in the park was a popular place with skaters. 'I first in my life, it being a great frost, did see people sliding with their skates, which is a very pretty art', recorded Samuel Pepys. A fortnight later, he mentions seeing the Duke of York, the King's brother, on the frozen canal and remarks of him that he 'slides very well'. John Evelyn, during the same great frost, was also impressed:

... Having seene the strange and wonderful dexterity of the
sliders in the new canal in St James's Park, performed before
their Majesties by divers gentlemen and others, with scheets, after
the manner of the Hollanders, with what swiftness as they pass,
how suddenly they stop in full career on the ice, I went home. . . .

Beside the new paved road near the Royal Pall Mall alley there
were at first no houses, except for St James's Palace with its Tennis
Court and Physic Garden at the western end, and at the eastern
end a small group of buildings which had faced on to the ancient
highway and therefore had their backs to Pall Mall. When King
Charles's enterprising friend Henry Jermyn started to develop the
fields to the north of Pall Mall and to build houses on them for
aristocrats and the very rich, some of the most percipient of the
people who wished to live near the Palace chose to live on the south
side of the new road, as they could enjoy from there an uninterrupted
view across St James's Park.

At the end of Nell Gwyn's garden was a low wall, from which
Among those who preferred to live on the sunny side of the old
avenue was the attractive, vulgar and impertinent actress Nell
Gwyn, mistress of the King, who moved into No. 79. All the buildings on the south side were on Crown land, no private person
owning the freehold. Nell Gwyn returned to the King her lease
and conveyances, saying, with a broad allusion to her own free and
easy ways where the Sovereign was concerned, that she would not
accept the place until it was conveyed free to her by an Act of
Parliament. She won her point, and No. 79 became a freehold
property.

At the end of Nell Gwyn's garden was a low wall, from which
she could look down into the Park. John Evelyn mentions this in an
entry in his *Diary*:

... I had a fair opportunity of talking to His Majesty ... in the
lobby next to the Queen's side ... where I presented him with
some sheets of my History. I thence walked with him through
St James's Park where I both saw and heard a very familiar
discourse between—— and Mrs Nelly, as they call an impudent
comedian, she looking out of her garden on a terrace at the top

of the wall, and——standing on the green walk under it. I was
heartily sorry at this scene. Thence the King walked to the
Duchess of Cleveland, another lady of pleasure, and curse of
our nation. . . .

The Duchess was the acknowledged mother of six of the King's
numerous illegitimate children.

Among the other seventeenth-century residents whose gardens
ran down to the Park was the Countess of Ranelagh, whose husband
the First Earl, a big-earning, big-spending man, owned houses in
King Street and St James's Square, as well as a large country mansion with beautiful grounds near the Hospital in Chelsea. At the
end of the century, a dark red brick house was built a few doors
from Nell Gwyn's, and this house – called 'Schomberg House',
after the Duke whose father acted as Second-in-Command to
William of Orange during the Glorious Revolution of 1688 – still
exists, though it has been partly reconstructed. During the last
four years of the painter Thomas Gainsborough's life, Schomberg
House was his home.

A little larger than Schomberg House was Marlborough House,
which can also be seen today. Designed by Sir Christopher Wren
for Sarah Churchill, the strong-willed Duchess of Marlborough,
and built between 1709 and 1711, the house has been much altered
and extended since, principally by Sir William Chambers in 1771
and Sir James Pennethorne (for Albert, Prince of Wales, later King
Edward VII) in the 1860s. Marlborough House is open to the public
now when it is not in use by the Commonwealth delegations for
which it is principally reserved, and as it contains early seventeenth-
century ceilings painted by Orazio Gentileschi for the Queen's
House at Greenwich, some fine eighteenth-century marble fireplaces,
and murals of Marlborough's victories painted by Louis Laguerre,
it may be found worth a visit.[3] Queen Mary, widow of King
George V, spent the last years of her life at Marlborough House.

In spite of the strictness of the regulations concerning quarrelling
and duelling in St James's Park – a gentleman's hand could be cut
off, it was said, if he were caught – standards of behaviour deterior-
ated there during the eighteenth century until the place became

really scandalous. As early as March 1712, Dean Swift was complaining that he had walked in the Park but had had to come home early 'to avoid the Mohocks'.[4] These unsavoury gallants, who derived their name from 'a sort of cannibals in India, who subsist by plundering and devouring all the nations about them',[5] would spend the early part of each evening in their clubs, drinking to inflame what little natural courage they had. Then they would sally forth, with their swords in their hands, looking for fun. Some of the Mohocks greatly fancied themselves as 'dancing masters', thrusting their rapiers between the legs of sober citizens in a way guaranteed to make them cut the most ridiculous capers. A day or two after Swift's walk in the Park, a party of these armed ruffians assaulted a female servant of Lady Winchilsea's, at her mistress's garden gate, 'cutting her face and beating her without provocation'.

The Park was also a noted haunt of whores of both sexes. (Ned Ward, a humorist 'of low extraction' who kept an infamous punch shop and tavern next door to Gray's Inn, said that it was 'a good place for a lady to furnish herself with a gallant whose faithfulness could be assured for a suit of clothes, three meals a day, and a little money for an occasional glass of usquebaugh'.) James Boswell went to the Park frequently – to watch the soldiers in the daytime, and after dark to look at the girls.[6] He was there one evening in December 1762 with his friend Andrew Erskine and was accosted

> . . . by several ladies of the town. Erskine was very humorous and said some very wild things to them. There was one in a red cloak of a good buxom person and comely face whom I marked as a future piece, in case of exigency. . . .

The following March, he was there again and 'picked up a whore . . . a young Shropshire girl, only seventeen, very well-looked . . . poor being, she has a sad time of it'. He went back in the same week and took the first whore he met, 'ugly and lean and her breath smelt of spirits'.

By the 1760s, the state of the Park was so scandalous that protests in the newspapers became frequent and insistent. The main burden of these complaints concerned the violence in the Park. Disorderly persons were said to 'infest' it, and the state of the place at night was particularly bitterly criticized. (Although the gates were locked at ten, thousands of people had keys for which they had paid a guinea, and many thousands more were known to have false keys. The unlighted grounds had become the nightly resort of soldiers who were off duty, and were not watched or guarded except when an occasional raid would be mounted from the Magistrates' Court at Bow Street.) Why could not an entrance fee of one penny be charged after 6 p.m., demanded one angry keyholder. The money could be used to put up lamps, and the expense would help to keep out undesirables.

There were other causes of complaint. The milkmaids who, for decades, had kept their troops of cows in the Park and had refreshed the wealthy and fashionable with their morning glasses of 'sillabub' – Spanish wine, topped up with milk of exquisite flavour, straight from the cow – were, by 1763, being described in the Press as 'the insolent milkwomen'. Rosamond's Pond, 'where so many have been drowned', should, said another correspondent, be filled up. And many writers drew the attention of the authorities to the stagnant channels that surrounded the duck decoy at the western end of the Canal,

> . . . which are so noxious to the health of the neighbouring inhabitations, especially in Downing Street and Duke Street, from the aquatic and stinking exhalations of those waters . . . which disagreeably and even dangerously affect all persons who walk or inhabit thereabouts. . . .

The Bow Street Magistrates, to give them their due, had been doing their best to cope with a situation that was clearly beyond their powers – a fact of London life of which the citizens must have been fully aware, to judge from an announcement in the *Public Advertiser*:[7]

> . . . Complaints having been made . . . of the notorious prophanation of the Lord's Day, the last time the Canals there were frozen over, by hundreds of skaiters and spectators shouting and

whooping in time of divine service, and in view and hearing of the royal family; we have the satisfaction to be informed, that for preventing this impious outrage tomorrow, if the Civil Power be too weak, a strong Press-gang will attend to make a draught of such of the skaiters &c. as may be thought proper for serving their country against the French, upon the frozen lakes of Canada. . . .

Reforms had started in a small way by the year 1766 when, according to the *Gazette*, the magistrates were taking steps 'to prevent the indecent practices in St James's Park by a set of disorderly persons, playing and betting at unlawful games, bathings, running of races naked, &c., particularly on the Sabbath Day'. The steps taken cannot have been particularly effective, for four years later a writer in the *Public Advertiser* was reporting sourly on 'the nuisance of beggars, gamblers and other disorderly persons' in the Park, 'the gamblers being those who set up teetotum tables, dice tables and other arts of gambling, such as throwing at oranges or pitching for halfpence on the top of a small stick'.

Some drastic changes were made in St James's Park in 1770 and 1771 when the landscape there was remodelled by Capability Brown, Rosamond's Pond and the foul ditches of the duck decoy being, under Brown's direction, drained and filled in. As if they were emboldened by these noticeable inprovements, the Bow Street Justices announced, in 1773, their intention of issuing warrants to take up the disorderly 'till St James's Park and its environs be brought into that state of decorum that his Majesty's subjects may enjoy the privilege of walking and passing through that delightful spot without nuisance or interruption'.

Officialdom took over the Park completely during the alarm and panic caused in 1780 by the Gordon Riots when, for a week, London was at the mercy of an enraged, fanatical and destructive mob. Several regiments of militia moved in and set up camp in the Park, with long lines of tents extending from east to west. King George III, believing that violence if met by firmness is commonly repelled, with remarkable coolness paid the encampment a daily visit.[8]

2

The King, at that time, was not living at St James's Palace which, after the Palace of Whitehall had been practically destroyed by a disastrous fire in 1698, had become the principal London home of the Royal Family. By 1762, King George had become thoroughly disenchanted with St James's, which he once referred to as 'this dust trap',[9] and, possibly at the suggestion of one of his Lords of the Bedchamber, he had purchased the town residence of the Dukes of Buckingham – a house that stood, surrounded at that time by fields, where Buckingham Palace stands now. (There is a delightful account by Mozart's father of a walk that the Mozart family was taking in the Mall when the new residents in Buckingham House came driving by 'and, although we were all differently dressed, they knew and saluted us; the King in particular threw open the carriage window, put out his head laughing, and greeted us with head and hands – particularly our Master Wolfgang'.) After the move, St James's Palace was used only for court ceremonies and as a home for junior members of the Royal Family.

Because for more than four centuries it has been almost literally on the doorstep of the Royal Family's principal London home, St James's Park has been for much of that time the most suitable place for holding royal processions (as, for example, to the State Opening of Parliament), for witnessing royal appearances on balconies (after Coronations, Royal Family weddings and other joyful ceremonies), and for the solemn funeral marches of dead Kings. (The proclamations of new Kings and Queens are still held more or less privately within the precincts of King Henry VIII's old palace.) One of the most extraordinary of these grand occasions was staged in the Park during the long hot summer of 1814.

At last, after nearly two decades of anxiety and effort, Napoleon Bonaparte had been defeated and was safely, it was thought, imprisoned on the Isle of Elba. To celebrate the Allies' success, and, incidentally, to commemorate the one hundredth anniversary of the accession of the first Monarch of the House of Hanover, the Prince Regent had invited the heads of all the friendly countries to London, and was determined to entertain them fittingly, without regard to expense. In any case he was heavily in debt, and he believed that a few lavish shows might make him more generally popular.

Over the Canal in St James's Park, within easy walking distance of Buckingham House, the Prince had a great Chinese-style bridge put up, to his own pet architect John Nash's design, and on this great bridge the Prince had a great seven-storeyed Chinese-type Pagoda built, not unlike the tower, scintillating at that time with coloured glass, which his grandmother had put up, with Sir William Chambers's help, in the gardens at Kew. Unlike the Kew Gardens Pagoda, though, the Prince Regent's Pagoda in St James's Park was to be (literally) aflame. In the words of the official programme:

> . . . The pagoda to be illuminated with gas lights; and brilliant fireworks, both fixed and missile, to be displayed from every division of the lofty Chinese structure. Copious and splendid girandoles of rockets to be occasionally displayed from the summit, and from other parts of this towering edifice, so covered with squibs, Roman candles, and *pots de brin* as to become in appearance one column of brilliant fire. Various smaller temples and columns on the bridge to be vividly illuminated; and fixed fireworks of different devices on the balustrade of the bridge to contribute to heighten the general effect. . . .

There were handsomely decorated boats on the Canal for those who wished to view the grand spectacle from the water. And the lawns of the Park were well supplied with open marquees with seats and other amenities.

From every one of the Prince Regent's Pagoda's seven storeys light poured at the appropriate moment, throwing a glorious sheet of flame, in reflection, on the serene surface of the Canal. Unfortunately no one in authority seems to have considered whether the system of gas lighting used would be entirely safe. It was not. While the assembled Top People of Victorious Europe were still congratulating their enterprising host, their host's Chinese Pagoda began to sway and, a moment later, it started to belch out smoke. Seconds after that, the Pagoda burst into flames and fell with a deafening crash into the Canal, which was still surrounded by admiring crowds. In this débâcle two of the spectators were killed, and a number of others were injured.

Despite this inauspicious start to his activities in St James's Park, John Nash was to play a large part, later, in giving the landscape there the appearance it has today. His opportunity came when he was invited in 1829 to improve the Park's layout. One of the most striking changes recommended by Nash, who was a lover of the romantic or 'picturesque' style favoured also by his Royal master, involved the alteration of the long, dead straight Canal of King Charles II's time into the less formal wrench-shaped lake that is so much admired today. (The oval-shaped peninsula between the 'jaws' of the wrench became known, almost inevitably, as 'Duck Island'.) The terraces that Nash built on the site and grounds of Carlton House, the grandiose mansion that his employer had given up, now provide a striking background to the pomp and pageantry that periodically brighten the Mall.

Half-way along Nash's Carlton House Terrace there is a wide gap that was left open on the instructions of King William IV to allow access to the Park from Waterloo Place. The 120-foot high Aberdeen granite column which stands at the top of the steps that here lead down into the Park was put up, in 1830–33, to the memory of the late Duke of York, son of King George III, who had been for many years Commander-in-Chief of the Army. The cost of the column, with the statue by Sir Richard Westmacott which surmounts it, was £26,000. This sum – very large in those days – was defrayed by public subscription, and every man in the Army was required to contribute one day's pay to the fund without the option of refusing, the amount being docked before he was given the rest. This arbitrary exaction led to a great deal of ill-feeling.

Two of King George III's other sons – Their Royal Highnesses the Duke of Sussex and the Duke of Cambridge – filled successively for many years the honourable and rewarding post of Ranger of the Metropolitan Royal Parks. When at last the Duke of Cambridge died in 1850, His Royal Highness Prince Albert wrote from Osborne to another grand old soldier, Field-Marshal the Duke of Wellington:

. . . The Queen wishes me to offer You, in Her name, the

Rangership of the Parks in London, which was held by the late
Duke of Cambridge and the Duke of Sussex before him.

Ever Yours truly,

Albert[10]

On the following day, 7 August, the Duke replied:

> ... He is very sensible of Her Majesty's precious consideration
> and favour in offering to appoint him Ranger of the London
> Parks. He is ready to serve Her Majesty in any capacity in which
> he can be considered useful to Her Majesty's Service. . . .[11]

Just over two years later, on 16 September 1852, the Queen and
Prince Albert were on an expedition from Alt-na-Giuthasach to
the Dhu Loch – 'One of the wildest and loneliest spots of the
Highlands', reported the Prince Consort – when sad news reached
them.

> ... The Death of the Duke of Wellington has deprived the
> Country of its greatest man, the Crown of its most valuable
> servant and adviser, the Army of its main strength and sup-
> port. . . .[12]

wrote the Prince next day, in a memorandum headed 'Balmoral', in
which he went on to suggest that the Rangership of the Parks in
London should pass to George, Duke of Cambridge, son of that
Adolphus who had been Ranger of the Parks before the Iron Duke.
This Duke of Cambridge held the Rangership of the London Parks
for nearly half a century, during which time, as we shall see, he
became heavily involved in a number of heated controversies.

The State funeral procession of the Duke of Wellington was
marshalled on the Horse Guards Parade in November 1852. On
the night before the funeral, the body of the victor of Waterloo was
removed from the Chelsea Hospital, where it had been lying in
state, and it was taken to the audience chamber at the Horse Guards.
On the following morning, the Duke's coffin was placed on the
monstrously heavy and ornate carriage which had been designed
for the hero's last journey to St Paul's Cathedral. The Horse

Guards Parade – screened by the Admiralty buildings to the east, by the Horse Guards in the centre, and by the back surfaces of the Treasury and Downing Street to the west – is now used for the annual ceremony of Trooping the Colour and some other occasional military functions such as 'Beating Retreat'. During the greater part of the year this historic expanse, which, as we have seen, was guarded originally by King Charles II's gentlemen when they returned with him from exile, now serves as a car park for selected officials.

Five years after the Duke of Wellington's funeral, the lake in St James's Park was spanned by a delightful suspension bridge which was intended to provide a more or less direct route for pedestrians who were moving between St James's Street on the north side of the Park and Queen Square on the south. For nearly a century after that, this attractive little bridge was one of the best-loved features of any of the London Parks. Proposals then were made that it should be pulled down, and in spite of many urgent and eloquent protests – in the correspondence columns of *The Times* and elsewhere – it was replaced in 1957 by the present 'Slim Line Bridge' which is at least elegant, though not nearly so romantic as the original structure.

Throughout the nineteenth century, Government officials of varying degrees of importance were almost continuously seeking, as persuasively as they could, to convert St James's Park from a private royal preserve into an enjoyable public amenity. Already in 1838, for instance, Lord John Russell was 'presenting his humble duty' to Her Majesty Queen Victoria and suggesting that the restriction which prevented soldiers from being admitted, with the rest of the public, into the Garden of St James's Park should be removed. It was, he submitted, an 'invidious distinction'.[13] Nor was Lord John afraid to press the new young Queen to allow more carriages to enter the St James's and Green Parks:[14]

. . . Lord John Russell humbly recommends to Your Majesty to grant the privilege of driving thro' the Parks to Lady Charlotte Greville and Lady Clinton – Lady Clinton enjoys it, so long as she remains in the household of Her Majesty Queen Adelaide[15] . . .

Requests of this sort reached the Queen in ever-increasing numbers. By November 1856, the time was ripe for a minor break-through:

> ... The Ranger of St James's Park (His Royal Highness the Duke of Cambridge) signified to the Board of Green Cloth[16] that the Queen had been pleased to order that the gates of St James's Palace that led into St James's Park from Pall Mall should be opened to the public for the passing and re-passing of private carriages and hackney cabs – but only to and from the Buckingham Gate[17] . . .

But the Queen was not going to give away any ground to the eager liberal reformers unless she was firmly convinced of the desirability of doing so. She kept a watchful eye on every possible development. A memorandum written in Her Majesty's Office of Works in January 1860 records that there was a public demand for covered seats to be placed in some of the Metropolitan Parks. Enough money was voted to have one covered seat put in either St James's Park, or the Green Park or Hyde Park, one in the Regent's Park, and one in the Victoria Park, East London. The execution of the work had to be delayed, however, until the design could be submitted, with other Park questions, for the Queen's approval.[18]

Later in the same year, Her Majesty's First Commissioner of Works, the Rt Hon. W. F. Cowper, suggested that the capabilities of the Parks for general amusement should be fully developed, and boating should be allowed on the lake in St James's Park. It was proposed to employ a Mr Renshaw, 'a very respectable boat builder who had charge of the boating of the Westminster boys'. He did not think it possible that any inconvenience would be occasioned to those in Buckingham Palace by the plying of boats in front of it. On the contrary, he thought that the scene would be 'enlivened and diversified'.[19] The Queen did not disapprove but, fortunately, perhaps, for the waterfowl on Mr Nash's lake, boating was never allowed to become one of St James's Park's important activities.

Anyone who tried to carry out an 'improvement' to St James's Park, even though it were quite a small one, without referring the

matter to Her Majesty would be liable to receive a crushing rebuke.
On 31 August 1864, for instance, Sir Charles Phipps, the Keeper
of the Privy Purse, wrote from Balmoral to the First Commissioner
of Works:

> . . . The Queen has heard that a considerable alteration is going
> on in the Birdcage Walk by which a portion of the ground
> hitherto enclosed in the gardens is converted into a ride, and the
> railings to that extent removed. Her Majesty directs me to say
> that she wishes no alteration to be made in the Royal Parks
> which has not been previously submitted for Her approval, and
> that a memorandum to this effect should be recorded in your
> office. . . . [20]

Early in the present century, the western end and the northern
side of St James's Park were altered considerably in appearance.
(Ironically, the changes were intended, in the first place, to form
part of a National Memorial to Her Majesty the late Queen Victoria,
who had been so reluctant to let anyone alter anything in the
Park.)

The changes involved, primarily, the laying out of the Mall, to
the designs of Sir Aston Webb, as a grand processional way. At the
eastern end of the Mall the ponderous Admiralty Arch was constructed – it was dedicated to the memory of the late King Edward
VII – and, at the western end, the great circular carriageway that
now carries the traffic round immediately in front of Buckingham
Palace. To make this carriageway, Sir Aston had to fill in part of
the western end of Nash's lake.

For the centre of the roundabout, the sculptor Thomas Brock
was commissioned to produce a suitable monument, and he did this
with great virtuosity, providing a wedding-cake-like concoction in
white marble and bronze that was only outdone in richness and
general magnificence by the memorial to His Royal Highness the
late Prince Consort in Kensington Gardens.

The principal feature of the Victoria Memorial is a thirteen-foot
high statue of the Monarch who sits, in her state robes, looking
down the Mall through which she has ridden in all her great

processions for more than sixty years, and which she has known only as a dignified kind of country lane.

Round the pedestal behind the Queen's throne are marble groups that represent Justice, Motherhood and Truth. Other groups, in dark bronze, represent Agriculture (a woman with a sickle gives the clue to this); Manufacture (a smith wearing a leather apron and wielding a hammer); Peace (a figure with an olive branch); and Progress (a figure with a torch). Naval and Military Power, which really existed in Queen Victoria's days, are fittingly suggested, and at the top, at a height of 82 feet, stands a gilded bronze figure of Victory with Courage and Constancy attending her. The stunning complexity of the whole seems to have entirely satisfied the taste of those in authority at the time, for Thomas Brock was knighted on the platform at the unveiling ceremony, in the presence of the Emperor of Germany.

The Renaissance-style Portland stone east front of Buckingham Palace which now faces St James's Park was built by Sir Aston Webb in 1912 with money that had been left over from the funds subscribed by the public for the Victoria Memorial, and it concealed an earlier front added to John Nash's Palace by Edward Blore in 1846. The transformation, which many people regretted, was carried out in the surprisingly short time of three months, the contractors having agreed in advance that they would do the work, if they possibly could, while Their Majesties King George V and Queen Mary were out of town.

Another Queen of England – Queen Alexandra, widow of King Edward VII – is commemorated by a less obtrusive memorial than Queen Victoria's. This – the last important work of Sir Alfred Gilbert, executed when he was nearly eighty – is situated at the Marlborough Gate of St James's Park, by the road that separates Marlborough House from Friary Court, the yard where each Sovereign of England is proclaimed on the first day after his or her accession. To pay for this memorial, a tiny fraction of the funds publicly subscribed for nursing charities on Alexandra Rose Day was annually set aside for twenty-one years, so that the founder of the Fund might eventually be suitably thanked, in marble and bronze.

Compared to the memorials to the Queens Victoria and Alexandra, the statue that comemorates the late King George VI, approached by steps on the north side of the Mall, is relatively modest and austere. Several other memorials in, and on the perimeter of, St James's Park are worthy of close inspection.

Near the Admiralty Arch, with its ornate gates that feature the royal lion and the unicorn, there stands by the Mall the figure of the British hero, Captain Cook. Below this much-admired bronze, which shows the Captain carrying a scroll and a telescope and wearing a three-cornered hat, passers-by can read this tribute to the man who did so much to make life safer and more comfortable for all those who had to travel long distances by sea:

. . . Circumnavigator of the Globe, explorer of the Pacific Ocean, he laid the foundation of the British Empire in Australia and New Zealand, he charted the shores of Newfoundland and traversed the ocean gates of Canada, both east and west. . . .

The statue was unveiled by His Royal Highness Prince Arthur of Connaught, on behalf of the British Empire League, in July 1914.

A little further along the Mall, facing the Duke of York's Steps, there is a lively bronze group set on a raised platform and screened, from the rear, by a curving stone bay. The memorial was erected by the officers and men of the Royal Artillery as a tribute to their honoured dead in South Africa in the years 1899–1902. The subject of the group is 'Peace controlling a War Horse', and the sculptor was William R. Colton. On the lower surfaces of the memorial there are some bronze relief panels that represent the firing of a gun, the transportation of munitions by horses and mules, and other military activities, and they give quite a dramatic impression of field warfare as it was at the beginning of this century.

Facing the Horse Guards Parade is the Guards' Memorial – the work, principally, of Gilbert Ledward, R.A. – which features five World War I guardsmen in front of a high stone cenotaph. They are cast in bronze provided by German guns captured by guardsmen in that war, and at one side there is a relief panel that shows a gun being brought into action.

Across the Horse Guards Parade, and near the gate that leads into the Park from the back garden of No. 10 Downing Street, stands the solitary figure, also in bronze, of Field-Marshal Lord Kitchener (1850–1916). The base of this statue is inscribed: 'Erected by Parliament'. In front of Robert Smirke's fine Horse Guards building stand two mounted figures – Lord Wolseley, the work of Sir William Goscombe John, R.A., and Lord Roberts, by Harry Bates.

Those are not the only sculptures for the visitor to St James's Park to see – there is a statue of Lord Clive (1725–74), for instance, by the steps that lead down to the Park from King Charles Street, and there is J. H. Mabey's stone figure of a boy kneeling with an urn, which was put up in 1863 by the path that leads from the Queen Anne's Gate entrance of the Park to the bridge over the lake – but no one is likely to leave the Horse Guards Parade for these without noticing, first, the two magnificent guns that stand there, protected now by heavy iron chains rather ineffectually from the numerous children who are unable to resist the temptation to clamber over them. (A photograph in the Royal Collection at Windsor, taken nearly a century ago, shows one of the guns protected by a bristly fence of sharp metal spikes.)

The first of these guns, to the north of the central archway in the Horse Guards Building, is, or was, Turkish. The gun was made by Murad, son of Abdullah, chief gunner of the Turkish army in 1524, and it was captured in Egypt by the British army in 1801. It is now mounted on a grandiose two-wheeled carriage constructed in the Royal Carriage Department, on the side of which Britannia, reclining by a somnolent lion, is threatened by a four-foot long crocodile. The gun is inscribed with this fearsome message:

The Solomon of the Age, the Great Sultan commanded the dragon guns to be made. When they breathe, roaring like thunder, may the enemy forces be razed to the ground. Year of the Hegira 931.

The second gun, a little to the south, is a stumpy mortar that now rests on the body of a grotesque gryphon. An inscription on the side of the carriage tells the gun's story:

To Commemorate the raising of the Siege of Cadiz, in consequence of the glorious VICTORY gained by the Duke of Wellington
over the French near Salamanca on the 22 July 1812 this MORTAR
cast for the destruction of that great port, with powers surpassing
all others, and abandoned by the BESEIGERS in their RETREAT was
presented as a token of respect and gratitude by the SPANISH
NATION to HIS ROYAL HIGHNESS the PRINCE REGENT . . .

A 'war memorial' of an almost unique kind still stands by the
Admiralty buildings just to the north of the Horse Guards Parade.
This is the massive concrete citadel put up, during World War II,
to protect the Prime Minister and his principal advisers from harm
from the air. The stronghold in which Mr (later Sir) Winston
Churchill spent so many historic hours has not, to date, been
removed, but its severe lines are now softened by Virginia creepers
and other growing things, and it has more than an acre of grass
lawn on its roof.

Another survival of a quite unique kind adds an unusual distinction to St James's Park – it is now the only Metropolitan Royal
Park to have a Master Gunner.

Before 1759, the senior Master Gunner was styled 'The Master
Gunner of England'. The first gentleman to hold this appointment
appears to have been one Roger de Leybourn, who was honoured in
1263 – during the reign of King Henry III.[21]

During the reign of King Edward VI (1547–53), the Master
Gunner's pay appears to have been two shillings a day, with
allowances – the rate of pay enjoyed by Members of Parliament at
the time. His residence lay in the Tower of London, and his duties
were concerned with the 'fee'd' gunners of that great stronghold,
but after Woolwich had been developed as a place with special
responsibility for Artillery detail, the Master Gunner was allotted
quarters in the Manor House at Woolwich. Even while living there,
he was required to take a parade of the 'fee'd' gunners at the Tower
twice a week and to teach them the science of gunnery.

The majority of the Master Gunners of England in the sixteenth
century held the appointment by Letters Patent from Queen
Elizabeth I. They do not all appear to have been soldiers, but were

chosen for their knowledge of laboratory duties and for their skill at the 'making of pleasaunt and warlike fireworks'. Bolton, in his *Present State of Great Britain and Ireland* published in 1758, recorded that further duties had been added by King James I:

> ... The Master Gunner of England is an Officer to teach all such as learn the art of gunnery and to certify to the Master General the ability of any person recommended to be one of the King's Gunners. To every scholar he administers an oath not to serve, without leave, any other Prince or State, or to teach anyone the art of Gunnery but such as have taken the oath, and these Artificers were not to quit the country without the King's leave. ...

According to the Artillery records, the duties of the Master Gunner of England (or of his 'Sufficient Deputy') were increased still further during the reigns of the Stuart Kings. From that time on, it was decreed, he would have to superintend the firing of salutes and the discharging of fireworks in London in honour of Royal Birthdays, to commemorate national victories, and for other celebrations, as required.

The last 'Master Gunner of England' died in 1758, and in 1759 the appointment was altered to that of 'Master Gunner Whitehall and St James's Park, London', one Captain Joseph Broome having been gazetted as such in the *London Gazette* of 5 January 1759. This officer was succeeded in 1796 by his son Major-General Joseph Walton as 'Master Gunner of St James's Park', Captain Broome having assumed, by that time, the name of Walton. The appointment has since then been reserved for the senior Artillery Officer or some other Artillery Officer of very high rank.

In 1881, the Master Gunners (Warrant Officers and Non-Commissioned Officers) were graded into 'classes', largely for the purpose of determining their pay, and Warrants were conferred on the First and Second Classes, but – probably by some oversight – the Master Gunner of St James's Park was relegated to the Third Class, which had the lowest rate of pay. Thus it followed that Field-Marshal Earl Roberts found himself junior to all the First,

Second and other Third Class Master Gunners. In 1910, it was decided that the pay of the Master Gunner of St James's Park, such as it was, should lapse on the death of Field-Marshal Roberts and that in the future the post should be honorary. The appointment has preserved its continuity up to the present time, the Master Gunner of St James's Park as this book goes to press being Field-Marshal Sir Geoffrey Baker, G.C.B., C.M.G., C.B.E., M.C.

St James's Park has provided a fitting background for a number of joyful royal occasions since World War II. Eight years after the end of the war, great stands were put up on both sides of the Mall so that as many privileged people as possible could see Her Majesty Queen Elizabeth II pass triumphantly through St James's Park on her way to her Coronation ceremony in Westminster Abbey. The year 1977 saw the vast, unforgettable crowds that pressed in a most orderly fashion along the Mall after Her Majesty had returned to Buckingham Palace from her Silver Jubilee Service of Thanksgiving at St Paul's Cathedral, from her memorable 'walk-about' in the City of London, on her way to luncheon at the Guildhall. On a less happy occasion, three years earlier, the Mall had been the scene of a most regrettable attack on two members of the Royal Family: Her Royal Highness Princess Anne and her husband Captain Mark Phillips were returning to Buckingham Palace from a function in the City when their car was stopped by an armed man who looked as though he was threatening them with physical injury. The Princess's personal detective and a police officer on duty in the Park moved swiftly, and in less time than it has taken to write this brief account of the incident the 'modern highwayman' had been disarmed and taken into custody.

It is difficult to imagine what St James's Park would be like, today, without its magnificent and carefully tended trees. As well as the weeping willows planted by the lake that give certain of the Park's vistas a curiously Chinese flavour, there are numerous fine specimens of the London Plane (*Platanus Hispanica*), some decorative groups of the Common Fig (*Ficus Carica*), and a few remaining elms (though these may well have disappeared by the time this book is published, as a result of the appalling Dutch elm disease). By Birdcage Walk, there are three well-grown examples of a choice and rare Chinese tree, the *Evodia Hupehensis*, which has very glossy dark leaves and smooth grey bark and produces, in early September, masses of subtly-tinted white flowers. The gardeners in this and the other Central Parks mount some ravishing floral displays, too – and have been known to exhibit with success at the Chelsea Flower Show.

So it is that the walk round the lake in St James's Park is now understandably one of the most popular promenades in London – famous politicians can be seen there, taking the air at moments of national crisis, as well as office workers enjoying a brief break in the daily routine. And, during the full cycle of the year, wild birds of as many as forty different species can be observed by people taking a little mild exercise in the Park.

The birds on the lake itself are packed, at times, so closely on the water's surface that there appears to be room for not one more! Among the commoner water birds to be seen are the slate-grey coot and the smaller moorhen; among the ducks, the mallard, pochard, shoveler, teal, tufted duck, and widgeon; and various gulls, including the herring gull, the black-headed gull, the lesser black-backed gull, and, more rarely, the greater black-backed gull. In November 1949, a single glaucous gull – normally an inhabitant of the Arctic Circle – made a brief appearance on the lake. Other surprising visitors in recent years have included the goldeneye, the long-tailed duck, and the smew.

But of course not all the birds to be seen on and near the lake in St James's Park are wild. Though the collections of exotic geese and ducks started by King Charles II had almost disappeared by the beginning of the eighteenth century, periodic attempts were made to re-stock the lake, and in 1837 the members of the Ornithological Society of London, recognizing the Park's great potentialities as a centre for bird life, provided a number of ornamental wildfowl of various kinds, and a cottage by the lake for a Bird Keeper. Today, there are several hundred pinioned waterfowl on the lake, drawn from as many as thirty different species.

Cormorants were introduced to the St James's Lake by King James I, but these highly individual seabirds have not been represented in the Park continuously since then. The modern colony – a small one at the best of times – was founded in 1888, when specimens were brought from the Megstone Rock in the Farne Islands, but the birds' successors failed to survive World War I. A new start was made in 1923, but the decision to do this was regretted after a few years when the cormorants were suspected by the authorities of preying on the Park's ducklings; the supposed assassins were quietly eliminated. Attempts made since World War II to re-introduce cormorants to the Park have met with only partial success. The sturdy members of the pelican colony continue, however, to thrive, having been reinforced from time to time by new recruits contributed by kind donors, including the Amir of Bahawalpur and the Lieutenant-Governor of Louisiana.

On and above the pleasant lawns in St James's Park there are other interesting birds to be seen, besides the resident and visiting waterfowl. There are, of course, the blackbirds, thrushes, pigeons, robins, starlings, tits and wrens that might appear at almost any time in a suburban garden. But there are rarer birds. Pied and spotted flycatchers are noticed in the Park occasionally, and warblers, wheatears and pied and grey wagtails turn up there from time to time. At least once, in recent years, a cuckoo has been heard in the Park.[22]

Chapter 3

Green Park

Green Park is a roughly triangular patch of timber and grass, bounded to the north by Piccadilly, now increasingly like a motorway; to the east by a line of stately buildings leading down from the Ritz Hotel; and to the south and west by Constitution Hill, also a busy road. As a park, it is too small to provide a really satisfactory refuge from the rush and roar of London's traffic, but it is appropriately named, for it is very well watered (though the Tyburn Stream, which once flowed through it on its way from Hampstead to the Thames, is now confined inside larger sewer pipes) and its trees are plentiful and leafy. Its gentle undulations, free from formal flower beds, provide many welcome resting places for those who may wish to enjoy, temporarily, a 'green thought in a green shade'.[1]

Until King Charles II returned from Europe and claimed his throne, the ground between the wall of St James's Palace and the Reading Road (known, ultimately, as 'Piccadilly') was waste ground or meadow. In old maps, its two shallow hills are shown as being planted with a few willow trees, and the ground between them appears to have been intersected by a variety of ditches. Here, in the reign of Queen Elizabeth I, children would come birds'-nesting, cutting across the sheep tracks that skirted the Royal Farm in St James's Fields. Here too, John Gerard, the distinguished botanist and author of *The Herball* (1597), used to wander, finding the small bugloss or 'ox-tongue' in the barren soil of the 'drie ditch banks about Pikadilla'.

King Charles quickly brought his civilizing touch to bear on this
unpromising territory, enclosing at least thirty-six acres with a high
brick wall so that the ground contained became known as 'The
Upper' – as opposed to 'The Lower' – St James's Park. On the
slow rising escarpment to the west, which had been previously
described as a 'Deer Park', the new monarch set up a deer harbour,
and that is the name, in fact, by which it is referred to thence-
forward in state documents.

Approximately in the centre of the new Park, the King had
built, before he had been on the throne many months, 'a snow-
house and an ice-house, as the mode is in some parts of France
and Italy, and other hot countries, for to cool wines and other
drinks for the summer season'.[2] (During the winter, snow and ice
would be collected in these deep pits and covered with a thick
thatch of straw, bracken, moss and other materials to provide the
necessary insulation.) Edmund Waller mentions these early sources
of refrigeration in his poem 'St James's Park':

> . . . Yonder the harvest of cold months laid up
>   Gives a fresh coolness to the royal cup;
> There ice, like crystal firm and never lost,
>   Tempers hot July with December's frost. . . .

The King's Snow and Ice Houses remained in the Park until the
early nineteenth century.

During King Charles's reign, many new houses were built on
St James's Fields, which flanked the Park on the east, and along
Piccadilly, to the north, some grand mansions appeared, most of
them in the newly popular 'classical' style. The ground between
these two rapidly developing areas and 'Constitution Hill' – which
got its name, it is believed, from the King's democratic habit of
taking his daily exercise there, among his subjects – was planted
with many splendid trees and laid out with extensive and useful
gravel paths, so that by the end of his reign the ground had the
makings of the pleasant oasis which it is today.

In one particular respect, however, the Upper and Lower St
James's Parks were unalike: in the Upper Park, the strict ban on

sword-drawing did not apply, so the place became, like two or three other lonely places a little way out of London, a favourite resort for duels. On Saturday, 11 January 1696, for instance, Sir Henry Colt, who had been challenged by 'Beau' Fielding, fought a duel with his adversary here in the late evening. The place appointed for the meeting was at the back of Cleveland Court (which was on the site of the present Bridgewater House), and this spot was probably chosen because Fielding would have wished to fight under the view of his mistress – and future wife – the notorious Duchess of Cleveland. Fielding is said to have run his opponent through the body before the baronet could even draw his sword, but in spite of this serious wound Sir Henry managed to disarm Fielding, and ended the fight.

In 1730, there was another duel in the Upper St James's Park which caused a considerable stir. The protagonists on this occasion were William Pulteney, who afterwards became Earl of Bath, and John, Lord Hervey. Hervey had been loyally writing defences of Sir Robert Walpole, the King's First Minister, in answer to attacks made on him in a journal called *The Craftsman*. To one of these defences, Pulteney had published an answer, entitling it *A Proper Reply to a Late Scurrilous Libel*. The *Proper Reply* was grossly and most improperly personal, and Hervey immediately challenged Pulteney. The two men met between three and four o'clock on a January afternoon behind Arlington Street, Mr Fox and Sir John Rushout acting as seconds. They fought with swords, but neither combatant suffered any grievous bodily harm.

At precisely the same time, Queen Caroline, wife of King George II, who, as we shall see, had been making many improvements around the Palace at Kensington, was beginning to take a great interest in the Upper St James's Park, and in February 1730 the Board of Works received orders to prepare a private walk along the eastern border of the Park, so that the members of the Royal Family might divert themselves there in the Spring, without being too much disturbed by the general public. Part of the path that runs from the north to the south of the Park on its eastern side is still known as 'The Queen's Walk'. A narrow passage near its southern end gives access to Pall Mall and St James's Palace.

Near her new walk, Queen Caroline had a summer pavilion put up – designed by William Kent, it is usually referred to as her 'Library'. The Queen's life may have been shortened, indirectly, by this building, for on 9 November 1737 she walked up to it from St James's Palace to take her breakfast. While she was there, she developed such a severe cold that no sooner had she returned to the Palace than she was obliged to retire to her bed. Ten days later, the Queen was dead. After her death, the Library was allowed to fall into disrepair.

During much of the eighteenth century, the Upper St James's Park was used extensively for military parades and manoeuvres. This activity became particularly intense during the most critical periods of the War of the Austrian Succession (1740–1748). The end of the war, which was marked by the publication of the Peace of Aix-la-Chapelle, was celebrated in England by a huge display of fireworks: the biggest show of the kind to be held anywhere in Europe – and probably in the world – during the whole of the eighteenth century. The centre of the Upper St James's Park was chosen as the most suitable site, and preparations were put in hand with the greatest enthusiasm.

To accommodate the engineers and the other necessary officers, a building called 'The Temple of Peace' was designed by a M. Servadoni, who had earned himself a considerable reputation in Paris. The Temple, 400 feet long and 114 feet high, would be fitted, at its centre, with a 'grand and extensive' musical gallery. Above this, there would be an allegorical figure of Peace attended by the massive figures of Neptune and Mars, and above that again a *basso-relievo*, which would represent the King – George II – in the act of bestowing peace upon a grateful Britannia. On a pole at the top of all there was to be an illumination representing the sun, which was to burn, somewhat improbably, almost throughout the night of the festivities. The style of the building, declared M. Servadoni, should be 'Doric'.

The performance was to begin with a grand military overture composed by Handel, to which one hundred cannon, fired from arcades in the Temple 'singly with the music', would provide an unforgettable punctuation. The music was to be stormy – representing, as vividly as possible, a sea swelling in anger and then as suddenly subsiding into a calm. (This was purely allegorical, the great composer was told: his theme, in more obvious terms, would be War giving way to Peace.)

In his house in Brook Street, Handel worked with zest on the necessary score – forty trumpets, twenty French horns, sixteen hautboys, twelve side drums and eight kettle drums were to compete with the hundred cannon as well as they could. The libretto provided the composer with certain difficulties. ('Vot are "billows"?' he is said to have asked, late one night, having knocked up the man responsible, and, on being informed, had returned to his carriage repeating 'Oh, de vave! De vave!')

At last, all was ready for the great display and the night of Thursday 27 April was appointed for the Grand Letting-Off. The fireworks, which were all Italian in origin, being made by Messrs Ruggieri and Sarti of Bologna, were to be ignited under the direction of 'Ch. Frederick, Esq., Comptroller, and Capt. Thomas Desaguliers, Chief Fire-Master of His Majesty's Laboratory'. The Comptroller and Chief Fire-Master had at their command:

87	air balloons
21	cascades
30	figured pieces
71	fixed suns
160	fountains
260	gerbes (jets in the form of wheatsheaves)
2,700	lances
5,000	marrons (maroons)
180	pots d'aigrettes (fireworks in the form of plumes)
12,200	pots de brin (fiery sprays)
21	regulated pieces
30	figured pieces
10,650	skyrockets
88	tourbillions (Catherine wheels) and
131	vertical suns and wheels

On the Monday before the day appointed, a daylight rehearsal was held. Some fireworks were let off, and a number of casualties were taken to the new St George's Hospital by Hyde Park Corner.

On the evening itself, all the entrances to the Park were opened, and a breach fifty feet long made in the park wall on the Piccadilly side in order to give admittance to the vast concourse of spectators awaited. (In their eagerness to see a Victory Parade after the 'Forty-five, the unruly citizens had taken the law into their own hands and had torn down the railings.) A special gallery had been erected for members of the Privy Council, the House of Commons, and the Peers. The rest of the seating room had been made available to the Lord Mayor.

As darkness fell, the King, who, earlier in the day, had reviewed the three regiments of Foot Guards from the garden wall of St James's Palace, went with a number of his courtiers to a special pavilion that had been put up for him by the Queen's Library in the Park. The Prince and Princess of Wales, who were on very bad terms with the King, did not join this party, preferring to watch the display from the home of the Earl of Middlesex in Arlington Street.

As soon as the King was in his place, the performance started with Handel's great overture. The cannon hidden inside the *chevaux de frise* were fired, and a hundred and one guns echoed the sound from Constitution Hill. Hardly had this deafening noise died away, when part of the Temple of Peace caught fire, and in the next few minutes the Upper St James's Park became a scene of the most appalling confusion. Several members of the crowd were injured in the excitement, and one at least is known to have perished. The Queen's Library, already dilapidated, was set fire to, and almost completely destroyed. ('An act of vandalism: it must never be repeated', declared a contemporary critic.)

In the following year, an extraordinarily macabre parade of the Dragoons took place in the Park. A complete turn-out of the force was insisted upon by those in command. To comply with this order, those who were 'absent sick' had to be represented by their boots which were fixed, on parade, in the stirrups of their riderless horses. Those who were absent because they were dead were similarly represented, except in one respect: the deceased dragoons' boots were fixed in their horses' stirrups with the toes pointing tailwards.

Several small but significant changes were made in the Upper St James's Park during the second half of the eighteenth century. In 1767, for instance, the Park was reduced slightly in size by King George III so that the gardens planned for the royal residence at Buckingham House could be enlarged. Moreover, after 1780 the Park became steadily less and less useful to the military, and in proportion became more and more of a social meeting place.

During these years, there were two notable incidents in the Upper St James's Park.

On the first occasion, Benjamin Franklin, the great American publisher and scientist, is said to have poured oil on the troubled waters of one of the Park ponds so that its soothing effect could be publicly demonstrated.

On the second – an evening in May 1771 – a duel was fought in the Park between Edward, Viscount Ligonier, nephew of the famous general, and Count Alfieri, the Italian poet, who was known to be having an *affaire* with Ligonier's wife. Alfieri came off worse, but he bravely returned to the Haymarket Theatre, despite the sword-wound he had received in his arm, so that he could be seen enjoying the last act of the play being then performed there. Later, the poet was reported to have said, 'My view is that Ligonier did not kill me because he did not want to, and I did not kill him because I did not know how.'

The grand junketings held by the Prince Regent in 1814 brought great crowds, once again, to the Upper St James's Park. The spectators were to be treated, first, to one of the most popular entertainments of the time – a balloon ascent. The star of this daring display was to be John Sadler, son of James Sadler, the celebrated aeronaut. (Two months earlier, Father James and another son, Windham, had made an ascent from the courtyard of Burlington House, ostensibly in honour of the Duke of Wellington. On that occasion, the two men had attained an altitude estimated at five miles, during which they had suffered severely from cold and pain in the ears, but they had made a perfect landing near Ockendon in Essex. Then, on 29 July 1814, Windham Sadler had ascended again from the same spot, accompanied by a Miss Thompson, who was described in the previous announcements as a young lady 'renowned in the Dramatic Corps'. After a flight of about three-quarters of an hour, the pair had descended safely near Coggeshall, which was forty-five miles away.)

In the ascent that John Sadler was to make, in celebration of Napoleon's defeat and in honour of the House of Hanover, the young balloonist was to be accompanied by a Mrs H. Johnstone, but when it was found that the fastening intended to secure the network of ropes to the valve at the top of the balloon was not sufficiently strong, the Duke of Wellington advised, or so it is alleged, that the ascent should be given up. The young aeronaut was not to be deterred, however, and he decided to 'go it alone'.

A thin drizzle of rain had been falling during the morning while Mr Sadler's balloon was being inflated, but this did nothing to discourage the thousands of people who were flocking, in the highest of spirits, to the Upper St James's Park. Shortly after midday the clouds lifted, the sun shone, and the revellers, elated, enjoyed themselves in singing and dancing during most of the afternoon.

Shortly after 5 p.m., Mr Sadler's balloon was judged to be sufficiently inflated to be capable of bearing the brave man aloft, and at twenty minutes to six precisely he took his place in the car. The mooring ropes were then cut, and the great sphere rose slowly and majestically into the air to the sound of loud cheers from the gentlemen among the crowd of spectators and of sobs, shrieks and screams, which were all that the ladies seemed to be able to manage. Clearly wishing to reassure his swooning female supporters, Mr Sadler leaned bravely out of the swaying basket and waved his cap to them.

The balloon gathered speed as it ascended, and soon Mr Sadler had passed right out of the view of the watchers in the Park. As he vanished from their sight, the ropes with which his balloon was enmeshed became displaced, the envelope started to burst through the inadequate netting, and he decided, with proper caution, that he ought to descend to earth without undue delay. To his horror, however, he found that the valve which should have allowed the gas to escape from the balloon had frozen up. Before he had managed

to make it work, the balloon was drifting away over the Thames
Estuary and the chances were high that it would be carried out to
sea and lost for ever. But Mr Sadler was not defeated. With admirable presence of mind he took out a knife and cut a hole in the
fabric of the balloon. As a result of his resourcefulness he managed
to land more or less safely, a few minutes later, in the suggestively
named Mucking Marshes.

But that was only a prelude. To provide a late night treat, the
Upper St James's Park was to be used, once again, as the setting
for a grand pyrotechnic display. On this occasion, the display was
centred on a romantic and picturesque 'castle', with a round tower
and ramparts a hundred feet square, that had been set up near
Constitution Hill. In spite of its massive size – with all its palings
and the cordon of sentries set up round it, the 'castle' covered
nearly one-third of the Park – the mock fortress had been specially
contrived so that it would revolve, enabling each of its surfaces to
be displayed in turn to every spectator. The building, designed by
Sir William Congreve and plainly an emblem of war, had been
given the name 'The Temple of Concord', which suggested that
some major transformation would take place in it before the
celebrations were over.

At midnight, then, the great fortress in the Upper St James's
Park, revolving merrily on its axis, changed suddenly and with a
deafening roar into the Temple of Concord that had been promised,
many hundreds of fireworks being ignited almost simultaneously
to produce a really spectacular effect. On this occasion, the display
seems to have gone off without mishap, and to have given a great
deal of pleasure. The materials used for building the Temple were
later sold by auction, together with the materials 'of the other
erections set up on that occasion'. They fetched only about £200.

Several more notable balloon ascents were made from the Green
Park, as the Upper St James's Park came to be called, during the
nineteenth century. (On one occasion, a man even made a balloon
ascent sitting on a horse and stayed aloft, still mounted, for an hour
and a half.) But the most advanced of these Green Park ascents
may have been the ascent made in 1821 by an innovator called
Charles Green.

Mr Green's earliest advertised ascent was arranged to take place from the Belvidere Gardens, Pentonville, on 18 July 1821 – about fourteen years, that is, after coal gas had first been specially manufactured for street lighting in London. Having demonstrated by actual experiments before the members of the 'Original Chartered Gas-Light Company' and 'other Scientific Characters' that their gas was of 'sufficient Levity for all the Purposes of Aerostation', Mr Green constructed a 'SUPERB BALLOON, of sufficient Capacity to contain One Hundred Thousand Gallons of Gas, and capable of raising into the Atmosphere Eight Hundred Weight' with which, he said in a handbill, he would ascend from the Pentonville beauty spot precisely at three o'clock in the afternoon. As his 'Stupendous BALLOON' would be inflated by a large pipe from the Company's Main, 'all Accidents to Ladies' Dresses, &c. from the action of Acid', he promised, would be avoided.

That ascent did not take place – probably because Pentonville was so far out. Instead, Mr Green was engaged by the Government to ascend on the following day from the Green Park, to make an exciting climax for the Coronation festivities. The inflation of the balloon – which was decorated with the royal arms, and inscribed 'George IV, Royal Coronation Balloon' – was effected from the gas main in Piccadilly, and on being released it rose to about 11,000 feet. Carried by a veering westerly wind and fearing that he might come down into the sea, Mr Green released a considerable quantity of gas, with the result that after about forty minutes he descended so rapidly into a field beyond Barnet that he was thrown out of his car and subsequently dragged along the ground for nearly a quarter of a mile holding on to the balloon's hoop.

There would not have been much, if any, of the Green Park left for balloonists to ascend from if Sir John Soane had had his way. This talented classicist, who had been appointed Architect to the Bank of England in 1788, and who was Professor of Architecture to the Royal Academy, was confident that when the Prince Regent at last became King, he himself would be invited to put up a suitably grand new home for him. Being a man of taste and sensibility, Soane did not take kindly to the King's proposal that the old Buckingham House should be altered and enlarged. Instead,

Sir John made drawings for a brand new palace to be set up in the Green Park. (These drawings can now be seen by permission, in Sir John's handsome house on the north side of Lincoln's Inn Fields.) All his work was wasted, for the King was determined to live on the site of Buckingham House, if not in the actual building. (The place had 'early associations', the new Sovereign explained, which made him especially fond of it.) Furthermore, the new Sovereign preferred buildings put up in the less academically correct style of his protégé John Nash. So the Green Park survived as a public open space, and, fortunately for us, it remains so to the present day.

After King George IV died and when King William IV, who was aesthetically less well trained, was nominally in charge of affairs, the Green Park was sadly neglected. The Chelsea Waterworks Company, for a start, had been allowed to take over almost the whole of the north-east corner of the Park, opposite Stratton Street, and had made a big reservoir there which was not to be drained and filled up for at least a quarter of a century. In 1835, however, a writer in *The Original* complained bitterly about the disgraceful state into which the Green Park had been allowed to sink. There had been talk some years before, the writer went on, of this conspicuously situated ground being partly terraced and wholly laid out in a highly ornamental style. His Majesty the King, the writer hoped, would give orders that these things should be done.

Before long, visible improvements were being made in the Park, though the hoped-for terraces were never actually brought into being. Almost the whole of the Park was to be adequately drained, however, and its surface was to be re-laid and re-planted. The decrepit Ranger's Lodge that used to stand at the Hyde Park Corner end of the Park, and which the writer in *The Original* had particularly condemned, was demolished at roughly the same time. (The young and inexperienced Queen Victoria was 'quite sure' that she had never given her consent, by signature or writing, to this old building being pulled down, but it was possible, she recorded, that sanction had been obtained in an unofficial way by a minister asking Lord Palmerston to mention the case to Her Majesty.)[3] The two bronze sculptures of stags which used to stand on the pillars at this Lodge's entrance may now be seen on either side of the Albert Gate, on the Knightsbridge side of Hyde Park.

The early years of Queen Victoria's long reign were marked by a number of alarming incidents that took place in or near the Green Park. In June 1838, for instance, the intrepid Mrs Graham – a female balloonist who was in the habit of attracting attention to her ascents by releasing model parachutes weighted with live monkeys – was engaged by the Government to make an ascent from the Green Park as part of the Queen's Coronation festivities. This ended in a fatal accident when the balloon's grapnel tore one of the coping stones off the roof of a house in Marylebone Lane, resulting in the death of a passer-by. (At the inquest, Charles Green gave evidence against Mrs Graham, his principal rival, on the ground that the silk of her balloon was unfit for flights in stormy weather. Mrs Graham retorted by producing, as she alleged, a piece of the silk of Mr Green's balloon, but Green denied angrily that the material was his.)

Then, in June 1840, a lunatic named Edward Oxford deliberately fired two shots at the young Queen as she was driving past in her carriage with Prince Albert. (Oxford was tried at the Central Criminal Court and found 'Guilty but insane'. He was accordingly ordered to be 'confined during Her Majesty's Pleasure'.) A second attempt on the life of the Queen was made in May 1842, by another lunatic named Francis, and a third attempt, by a half-wit named Hamilton, shocked the nation in 1849. On the twenty-ninth day of June in the following year Sir Robert Peel was thrown from his horse at the upper end of Constitution Hill and very severely injured. He died at his house in Whitehall Gardens a few days later.

All through the latter decades of the nineteenth century, there was controversy over the question of who really controlled the Central Royal Parks of London – the Ranger, who had been appointed by the Crown, or the Chief Commissioner of Works, who was a Government official. Which of these two men, ran the Great Debate, was really responsible for submitting to the Sovereign, for her consideration, proposals for any changes that

might have to be made? By July 1850, Lord Seymour, the Chief
Commissioner of Works, was writing to explain to Lord John
Russell, the Prime Minister, that in former days

> . . . The Ranger [of St James's, the Green and Hyde Parks] had
> the complete management of those parks; he directed the
> planting, the improvement of the herbage, the making of roads,
> paths, seats, etc. . . .[4]

Those duties had been transferred to the Office of Works, Lord
Seymour pointed out, but nevertheless everything appertaining
to the custody of the Parks was still said to be under the Ranger:

> . . . The Keys of private Gates have been sometimes given by
> the Ranger and sometimes by the Chief Commissioner.
> The Ranger determines the hours for opening and closing the
> gates, but as the constables within the park are under this office,
> unless regulations are made in concert some inconveniences
> arise. For instance persons have complained of being locked in
> the Green Park for half the night. All workmen employed in
> the park are under this office, therefore though the Ranger has
> nominally the custody of the Park, it is obviously [sic] that he has
> responsibility without any power. . . .[5]

When Her Majesty the Queen's views were sought on the matter,
in 1865, she made it known firmly from Osborne:

> . . . The Queen never has wished in any way to curtail the
> proper duties and management of the Chief Commissioner in
> these parks. Where an expenditure of public money is to take
> place, it is absolutely necessary that a Minister should intervene,
> but the Queen would wish it to be remembered that these Parks
> are the property of the Crown and that whilst the greatest
> facility for the enjoyment of them for the purpose of exercise
> and recreation which is compatible with good order, the regula-
> tions with respect to them emanate from the Sovereign. Her
> Majesty considers the Ranger as Her own officer appointed by

Herself representing Her authority and has always regarded it as his duty to submit to Her any proposed alteration or new regulations.

The Chief Commissioner of Works as a Minister and Privy Councillor can always lay before Her Majesty, whilst submitting the details by which the measure would have to be carried out, his opinion and advice upon these subjects and thus fulfill the constitutional duties of his office, but it seems hardly necessary to quote instances in which the personal orders of the Sovereign have been adduced both for authorizing and preventing alterations.

It does not appear to Her Majesty that there is any necessity for any collision or confusion of authority . . .[6]

Her Majesty regarded the correspondence, after that, as closed, but in spite of the confidence with which she had dealt with the matter, relations between the warring parties remained strained.

In 1889, the roadway at Constitution Hill was thrown open to the public as a thoroughfare for carriages, but the highly prized privilege, granted to a limited number of specially favoured persons, of being allowed to pass in their vehicles through the gates of St James's and the Green Parks did not fall entirely into abeyance – the lists of those Officers of State and 'such other persons as the Sovereign was pleased to direct' who had previously held the coveted honour were re-scrutinized, and new ivory tickets were issued to those still thought worthy of the honour. This was done so that the right should be retained of closing the road if and whenever it might be thought necessary to do so.[7]

The Green Park emerged almost unscathed from the orgy of fountain-planting and statue-raising that affected the other Royal Parks of London during the later days of Queen Victoria's reign – it is, in fact, a pleasantly uncluttered place today, resembling a small expanse of well-wooded countryside rather than a public amenity in the heart of a great city. Almost the only touch of formality in the Park is provided by the 'Broad Walk' designed, like Sir Aston Webb's The Mall, to draw as much public attention as possible to the Queen Victoria Memorial in front of Buckingham

Palace. There are ornamental iron gates at each end of this stately avenue, those near the Memorial itself having been presented by the British Dominions.

The gates at the north end of the Broad Walk have a longer history. They were probably made by a craftsman named Warren about 1735, and they originally stood at Lord Heathfield's house at Turnham Green. They were acquired by the Duke of Devonshire in 1837 and put up at his Chiswick House, the Devonshire arms being substituted for those of Lord Egmont, who had occupied Heathfield House from 1765 to 1771. In 1898 the gates were removed from Chiswick and put up again outside the great mansion called Devonshire House which used to grace the north side of Piccadilly, near the present corner of Berkeley Street. In 1921, when Devonshire House was demolished, the gates were purchased out of the Queen Victoria Memorial Fund by the Commissioners of His Majesty's Works and re-erected on their present site.

It is hardly surprising that the Green Park, hemmed in closely as it is by busy roads, is less often visited by birds of rare species than the neighbouring Royal Parks, and there are few nests to be found in it (though great tits, it is said, sometimes build in the bases of the lamp standards near one of the walks).[8] The absence of a large pond or lake, too, tends to reduce the bird life of 'the romantic modulations of the green hills along the Piccadilly areas', to use the novelist Goerge Moore's description of the Park's slopes and valleys.

Chapter 4

Hyde Park – the early days

It is interesting to wonder how much money Hyde Park would fetch today, if it were divided into plots and sold for 'improvement'. The Park's value to the Londoner, just as it is, is incalculable – within two or three minutes' walk of the rush and roar of Oxford Street, and the din of Park Lane, anyone tired of this dynamic part of the metropolis can find gently sloping expanses of grass land that lead down into valleys and dells where cars and pavements can be temporarily forgotten. For this heavenly peace, not even one penny is charged, by the Crown or anyone else.

In Saxon times, the site of the future Hyde Park was little more than an overgrown wilderness. It was bounded on the north by the Via Trinobantina, one of the great Roman military roads, which followed the course of the present-day Oxford Street and the Bayswater (or Uxbridge) Road. Another Roman road lay to the east: the old 'Watling Street', which crossed the other at Tyburn (now 'Marble Arch') and sloped off to the south-east. On the west and south its limits were not so clearly defined.

Under the Saxon Kings, the Manor of Eia, of which the land forms a part, belonged to the Royal Master of the Horse. About the time of Domesday, the manor was subdivided into three smaller manors called, respectively, Neyte (Pimlico), Eabury (Chelsea) and Hyde. After the death of Geoffrey de Mandeville, the Manor of Hyde passed, by his will, to the Benedictine monks of Westminster. The monks, in exchange, were required to say masses for the repose of Geoffrey's soul.

(*Above*) The Promenade of Grace and Fashion in St James's Park, as seen in an eighteenth century print. (The old Buckingham House is shown in the background) (*Below*) The ill-fated Pagoda set up in St James's Park during the Peace Celebrations of 1814

(*Above*) Keep away! A photograph from the Royal Collection at Windsor shows the deterrent fencing that used to keep members of the public away from the great gun of Murad, son of Abdullah, on Horse Guards Parade (*Below*) The graceful suspension bridge, beloved by Victorian artists, that used to span the lake in St James's Park

(*Above*) The execution of Earl Ferrers at Tyburn on 5 May 1760. (From a print of time) (*Below*) Police waiting in Kensington Gardens on the occasion of the great Reform Meeting of 1867

The Memorial to Albert the Prince Consort in Kensington Gardens

The 'Peter Pan' statue in Kensington Gardens – with a small admirer

(*Above*) Mr Henry Hunt, Junr., drives his father's 'Matchless Blacking' van, drawn by four blood horses, over the frozen Serpentine on 17 January 1826. By this exploit the young man won from 'a Noble Lord of sporting celebrity' a wager of one hundred guineas (*Below*) The Ornithological Society's cottage in St James's Park

(*Above*) The 'Crystal Palace' put up for the Great Exhibition – as seen from the Serpentine in 1851 (*Below*) Queen Victoria at a Review of the Volunteer Troops in Hyde Park, 23 June 1860

(*Above*) Queen Mary at the Inspection of the Household Batallion in Hyde Park, 2 November 1916. King George V is in the middle distance, and Princess Victoria, Princess Mary and Queen Alexandra in the background (*Below*) Queen Mary admires a display of country dancing in Hyde Park, in June 1928

Before the monks could make any good use of the land they had acquired, they had to clear away much timber and thick under-growth, and make fields, which they cultivated in strict rotation. The higher fields, which were nearest to the old Via Trinobantina, were comparatively dry, and were usually known as 'folds'. The lower fields. to the south, were designated as 'drips', from their marshy nature, and from the difficulty the monks had in draining them. In the woods and thickets that the monks left uncleared there were deer ready to be hunted and wildfowl waiting to be shot, netted, trapped, or flown down, and these had a regrettable tendency to distract from their devotions the Abbots who, in Chaucer's words, 'loved venerie', or

> . . . To ryde on hawkings by the ryver
> With grey goshawke in hande . . .

At last the time came, in the sixteenth century, when King Henry VIII, who also loved venerie, 'drove the poor monks from their snuggeries and claimed the church lands'.[1] Henry's main object in appropriating to himself the Benedictines' Hyde estate seems to have been the extension of his hunting grounds to the north and west of London. As we have seen, he had already taken over the Leper Hospital grounds which afterwards became St James's Park. Marylebone Park (now the Regent's Park and sur-rounding districts) already formed part of the royal domains. So King Henry saw that by using the Manor of Hyde to connect these he would have a hunting ground which would extend without interruption all the way from his Palace at Westminster to the high slopes of Hampstead. The King's intentions were made clear by a proclamation concerning the preservation of the royal game, issued in July 1536, in which it was stated:

> As the King's most royal Majesty is desirous to have the games of hare, partridge, pheasant and heron preserved, in and about the honour of his palace of Westminster, for his own disport and pastime, no person, on the pain of imprisonment of their bodies, and further punishment at his Majesty's will and pleasure,

3

is to presume to hunt or hawk, from the palace of Westminster to St Giles'-in-the-Fields, and from thence to Islington, to Our Lady of the Oak, to Highgate, to Hornsey Park, and to Hampstead Heath.

At roughly the same time, the ground at Hyde seems to have been enclosed with a high fence or paling.

As soon as the Abbey manor was turned into a royal hunting ground, it followed, as a matter of course, that the King had to appoint a Ranger or Keeper. The first man to hold this post was named George Roper – related, perhaps, to the William Roper who married the daughter of Sir Thomas More. When he died, two Keepers were appointed, and a lodge was assigned to each. One lived in the south-east corner of the Park; the other, in a building afterwards known as 'The Banqueting House' or 'The Old Lodge', which remained in existence until the Serpentine was made, in the 1730s.

In the reigns of King Edward VI, Queen Elizabeth and King James I, then, Hyde Park was used almost exclusively as a hunting ground. In 1550, the boy King Edward hunted in it with the French ambassadors. In January 1578, John Casimir, Count Palatine of the Rhine and Duke of Bavaria, who paid a visit to Queen Elizabeth I, was lodged in Somerset House, made by Her Majesty a Knight of the Garter, and entertained by being taken hunting at Hampton Court and shooting in Hyde Park. Old chronicles relate that on the latter occasion the Count 'killed a barren doe with his piece from amongst three hundred other deer'. In 1592, new stands were put up in Marylebone and Hyde Park so that from there Queen Elizabeth and the Duke of Anjou, from France – a possible husband for Her Majesty – could watch the sport.

At the north-east corner of the Park – called 'Tyburn' because the bourn or stream of the Manor of Eia ran past there – criminals, from very early times, had been executed, being taken there for the purpose from the London prisons. Before 1571, the fatal rope would be tied to the branch of a tree, or a gallows would be put up as and when it was needed. From 1571 until 1759, the execution would be done under a raised timber triangle, the whole framework being known as 'Tyburn Tree'. (From this 'tree' a dozen victims could be suspended simultaneously.) After 1759, and for as long as that corner of the Park was used for public killings, a temporary gallows would be re-erected whenever one was needed – which was frequently.

During the reigns of the Tudors and of the early Stuart Kings, Hyde Park contained a number of ponds or pools – as many as ten or twelve, according to some authorities – which communicated with each other and were fed by a small stream (the 'West Bourn') which rose on the western slopes of Hampstead and passed through Kilburn and Bayswater before intersecting Hyde Park, which it left at Knightsbridge on its way to join the Thames at Millbank and Chelsea. These pools were the favourite haunts of heron (which King Henry VIII included among the game to be preserved in the neighbourhood of his palace) and other waterfowl, but they were also used to supply the western parts of London with water until a complaint was made by the Keepers of the Park in the time of King Charles I that there was insufficient water for the deer. This was stoutly denied by the citizens of London, who petitioned the King to allow the supply to continue. King Charles rejected their petition, however – a step which greatly increased his already marked unpopularity.

It was King Charles, though, who first admitted the citizens of London freely to Hyde Park, and it was also in his reign that the 'Ring' was laid out. This was a circular, or semicircular, carriage track and racecourse, two or three hundred paces in diameter, and bounded by posts, with rails about three feet from the ground. It was situated on level ground just to the north of the West Bourn pools – approximately where the present Serpentine boathouse stands – and fashionable people drove, or were driven, out there to see and be seen. The King was a doomed man, however, and after he gave up his attempts to control the Parliamentarians and left London, Hyde Park was used principally as an exercise ground for the 'Trained Bands', as the earnest regular forces of the City were called.

When the Civil War was over, and the Parliamentarians had won, Hyde Park became a mournful place, enjoyment being temporarily out of fashion. But worse was to come: on 1 December 1652, the Commonwealth Government, having decided to sell off most of the Crown lands, passed a special resolution: 'That Hyde Park be sold for ready money'. The Park, at that time, extended over about 621 acres, and the sale of the land, in three lots, realized £17,068 2s. 8d., the purchasers being named Richard Wilson, John Lacey and Anthony Deane. John Evelyn, in his *Diary*, recorded on 11 April 1653: 'I went to take the aire in Hyde Park, when every coach was made to pay a shilling, and horse sixpence, by the sordid fellow who purchased it of the State, as they were called.' Ironically, it was in the Park of the same 'sordid fellow' that Oliver Cromwell suffered, in Thomas Carlyle's words, a 'humiliating accident':

> ... The horses, beautiful animals, tasting of the whip, became unruly; galloped would not be checked, but took to plunging; plunged the postillion down; plunged or shook his Highness down, dragging him by the foot for some time so that 'a pistol went off in his pocket', to the amazement of men. Whereupon? Whereupon – his Highness got up again, little the worse; was let blood; and went about his affairs much as usual. ...

As soon as King Charles II returned to London at the Restoration, the whole of Hyde Park was taken back into royal ownership, the sales that had been made of parts of it to private individuals being treated as null and void. Almost immediately, the ground was once more opened to the public without charge, but the royal rights were entirely and most firmly reserved. When, for instance, Mr James Hamilton, one of the King's Grooms of the Bedchamber, who had been appointed Ranger of the Park, wished to make an orchard there, he was required to deliver to the Lord Steward or to the Treasurer of the Household

> one half of the pippins or red streaks, either in apples or cider, as his Majesty may prefer, the produce of the trees he is authorised to plant in fifty-five acres of the north-west corner of the Park, on the Uxbridge Road.[2]

Being, though, generally in the King's favour, Hamilton received various additional grants, including the triangular piece of ground between his lodge, which stood where Apsley House stands now, and the present Park Lane. Hamilton started to build houses on this land – hence the name it still bears: 'Hamilton Place'.

Early in June 1660, only a few days after the Restoration of the Monarchy, Samuel Pepys heard from friends that the two Royal Dukes of York and Gloucester 'do haunt the Park much', but he had not yet seen them there with his own eyes. On the 9th of the month, however, the Clerk of the Admiralty had the happiness of seeing His Majesty there face to face – a sight which he recorded as 'gallantly great'. John Evelyn, in his *Diary*, also described the gay appearance which the Park presented after the Restoration, especially on May Day. On 1 May 1661, Evelyn went to the Park to take the air, and 'there was his Majesty and an innumerable appearance of gallants and rich coaches, being now a time of universal festivity and joy'.

By 1663, Hyde Park had become so popular a meeting place on each May Day that it met with Mr Pepys's disapproval:

> . . . Here I saw nothing good – neither the King, nor my Lady Castlemaine nor any great ladies or beauties being there, there being a great deal more pleasure on an ordinary day; or else those good faces that were there being choked up with many bad ones, there being people of all sorts in coaches there to some thousands . . .

There had been foot races round the Ring, and other attractions, but the only part of the day's festivities for which Mr Pepys could raise any enthusiasm was 'the King's riders showing tricks'. During the next few years, some impressive displays of horsemanship were given in Hyde Park.

By 1664, Colonel Hamilton, the enterprising Ranger, had advised King Charles that he should enclose Hyde Park with a brick wall and re-stock it with deer. (In that year, the Surveyor General observed in a report that the King was 'very earnest' with him for walling Hyde Park, 'as well for the honour of his palace and great city as for his own disport and recreation'.) Within ten years, a good part of the Park had been so well fenced in that it could be safely replenished with game.

The great outbreak of plague that hit London in 1665 brought to a temporary halt the developments that were being made in the Park for everyone's pleasure, for in that fatal and fearful summer a regiment of the Guards was quartered there, under the command of General Monck, Duke of Albemarle, who had resolutely refused to move right away from the stricken city. During the August and September of that terrible year, a large number of the poorer inhabitants of London who could not escape into the country moved into the Park with their household goods and set up tents, forming a kind of camp. Their attempts to isolate themselves were vain. An old ballad or broadside preserved in a *Volume of London Songs* in the British Library describes their agony:

> . . . At length the plague amongst us 'gan to spread,
> When every morning some were found stark dead.
> Down to another field the sick were ta'en,
> But few went down that e'er came up again.
> But that which most of all did grieve my soul,
> To see poor Christians dragg'd into a hole . . .

At the end of that October the poor survivors encamped in the Park heard that the virulence of the Plague in the City was lessening, and they decided to return to their homes.

The lively company of the rich and fashionable soon reappeared in Hyde Park after the tribulations of the Plague and the Fire of London. On St George's Day in the year following the latter disaster the King and the Knights of the Garter had the 'ridiculous humour'[3] of keeping on their robes all the day, and in the evening made their appearance in the Ring, still wearing their insignia – cloaks, coronets and all. The Duke of Monmouth and another noble lord indulged in an action more freakish even than that, for dressed in their fullest apparel they drove about the Park in a hackney coach.

By 1668, the Ring was being used, almost exclusively, by the superlatively well turned out, the *beau monde* being carried in magnificent equipages mostly drawn by six grey Flanders mares, and having the owner's coat of arms emblazoned conspicuously on the panels, and, according to Thomas Pennant, 'exchanging, as they passed, smiles and nods, compliments or smart repartees'. Sometimes, the Ring was called 'the Tour', and in this sense Pepys uses the words in his diary entry for 31 March 1668:

> . . . Took up my wife and Deb, and to the Park, where being in a hackney [hired carriage] and they undressed, was ashamed to go into the Tour, but went round the Park, and so with pleasure home. . . .

Just over two months later (3 June 1668), Mr Pepys had another reason for feeling a little embarrassed:

> . . . To the Park, where much company and many fine ladies; and in so handsome a hackney I was that I believe Sir W. Coventry and others who looked on me did take me to be in one of my own, which I was a little troubled for; so to the Lodge and drank a cup of new milk and so home. . . .

The Lodge referred to by Mr Pepys stood in the middle of the Park and was used for the sale of refreshments. It was sometimes called 'Price's Lodge', from the name of Gervase Price, the chief Under Keeper.

During the reigns of King Charles I and King James II the mania for duelling was at its height – with gentlemen wearing their swords in everyday life as part of their costume the custom was unlikely to pass away – and many bloody and fatal encounters took place in Hyde Park. The duel in which the Duke of Grafton killed Mr Stanley, brother of the Earl of Derby, 'upon an almost insufferable provocation', was recorded with the greatest disapproval by John Evelyn in 1686. 'It is to be hoped', he added, 'that his Majesty will at last severely remedy this unchristian custom.' But the 'unchristian custom' went on, and on 15 November 1712 one of the most sensational duels of all was fought in the Park, between Lord Mohun, a notorious profligate who had frequently been engaged in duels and midnight brawls and had twice been tried for murder, and the Duke of Hamilton. Sir Bernard Burke, in his *Anecdotes of the Aristocracy*, gave this graphic and probably reasonably accurate account of the affair:

... This sanguinary duel, originating in a political intrigue, was fought early one morning at the Ring, in Hyde Park, then the usual spot for settling these so-called affairs of honour. The duke and his second, Colonel Hamilton of the Foot Guards, were the first in the field. Soon after, came Lord Mohun and his second, Major Macartney. No sooner had the second party reached the ground, than the duke, unable to conceal his feelings, turned sharply round on Major Macartney and remarked 'I am well assured, sir, that all this is by your contrivance, and therefore you shall have your share in the dance; my friend here, Colonel Hamilton, will entertain you.' 'I wish no better partner,' replied Macartney; 'the colonel may command me.' Little more passed between them, and the fight began with infinite fury, each being too intent upon doing mischief to his opponent to look sufficiently to his own defence. Macartney had the misfortune to be speedily disarmed, though not before he had wounded his adversary in the right leg; but luckily for him, at this very moment the attention of the colonel was drawn off to the condition of his friend, and, flinging both the swords to a distance, he hastened to his assistance. The combat, indeed, had been carried on between the principals with uncommon ferocity, the loud and angry clashing of the steel having called to the spot the few stragglers that were abroad in the Park at so early an hour. In a very short time the duke was wounded in both legs, which he returned with interest, piercing his antagonist in the groin, through the arm, and in sundry other parts of his body. The blood flowed freely on both sides, their swords, their faces, and even the grass about them being reddened with it; but rage lent them that almost supernatural strength which is so often seen in madmen. If they had thought little enough before of attending to their self-defence, they now seemed to have abandoned the idea altogether. Each at the same time made a desperate lunge at the other; the duke's weapon passed right through his adversary, up to the very hilt; and the latter, shortening his sword, plunged it into the upper part of the duke's left breast, the wound running down into his body, when his grace fell upon him. It was now that the colonel came to his aid, and raised him in his arms. Such a blow, it is probable, would have been fatal of itself; but Macartney had by this time picked up one of the swords, and stabbing the duke to the heart over Hamilton's shoulder, immediately fled, and made his escape to Holland. . . .

When the Duke fell to the ground, the spectators of this bloody affray, who do not appear to have interfered before in any way, then came forward to carry him to the Cake House, as the old Lodge was by that time called, so that a surgeon might be called and his wounds be attended to. Before they could raise him from the grass, however, the injured Duke expired. Lord Mohun also died of his wounds on the spot. Mohun's widow does not seem to have been particularly surprised or saddened when her husband's corpse was taken to their home. She is said to have rebuked the men who laid the body on the best bed for ruining with blood her fine and expensive sheets.

In 1724, one of the greatest crowds ever to be seen at Tyburn assembled to watch the execution of Jack Sheppard, the young thief who had made himself famous by his daring escapes from prison, culminating in his greatest escape of all – from the condemned cell in Newgate, after he had been loaded with heavy iron weights, handcuffed, and attached by strong chains to staples fixed in the floor. Arrangements had been made by his confederates for Sheppard to be cut down from the gallows before he was properly dead, so that he could be operated on, and if possible revived, by a surgeon who had been specially engaged for the purpose and who was waiting in the immediate vicinity. The revivalists' plans miscarried, however, for the members of the crowd, thinking that Sheppard's apparently lifeless body was being taken off to the Surgeons' Hall to be anatomized and dissected, started to fight those who were carrying it away and each other for the body, so that eventually it was literally pulled to pieces. The execution of the Thief-Taker General, Jonathan Wild, at Tyburn only a few months later was just as dramatic, for the mob of spectators did not show the wretched man in his last moments any sign of pity or sympathy. Instead, they reviled and cursed him on his way to the fatal tree and pelted him with stones and dirt continuously, until he was 'turned off'.

By 1730, the Ring in Hyde Park had ceased to be a popular meeting place for the wealthy and stylish, since the aimless circuits that the carriages made in the old arena had eventually proved to be boring – 'When they [the coaches] have turned for some time round one way, they face about and turn t'other', complained the French traveller and author Francis Maximilian Misson, in his *Memories and Observations in his Travels through England*, published in an English translation in 1719 – and the affected mannerisms of the drivers and driven were no longer much to anyone's taste. In the Mall one at least met with a little conversation now and then, pointed out a Young Lady of Quality in one of Sir George Etheredge's plays, and the audience who heard her must have agreed. In December 1736 the *London Spy* announced that, 'The Ring' . . . being quite disused by the quality and gentry, we hear that the ground will be taken in for enlarging the Kensington Gardens'.

But Hyde Park was not to lose completely its centre of equestrianism, for while his wife had been planning a new Serpentine Lake as one of her personal improvements to Kensington Gardens, King George II had been planning a new carriage road or 'Route du Roi' – the 'Rotten Row' of the future. The Row was mentioned for the first time in *The London Spy Revisited* in 1737:

The King's Road . . . is almost gravelled and finished, and lamp-posts are fixed up. It will soon be levelled, and the old road [the present South Carriage Drive] levelled with the Park.

When the King's road was supposedly complete, it was anything but safe, the surface being notable for its big pits and holes. The King's four daughters were in a chaise that crashed at one particularly dangerous spot. (The Princesses were taken quickly to Kensington Palace, where their Gentlewomen bathed their hurts with Eau de Carne, Eau de Luce and Hungary Water.) Very shortly after, the Duke of Grafton's carriage was upset at exactly the same place, and His Grace's collar-bone was dislocated. The track could not be considered even reasonably safe until after all the boulders had been dug out of it, the pot-holes filled and the mud-flats drained. By that time, however – and it was quite late in the eighteenth century before all this had been done – a new surface of fine gravel mixed with tan had been laid over the road to make its surface more suitable for the horses and, incidentally, to soften the fall of anyone – either novice or dare-devil – who might come prematurely to grief.

During the whole of the eighteenth century, Hyde Park was quite rural, having the same kind of character, in fact, that parts of Richmond Park have to this day. In the Park's lonelier groves and thickets there lurked, as was only to be expected, numerous thieves and footpads. Horace Walpole, son of the King's First Minister, suffered in 1749 at the hands of the notorious highwayman Maclean. Maclean had once kept a grocer's shop in the West End, but on losing his only child, of whom he was very fond, he had sold his business and had 'taken to the road'. Walpole had a narrow escape:

> . . . One night, in the beginning of November, as I was returning from Holland House by moonlight, about ten o'clock, I was attacked by two highwaymen in Hyde Park, and the pistol of one of them going off accidentally, razed the skin under my eye, left some marks of shot on my face, and stunned me. The ball went through the top of the chariot, and if I had sat an inch nearer to the left side, must have gone through my head. . . .

Maclean was hanged at Tyburn in the following year, mourned more or less secretly – since he was an unusually handsome man – by many a lady of fashion.

Laurence Shirley, Fourth Earl Ferrers, born in 1720, was one of the most superlatively turned out men ever to be hanged at Tyburn. Parted from his wife in 1758 – she obtained an Act of Separation from him, on the grounds of cruelty – the Earl was to see the Ferrers estates, in the same year, being vested in Trustees, a certain John Johnson, the Earl's steward, being appointed receiver of the rents. Up to that time, the Earl had been on more or less friendly terms with Johnson, but relations between the two then cooled rapidly.

At last, on 18 January 1760, after Ferrers had failed to turn Johnson out of a farm of which the Ferrers Trustees had granted him a lease, the Earl deliberately shot the steward, with a pistol, at his house at Staunton Harold in Leicestershire. Johnson died of his wounds next day, and the Earl was arrested. He was imprisoned in the Tower of London and tried before his peers in Westminster Hall on 16 April 1760 and the following days. Ferrers pleaded Not Guilty and claimed that he suffered from occasional bouts of insanity. Though he called many witnesses, including two of his brothers, he failed completely to prove that he was not responsible for his actions and he was unanimously found Guilty of murder and sentenced to death.

On 5 May 1760, then, the Earl, dressed in a suit of light clothes magnificently embroidered with silver, was driven from the Tower in his own landau drawn by six horses to the gallows at Tyburn, where he was hanged in the presence of another enormous crowd. He is said (in *All The Year Round*, New Series, VII) to have been the first person in England to have been executed by the relatively humane 'new drop' introduced to replace the barbarous cart, ladder and gibbet method by which the victim was horribly strangled to death, but there appears to be little foundation for the often-repeated statement that he was hanged with a silken cord instead of a hempen rope.

Sooner or later, inevitably, as increasing numbers of well-to-do people moved into the houses that were springing up round Hyde Park, the new residents of the area came to resent the noisy crowds of excited and usually drunken Londoners who gathered at Tyburn to enjoy the hangings that were held there. So another place had

to be found for London's public executions, and before the eighteenth century ended they were being carried out in the street
outside Newgate Jail. Hyde Park, for some time after that, was the
scene of fewer disorders, and as the 'Tyburn Gate' was renamed
the 'Cumberland Gate' in honour of the hero of the Battle of
Culloden the old associations of the place soon began to fade.

Deer were hunted by Royalty in Hyde Park for the last time in
1768, when King Christian VII of Denmark joined his brother-
in-law King George III for a final chase, only a single buck being
allowed to be shot. By this time, though, it was hardly possible to
think of 'Hyde Park' without taking into account the gardens and
grounds of the Royal Palace of Kensington, which lay immediately
to the west.

Chapter 5

Kensington Gardens

More lines of poetry have been written about Kensington Gardens than about any other Royal Park in or near London. Usually, the poet is content, like Matthew Arnold, to savour the contrast between the beautiful peace of the scene and 'the huge world which roars hard by', but Arthur Symons, writing in 1892, was a little more outspoken with his

> Love and the Spring and Kensington Gardens,
> Hey for the heart's delight!

Prose writers, too, have covered many hundreds of pages with material inspired more or less directly by the Gardens. Sir James Barrie, possibly the most devoted Gardens-lover of them all, chose the Gardens as a principal playground of his most famous creation Peter Pan. The Gardens, Barrie saw, made an ideal place for West London children and their nannies to take the air:

> ... The Gardens are bounded on one side by a never-ending line of omnibuses, over which your nurse has such authority that if she holds up her finger to any one of them it stops immediately. She then crosses with you in safety to the other side...[1]

Just outside the gate of the Gardens, Barrie recorded, there sat an old lady selling balloons.

The life of the lovely Gardens may be said to have begun when King William III, newly arrived from Holland, began to look for a house in which he could live at a convenient distance from the mists of riverside Westminster and from the crowds that thronged the Palace of Whitehall. Being asthmatic, and not caring to take his dinner in public before the inquisitive eyes of his curious new subjects, the King wanted a place where the air would be better and where his quarters and the Queen's would be more private. So he inspected the little country village of Kensington, between two and three miles to the west.

He is said to have looked first at Holland House, but, deciding that that mansion was too rambling for his liking, and too draughty, he turned it down.

Next, he looked at Nottingham House, which stood where Kensington Palace stands now. This small mansion had been bought by Sir Heneage Finch from his younger brother when Finch – called by his contemporaries 'Old Dismal' – had been Member of Parliament for Oxford University. Then, in 1681, Finch had been made Lord Chancellor and Earl of Nottingham, upon which he had partly reconstructed his home and had re-named it 'Nottingham House'. John Evelyn, in his *Diary*, referred disparagingly to the property as 'a patched up building with gardens'. The King looked over the patched-up building, liked its position and gardens, and bought it, with 26 acres of land, for £18,000.

King William then commissioned Sir Christopher Wren to rebuild and enlarge the country seat he had just acquired, and the great architect drew up his plans with, as we can see today, consummate success. To make travelling between Kensington and Westminster a little easier for everyone, the King, no doubt prompted by Sir Christopher, had a high road cut through the well-timbered land to the east of his gardens. This road, the 'South Carriage Drive', which led through Hyde Park and then continued past the Upper St James's Park to St James's Palace, was lit during the winter months by three hundred lanterns, and was one of the first illuminated highways of its kind. (During the summer months the lanterns were taken down and stored in the Kensington Palace woodyard until such time as they would be needed for 'their Majesties' further service'.)

Fortunately for us, Queen Mary II was fond of gardens – gardens in the formal Dutch style, that is – and the immediate surroundings of the Palace that Sir Christopher Wren produced for her husband were at once tidily and permanently laid out and scrupulously maintained. But the time came all too soon when the virtuous and devoted Queen felt ill for two or three days – she vomited more than once, and suffered from other distressing discomforts. Then more serious symptoms appeared. Sir Thomas Millington, Physician in Ordinary to the King, thought that the Queen might have caught the measles. John Radcliffe, a man of humble birth who was by that time one of the most skilled diagnosticians in London, thought otherwise. Observing that the red spots on his royal patient's brow were turning into pustules, he pronounced the terrifying verdict: 'It could be smallpox . . .'

The Queen received the news that she was in the gravest danger with true greatness of soul, according to Lord Macaulay. Immediately, she sent away from Kensington Palace every lady of her household and every servant who had not previously had the smallpox. Then she shut herself away in her room and went through her papers, destroying all the documents that she did not wish to leave behind, and calmly awaiting her fate.

After his wife's death, King William spent less and less time at Kensington and more and more at the remoter Hampton Court, where he could not easily be bothered by politicians and other undesirable people. When, however, the new Queen, Mary's sister Anne, came to the throne, helped by the royal gardener Henry Wise, she extended the gardens considerably, converting some of the parkland of the old Nottingham House in the process. Queen Anne spent her Easter recess each year at Kensington, and by the end of her reign the pleasure grounds of the Palace had several features that are familiar to visitors today – the red brick Orangery, for example (designed not by Wren, as was supposed until recently, but by Sir John Vanbrugh, possibly with the assistance of Nicholas Hawksmoor). The Queen used this charming building – one of the finest baroque buildings in the whole of

England, it has been said – for her summer supper parties, and for taking tea; she even tried to grow oranges in it, but with very little success.

Recently, the Orangery has been most skilfully restored and refurnished, and, to replace some unsightly concrete, has been given a stone floor not unlike the one there originally. Her Majesty Queen Elizabeth II has helped this refurbishment by providing a number of handsome and historic vases and statues from her gardens at Windsor – among other works, she has sent four rustic deities sculpted during the reign of the first Elizabeth by Francavilla, pupil of Giovanni da Bologna, who after Michelangelo's death was the most celebrated sculptor in Florence. These had been bought from the Abate di Bracci for Frederick, Prince of Wales, and were taken to Windsor by King William IV when he was rebuilding the Castle.[2]

Not far from this wholly delightful Orangery – in fact, just across a small green, shaded by clipped hawthorn, holly and other trees – is the celebrated Sunken Garden which recalls the original Sunken Garden planned here for Queen Anne. The modern garden is nearly surrounded by a walk enclosed by pleached lime trees – in the Summer it resembles a cool green tunnel – and is graced by a charming rectangular pond. Joseph Addison, writing in the *Spectator*, approved of the work done in the upper garden of the Palace, which was at first, he said, nothing but a gravel pit. It must have been a fine genius for gardening, he went on, that could have thought of forming such an unsightly hollow into so beautiful an area, 'and to have hit the eye with so uncommon and agreeable a scene as that which it is now wrought into'.

Queen Anne's improvements to the gardens at Kensington, notable as they were, were soon radically affected by the changes made in and around the Palace about 1723 for King George I by William Kent. Kent, a Yorkshireman, had been 'discovered', when he was studying in Rome, by Richard Boyle, the Third Earl of Burlington, who was making the Grand Tour. When he returned to England filled with enthusiasm for Italy and for the classical architecture and sculpture he had seen there, the Earl had brought

Kent back with him to this country as a kind of domesticated Arbiter of Good Taste. Not everyone, however, approved of the alterations that Kent made at Kensington – Augustus Hare, for one, comments frequently in his *Journals* on the features of the place that were 'much spoilt by Kent'.

It was King George II's wife, Queen Caroline of Ansbach, who was principally responsible for the grandeurs of Kensington Gardens as we know them today. Queen Caroline was the daughter of John Frederick, Margrave of Brandenburg-Ansbach. She was an ambitious and bold landscape gardener who could think on the same grand scale as King Charles II. Like King Charles, Caroline ran into certain difficulties over money, but she was more fortunate than her predecessor in that she was aided and abetted in her schemes by Sir Robert Walpole, who happened to be in charge of the Treasury. The King was led to believe that the Queen was paying out of her own pocket for the work she was having done, and, like many affectionate husbands before and since, he adopted a 'let the dear thing get on with it' attitude. It was only after her death that the King discovered that his wife had, in fact, spent over £20,000 of the royal finances – several millions, in today's terms – on her projects. By that time, fortunately, it was much too late for the work to be undone.

The Queen's improvements and embellishments were in full fling by about 1728, when, after some lengthy discussions with Charles Bridgman, Thomas Wise's successor as royal gardener, she decided to plant trees in a series of magnificent avenues in the parkland outside the gardens of the palace at Kensington. These avenues were to be wide and straight, she decreed, like the avenues of lime trees outside the east front of the palace at Hampton Court which had been planted sixty years before by King Charles II, and which would by that time have grown just high enough for their future magnificence to be easily appreciated by anyone with a good eye for landscape, and for gardens. As the ground between the trees would be interrupted only where necessary by a ha-ha, one of the newly fashionable sunken fences, they would open up, she hoped, some incomparable vistas from the gardens into Hyde Park. She consulted the Surveyor General of Woods and Forests,

Charles Withers; he approved, and so one of the greatest of all royal planting operations began.

Most splendid of all Queen Caroline's avenues was, until recently, the 50-foot wide Broad Walk which led one in a southerly direction from the Black Lion Gate in the Bayswater Road, past Kensington Palace, and then down towards the stone at which, in the days when the trees were planted, coaches using the Kensington Road stopped on their way to Hammersmith. (The Broad Walk now meets the Kensington Road near the entrance to the thoroughfare known as 'Palace Gate'.) Barrie, assembling his *Peter Pan in Kensington Gardens*, used the Broad Walk ('such a fascinating slide-down kind of place') as the setting for one of his most daunting *contes terribles*:

> . . . There is no more awful story of the Gardens than this of Marmaduke Perry, who had been Mary-Annish three days in succession, and was sentenced to appear in the Broad Walk dressed in his sister's clothes. He hid in the little wooden house, and refused to emerge until they brought him knickerbockers with pockets. . . .

(To be 'Mary-Annish', Barrie explained, was to behave like a girl, whimpering because Nurse wouldn't carry one, or simpering with one's thumb in one's mouth. It was, he added censoriously, a hateful quality.) Sadly in 1953 the noble and ancient elms of Queen Caroline's Broad Walk – planted, it has been said, according to the disposition of the Guards at the Battle of Blenheim – were judged to be dangerous, and, to the sound of a storm of protest from the public, they were cut down. The limes and Norway maples planted in their place have already grown to significant heights.

Outside Kensington Palace, and near the Broad Walk, Queen Caroline and her advisers decided to have a more or less circular basin excavated and kept filled with water. (Again, the Queen was probably stimulated to do this by the pleasure she derived from the round basin that Sir Christopher Wren had devised to punctuate the greatest of all British tree-lined avenues – the Grand Approach he had designed for King William III in Bushey Park, to lead from the Teddington Gate to King William's magnificently re-appointed Hampton Court Palace.) The basin at Kensington is known usually now as 'The Round Pond', and it is still one of the most attractive features of Kensington Gardens – literally attractive, for it draws like a magnet scores of those who have model boats and yachts to sail, especially on summer Sunday mornings. Sir James Barrie naturally viewed these visitors and their offspring with his usual quizzical interest:

> ... There are men who sail boats on the Round Pond, such big boats that they bring them in barrows, and sometimes in perambulators, and then the baby has to walk. The bow-legged children in the Gardens are those who had to walk too soon because their father needed the perambulator. . . .[3]

For a spot a little farther from Kensington Palace than the Round Pond, Queen Caroline got her protégé William Kent to design a small and charming classical temple. In later years, this building fell out of favour, and was used as a toolshed. In Victorian times, it was converted into a keeper's cottage by the building of a house, in haphazard fashion, around and over it. Recently, experts employed by the Department of the Environment have lovingly unpicked Kent's temple from its rambling and unattractive extensions, they have restored its overburdened structure and stonework, and they have reconstructed the roof so that it corresponds once more to Kent's designs. (The interior mouldings were reconstructed according to the faint traces of the originals that survived, like ghosts, beneath the nineteenth-century plaster and layers of paper.) So, the building has been most successfully revived as an elegant and historic piece of garden architecture, and visitors to the Gardens are welcome to shelter in it, when shelter is necessary. Already, *graffiti* are appearing on its walls.[4]

The most ambitious and imaginative of all Queen Caroline's schemes at Kensington was, without any doubt, the creation of the splendid lake usually known as 'The Long Water' (where it adjoins Kensington Gardens) and 'The Serpentine' (where it is an important feature of Hyde Park). If a great sheet of ornamental water were to be made for her massively extended grounds, the Queen saw that she would have to enlarge and join up the various pools through which the little West Bourn flowed. Moreover, she would have to have this done in an entirely 'natural' and adventurous way. For several decades, most of the large ornamental water surfaces introduced artificially into English gardens had been perfectly straight and square, according to the traditional Dutch system, but now these long canals were being denounced as old-fashioned by William Kent, the reigning authority on Good Taste, who stated categorically that Nature abhors a straight line, and who favoured the alternative of gently curving lakes like the one he had introduced into the gardens of Lord Burlington's Italianate villa at Chiswick. So, Queen Caroline's new lake, which was to be approached partly from Hyde Park and partly from Kensington Gardens, had to have a slight bend at its centre – just sufficient to justify its reptilian name and to earn the approval of Kent and his increasingly numerous followers.

Although there is now nothing much to show for her proposals, except a model preserved at Hampton Court, the Queen seems to have planned the building of a new royal palace in Hyde Park, somewhere beside or overlooking her new lake. The *London Journal* of 26 September 1730 reported her intentions:

> . . . Next Monday they begin the Serpentine River and Royal Mansion in Hyde Park. Mr Ripley is to build the house, and Mr Jepherson to make the river, under the direction of Charles Withers Esq. . . . .

Before the lake could be made, the Old Lodge at the centre of Hyde Park had to be sacrificed, and the Directors of the Chelsea Waterworks Company had to be given £2,500 to induce them to give up their right to carry waterpipes through the Park. (The King, believing somewhat ingenuously that all this was being paid out of the Queen's own money, declined to look at her plans, saying in his good-humoured way that he did not care how much of her own revenue she might be willing to fling away.) Two hundred men had to be employed on the work, and the total cost of the whole project was more than £6,000.

In the course of constructing the lake, the two hundred men uncovered a number of the great timber trunks which the monks, in medieval times, had driven into the swampy ground in their attempts to provide proper embankments for their fishponds. (The trunks now lie deep beneath the waters of our present Serpentine.) Across the valley of the little West Bourn the men then threw a strong dike or dam. With the soil that the men dug out of the new lake's intended bed a great mound was raised near the south-east corner of Kensington Gardens. On the apex of this mound – called, rather grandly, 'The Mount' – the Queen had a revolving shelter placed. The shelter, shaped like a temple, contained a seat, the occupant or occupants of which would be protected, it was hoped, from the prevailing wind. The political commentators of the day were quick to make fun of the Queen's ingenious little summerhouse. The seat, they said, was the King's chair, and it would be turned due south 'by a certain corpulent man who seemed to be his chief minister' so that his Majesty's attention would be drawn to the corpulent man's own villa in Chelsea, although the King himself desired to look 'to the left'.

When all the necessary digging was finished, the dike that held back the waters of the West Bourn was opened, and within a few days the new lake was sufficiently filled with water for two yachts to be launched, for the diversion of the Royal Family. The King's children were by no means the only people to be delighted by Queen Caroline's improvements at Kensington; her work attracted international attention. The Doge of Genoa sent the Queen, as a present, a large number of tortoises for her refurbished Park. With these, Queen Caroline introduced a number of red squirrels. The tortoises soon disappeared, but the squirrels continued to populate the groves and thickets until early in the present century, when a mysterious epidemic broke out among them, and exterminated all but a few.

Not so welcome was a flock of geese which, in the 1730s, migrated from St James's Park to Kensington and there started to scratch and peck holes in the gravel paths. Lord Essex, who was Keeper to the Royal House at the time, ordered the offending geese to be shot. (In 1739, Lord Essex was appointed to a Captaincy in the Yeoman of the Guard, but this may have been for other reasons.)

During the rest of the reign of King George II and in fact for the remainder of the eighteenth century the transformed Gardens at Kensington were opened to the public at week-ends, when the King and the Court were away at Richmond or elsewhere. Formal dress was required, however, and all soldiers, sailors and liveried servants were excluded, as well as those whose appearance the gatekeepers did not consider to be sufficiently respectable. This favouritism, as it was called, caused much bad feeling among those who were shut out from the Gardens, though those who were allowed in warmly appreciated their freedom from the company of the less genteel and the less frequently washed. Soon it became a pastime of the excluded servants to band together outside the Gardens gate to mock in the most embarrassing fashion those who were permitted to pass the hallowed threshold. An irate protest at this disgraceful practice was sent to the *Morning Herald* by a gentleman who signed himself, merely, 'Reformer':

... Your paper being circulated in the most polite part of the town, I beg leave, through the channel thereof, to recommend to the ladies and gentlemen who visit Kensington Gardens on Sunday, to give notice to their servants that they behave themselves decently. Yesterday it was hardly possible to get near the gate leading into the Gardens for the crowd of servants who gathered round there, and who insulted every person not particularly known to them, going in, or coming out of the Gardens. Unfortunately for my servant, I found him one of those gentry, and have already discharged him, and if the like is practised on any future day when I am present, I shall take the liberty of giving the discipline of the horse whip to such as I may catch pursuing the like line of conduct, and that I may not be under the necessity of doing so, beg you will give them notice thereof by inserting this. ...

Attractive as the Gardens at Kensington were to those who enjoyed their relative exclusiveness, their remoteness from London and the dangers of the countryside that lay between made any expedition to them something of an adventure. (King George II himself was once robbed at Kensington by a highwayman who climbed over the wall and 'with a manner of much deference' deprived the King of his purse, his watch and his buckles.) At the end of each day, when the Gardens were open, a bell would be sounded 'to muster people returning to town'. Then as soon as a party numerous enough to provide mutual protection had formed, they would start the long hazardous journey through the Gardens and woodland either to the Tyburn end of the Uxbridge Road or to the relative safety of the paving stones at Piccadilly. In the reign of King George III, scarcely a single week would pass without at least one notable robbery being heard of, the victims being almost invariably from among those who failed to take this elementary precaution.

An important chapter in the story of Kensington Gardens may be said to have been ending in October 1760 when, after the conquest of Montreal and the virtual annihilation of the hostile fleet, the French domination of Canada was finally brought to an end. Wildly elated by the brilliant military and naval triumphs of which they had been hearing, a great crowd flocked out to see King George II, from a grand pavilion or tent that had been put up under the Kensington Gardens wall, review Colonel Burgoyne's Regiment of Light Horse. As soon as this display was over, some military appliances of an entirely new kind were set on fire, occasioning 'such a smoke as to render all persons within a considerable distance entirely invisible, and thereby the better enabled in time of action to secure a retreat'. It was the last public appearance of the King who had unwittingly paid so much towards the development of those Gardens. Less than forty-eight hours later, between 7 and 8 o'clock in the morning, as he was preparing to take a walk in the Gardens, the King died suddenly, from a rupture of the right ventricle of the heart.

From that day on, Kensington Palace ceased to be a principal royal residence. When the Court was no longer centred there, the grounds were opened more frequently in the Spring and Summer, and by the time of King William IV they were opened all

the year round 'to all respectably dressed persons' from sunrise
to sunset. Gradually, as the Gardens of the Palace were made
more generally available, they tended to merge, in the minds of
the public, with Hyde Park. The later histories of these neighbouring estates must therefore be treated as if they were one.

Chapter 6

Hyde Park and Kensington Gardens – their further history

Hyde Park continued to be a favourite duelling ground during the latter part of the eighteenth century. Among the more humanely conducted encounters that took place there was the duel, in 1762, between John Wilkes, the notorious agitator, and Samuel Martin, a truculent Member of Parliament who had referred to Wilkes in the House as a 'stabber in the dark, a cowardly and malignant scoundrel'. Wilkes challenged Martin as soon as the House adjourned and the parties repaired at once, with a brace of pistols, to a copse in the Park. They fired four times before Wilkes fell, wounded in the abdomen. Martin, somewhat chastened, then hurried up and insisted on helping his adversary to rise from the ground. Wilkes, not to be outdone in courtesy, urged Martin to hurry away so that he might avoid being 'taken up'. It was learned afterwards that Martin had practised for six months in a shooting gallery before he made his offensive speech.

Even after that, there were further fights in the Park. In 1772, Richard Brinsley Sheridan went there with a Captain Matthews to fight a duel, but, finding the crowd too great, the two men repaired to the Castle Tavern in Covent Garden and fought there instead, it is said, with swords. In 1780, a duel was fought in the Park between the Earl of Shelburne and a certain Colonel Fullarton; in 1783, a Lieutenant-Colonel Thomas and a Colonel Gordon met in the Park in deadly combat and the former was killed; in 1797, a Colonel Fitzgerald was similarly killed there. The last really spectacular duel in the Park of which there is certain evidence was that between a Captain MacNamara and a Colonel Montgomery in 1803 – Edmund Blunden has written a long and very fine narrative poem about this duel[1] – though some kind of a fight between the Dukes of Bedford and Buckingham seems to have taken place there as lately as 1822.

Much of the popular activity in Hyde Park was centred, then as now, on the ground adjoining the Serpentine Lake. Then also, as now, where there tended to be crowds in London there tended to be pickpockets and other petty criminals. One handkerchief thief caught by the crowd in 1771 was handed to a soldier to be given a ducking in the Serpentine. One extra dousing was to be given to the wretch for each handkerchief improperly found on him.

In really hard winters, when the Serpentine froze over completely, Rotten Row would be quite deserted, and for as long as the cold spell lasted the ice on Queen Caroline's lake would become an arena on which deeds of the greatest skill and daring would be performed. In 1776, for example, the sum of £50, very large for those times, was offered to the first man who could manage to skate a mile in less than a minute. (The speed record was said to be held by an Irish footman who, it was alleged, had skated eight miles in only ten minutes.) In the last year of the eighteenth century there was another Great Frost, and a new crop of skaters, determined not to be outdone by the daredevils of their fathers' generation, devised some breathtaking exploits of their own.

Meanwhile, the crowds who strolled in the Spring and Summer to and fro along the sides of Rotten Row would see there, as likely as not, some prominent member of the Royal Family out for a horse-drawn airing. The Prince of Wales, for instance, drove frequently in the Park with the lovely actress Mrs 'Perdita' Robinson during their brief *affaire*. (The lady's carriage, painted scarlet and panelled with silver, had cost the Prince nine hundred guineas.) When the Prince wished to see the lady no more, he chose the Park as the most suitable place for publicly cutting her dead. His father, the King, hearing of the *affaire*, wrote to Lord North, the Prime Minister:

My eldest son got last year into a very improper association with an Actress, a woman of indifferent character. Through the *friendly* assistance of Lord Malden, a multitude of letters passed which she has threatened to publish unless He, in short, bought them of Her . . .

For King George III, Hyde Park had other unhappy associations, for an attempt on his life was made when he was reviewing his troops there – an onlooker received a musket shot in his thigh, but it was clearly intended for the King. Later in the same day, when the King, the Queen and the Princesses attended a performance of Colly Cibber's *She Would and She Would Not* at Drury Lane, the audience gave him a tremendous ovation.

Although it had ceased to be a principal royal residence, Kensington Palace was still used by members of the family who were of lesser importance than the Monarch – Caroline, for example, the estranged wife of the Prince of Wales, lived there for four years between 1810 and 1814. Caroline wandered about in Kensington Gardens with no marked royal dignity, surprising and deeply shocking Lady Brownlow who saw her sit down on a bench occupied by 'two old persons' and chatter to them with the utmost freedom.

When the Prince Regent invited the Allied Sovereigns to London in 1814 to celebrate, somewhat prematurely, the defeat of Napoleon Bonaparte, he gave orders that Hyde Park should be converted, as far as possible, into one great traditional fairground where, among other amusements, his father's subjects could watch performing dogs and monkeys, marvel at stalwart men who ate fire or swallowed swords or executed other prodigious feats, or gape in wonder and admiration at the fattest ladies of forty in the world. To add zest to the merriment, brewers' drays laden with hogsheads of draught porter were kept circulating from stall to stall, and there was more drunkenness in the Park than had ever been seen before.

Such revelry inevitably led to debauchery, at which the Protestant Bishops protested. At the height of the excitement, a young woman stripped off her clothes and prepared to bathe in the Serpentine in a state of complete nudity. There were encouraging shouts from the men standing around, but before the rash female could immerse herself in the foul water she was hustled from the scene by a group of older ladies who were dressed fully and properly in black.

As a grand climax to the celebrations in Hyde Park, the authorities had arranged that one of Admiral Lord Nelson's naval victories should be re-enacted, on a very small scale, on the Serpentine. For this exciting miniature engagement, models of the upper parts of fourteen ships-of-the-line were made with wood and canvas, embellished with tiny guns and figureheads and other details that added to their general realism, and each was mounted on a rowing boat. On the chosen day, as the setting sun approached the horizon, the foremost ship-of-the-line started to move, and within a few minutes its little guns had opened fire, in spectacular fashion, on the despicable French.

In less than an hour, the simulated battle was over. The spectators then turned away from the Serpentine and started to move off towards the further pleasures that had been promised a little to the east. The crush was so great, however, that few could move with any speed. Suddenly, one of the model men-of-war was seen to have caught alight, and the crowd turned round again. For a moment there was a dreadful hush, and then the spectators, realizing that the real excitement on the Serpentine was yet to come, gave a triumphant roar. The blazing vessel, adrift from her moorings, bore down remorselessly on the remaining ships of the stricken French fleet and, to the great delight of all who saw, the enemy squadron burst into flames.

Altogether, the Prince Regent's Fair had cost the Government over £40,000, and speaker after speaker rose in the House of Commons to protest at the disgusting scenes of vice it had engendered and to express 'the infinite annoyance it had caused all the middle classes of society'. The young woman who had undressed and had tried to plunge into the Serpentine had not only shamed her sex, claimed one censorious person, but she had also spoiled the nation's tribute to Admiral Lord Nelson and His Grace the Duke of Wellington. Amends would be made, declared the Countess Spencer – amends in the name of the Ladies of Britain.

So, a Committee of Ladies under the leadership of the Countess set to work upon a project which would, they felt sure, efface from the minds of the Great British Public the memory of the disgraceful incident by the Serpentine. They would have a magnificent statue put up in Hyde Park, they decided – the idea of doing such a thing had been in the Countess's mind for some time, it had been suggested, but she had not had such an excellent reason before for acting upon it. At first, no one seems to have known what the statue was to be like, for a letter was sent out announcing that the figure 'would be a facsimile of a statue of Phidias, representing Alexander the Great taming Bucephalus'. None of the Ladies of Britain to whom this letter was sent ventured to point out – perhaps none of them had realized – that Phidias had died almost a century before Alexander the Great. The statue was to be erected in honour of the great Duke of Wellington and his brave companions in arms, and that was enough; subscriptions began to pour in.

Enthusiasm for the Countess's project rapidly snowballed. The Ordnance Office handed over twelve 24-pounder guns that had been captured from the French at the battles of Salamanca, Vittoria, Toulouse and Waterloo, so that they could be melted down to provide the metal needed for the statue. The Pope allowed the sculptor, Sir Richard Westmacott, to use casts taken from one of the great antique figures, a horse-tamer, that stood on the Monte Cavallo at Rome. The King – before the work was complete the Regent had become King George IV – allowed fifty feet of good Park land, within sight of Apsley House, to be used for the granite base. The statue, when at last it was finished, had cost over £10,000, and its size was such that it would not pass through any of the Park gates. So, part of the Park wall had to be knocked down so that the statue could be taken through the gap.

From the first, even before it was set up, the statue was bitterly criticized. Everyone realized, more or less, that the sculptor had been trying to evoke the image of an heroic male figure – allegedly, Achilles – caught in the act of raising a shield and striking at an unspecified target. But Westmacott had not been single-minded. In an attempt, which proved vain, to please all the Ladies who had subscribed to the cost of the statue, the sculptor had placed

on the Homeric body a head that might have been taken, if one
did not look at it too closely, for that of the Iron Duke. Lower down,
the undraped figure was, for a muscular male, all too obviously
under-endowed. The sum of all these ill-assorted parts was wholly
regrettable. Cruikshank and other cartoonists rushed to their
drawing boards in a race to see who could lampoon it first, and
most cruelly. Sheriff Perkins in the columns of the *Morning Herald*
told his readers that if his mother, who was a God-fearing New-
castle woman, 'had caught any of her children looking at such an
object, she would have soundly whipped them'. Another critic
declared that Westmacott, from that time on, ought to devote
himself solely to the representation of nymphs. The Ladies who
had raised the subscription, abashed by the storm of abuse, claimed
that the sculptor had not consulted them about the allegorical
statue and, indeed, had completed it before the subscription had
even been set on foot. (The fig-leaf fitted to the statue at a later
date was torn off by vandals in 1961. It has since been replaced
with an oak-leaf.)

As the land to the north and north-west of Hyde Park and
Kensington Gardens became ever more heavily built upon, the
little West Bourn which flowed through it and acted as a general
sewer became ever more heavily polluted. Accordingly, as it was
the West Bourn that principally fed the Serpentine, the waters
of that lake became increasingly foul, until in the warmest days
of Summer it was difficult for anyone to approach the lake's edge
unless he, or she, were determined to commit suicide. Harriet
Westbrook, the ill-fated first wife of the poet Shelley, chose a dark
December day in 1816 on which to drown herself in the Long
Water. By June 1820, the Princess Lieven was writing to Prince
Metternich:

... I am melting in the heat ... Only in Kensington Gardens
can one breathe. But for some years that lovely garden has been
annexed as a middle-class rendezvous, and good society no
longer goes there, except to drown itself. Last year they took
from its lake the body of a very beautiful woman, expensively
dressed, who had probably been a whole week in the water ...

Disgustingly polluted as the Serpentine was, it still froze over most satisfactorily in the very hardest winters. During the winter of 1814, a great fair was held on the ice, and in 1826, during another great frost, there was carried out there an exploit that was referred to as 'the most daring feat of all times'. Beneath a lithograph picture made and sold after the event by Messrs Ingrey and Madeley, there can be read this description:

> On Tuesday, the 17th January 1826, Mr Henry Hunt for a bet of 100 guineas made with a Noble Lord of Sporting Celebrity drove his Father's Matchless Blacking Van with four blood horses upon the ice of the Serpentine at the broadest part:– he accomplished the hazardous task in the grandest style without the smallest accident:– The Picture represents his return to the North Bank from which he had set out amid the acclamations of the multitude.

In 1819, the baby who was to become Queen Victoria was born in Kensington Palace. Victoria's mother, the Duchess of Kent, guided by her Major-Domo Sir John Conroy, was determined to keep the child away from the surviving members of King George III's family and her other disreputable Hanoverian relatives, and the little Princess was brought up in comparative seclusion, the Gardens at Kensington being her principal playground, outside the immediate surroundings of her home.

Before she was in her teens, Princess Victoria would have seen some important additions made to the architectural features of the domestic landscape. In 1825, for instance, Decimus Burton – so called because he was the tenth child of James Burton, the well-known and successful London builder – was commissioned by the Government to carry out various improvements in Hyde Park, including the laying down of roads in and around the park, and the re-modelling of the old Guard House (still known by many people as 'The Magazine') that stands on the north bank of the Serpentine. He was also asked to plan the western approaches to Buckingham Palace. In the following year, the brothers Rennie started to put up the massive but elegant bridge that now spans the Serpentine with such distinction, carrying the road that marks the division, at that part of the boundary, between Kensington Gardens and Hyde Park.

In planning the approaches to King George IV's principal London home, Burton set out to make a grand sweep from the forecourt of the Palace, through the 'Marble Arch', which John Nash had designed as its main entrance, up Constitution Hill, through a new and grand Corinthian arch at Hyde Park Corner, and then between the columns of an Ionic screen, based on Robert Adam's screen at Syon House, into Hyde Park.

But Burton was unlucky, and his splendid intentions were never to be fully realized. In his design, his new Corinthian arch at the top of Constitution Hill was intended to support a quadriga, or massive sculpture showing a rider in a chariot drawn by four horses, harnessed abreast. With callous indifference to the young architect's feelings, the Government decided instead to disfigure the arch with an equestrian statue of the Duke of Wellington, which looked so ludicrously out of place in its setting that it drew from a French officer the cutting comment, 'Nous sommes vengés!' Desperately disappointed, Burton made a will in which he offered to leave the nation the sum of £2,000 if only the nation would have the offending statue removed. (It was, in fact, taken down and moved to Aldershot in 1885, four years after Burton's death, but long before then he had given up hope and had re-made his will.) Little of Burton's ambitious scheme survives today, apart from the delightful dove-grey screen – a miracle of lightness and elegance – that still adjoins Apsley House (now the 'Wellington Museum'), and his Constitution Arch, which was rebuilt slantwise during the 1880s, destroying the austere simplicity of Burton's design. But the Cumberland Gate Lodge, the Grosvenor Gate Lodge, the Stanhope Gate Lodges, and the lodge to the west of the Hyde Park Corner screen for which he was largely responsible, still enhance, with their fine proportions and correctness of detail, some of the Park's most extraordinarily attractive entrances.

Architectural history was made in Hyde Park in 1850–1 after Queen Victoria's consort, Prince Albert of Saxe-Coburg-Gotha, had the idea of holding a great international exhibition of the arts and sciences – largely, to promote trade. Right from the start, Sir Robert Peel favoured the use of a site in the Park for the building that was to house the exhibition. Other people were not so enthusiastic: a suburb would be more suitable, suggested one reader of *The Times*, naming, prophetically, Sydenham. A body of Protestants protested volubly against the Prince's scheme, saying that the exhibition would be used as a rallying-point by the riff-raff of any revolution and would in any case encourage a Papist invasion. Confusion, disorder, famine and pestilence would inevitably result, prophesied some other Jeremiahs.[2] A group of Nonconformists dismissed the whole enterprise as 'Satanic', and prayed that some Act of God might intervene. Undaunted, Prince Albert and the members of his organizing committee pressed inexorably ahead.

At first, the organizers intended to erect for their exhibition a building constructed mainly of bricks. Then, the Bedfordshire gardener who was later to become Sir Joseph Paxton, and who had already had some experience of designing large conservatories for the Duke of Devonshire at Chatsworth and Chiswick, produced a design resembling an enormous hothouse. The members of the committee, realizing that by the use of iron and glass they might save a considerable amount of money, welcomed the new scheme, and they warmed to it even more when they obtained a satisfactory tender of a mere £80,000 for its construction.

By the end of 1850, more than two thousand workmen were engaged on the raising of Prince Albert's Crystal Palace. (It went up, on a nineteen-acre site, between Rotten Row and the Kensington Road.) To make the great greenhouse, which was nearly two thousand feet long and over four hundred feet wide, cast-iron girders and wrought-iron trusses weighing altogether four thousand tons were needed, with 900,000 square feet of glass weighing at least four hundred tons, thirty miles of guttering, and two hundred miles of wooden sash.[3] From time to time the men working on the site would be entertained to a free dinner at which speeches would be made and the advantages of temperance extolled.

By the end of April 1851, the Crystal Palace was virtually complete and most of the 14,000 remarkable exhibits, valued at more than two million pounds, had been unpacked and suitably

displayed. On the first day of May, the Queen went to Hyde Park
to declare the Great Exhibition open. There was a short ceremony,
during the course of which (actually, while the 'Hallelujah Chorus'
was being sung) a curious incident occurred. This is how it was
described by Lord Playfair, who was feeling responsible:

> . . . A Chinaman, dressed in magnificent robes, suddenly emerged
> from the crowd and prostrated himself before the throne. Who
> he was, nobody knew. He might possibly be the Emperor of
> China himself, who had come secretly to the ceremony, but it
> was certain that he was not in the programme of the procession,
> and we who were in charge of the ceremony did not know where
> to place His Celestial Highness. The Lord Chamberlain was
> equally perplexed, and asked the Queen and the Prince Consort
> for instructions. We were then told that there must be no mistake
> as to his rank, and that it would be best to place him between the
> Archbishop of Canterbury and the Duke of Wellington. In this
> dignified position he marched through the building, to the
> delight and amazement of all beholders. . . .

The next day, it was ascertained that this 'illustrious Chinaman'
was merely the Captain of a Chinese junk which happened to
be lying in the Thames for public inspection at one shilling per
head.

Like nearly all her subjects who saw Paxton's great gleaming
structure with its splendid contents, the Queen was enormously
impressed. This was the triumph of her beloved Albert, she wrote
confidently in her *Journal*. The Crystal Palace was 'the most
beautiful and *imposing* and *touching* spectacle ever seen'. May Day
1851 was 'the *greatest* day in our history'. Lord Macaulay was
also ready to sing the Prince Consort's praises. On the night after
the opening, he wrote in his *Journal*:

> [The Crystal Palace] is a most gorgeous sight; vast; graceful;
> beyond the dreams of Arabian romances. I cannot think that
> the Caesars ever exhibited a more splendid spectacle. I was
> quite dazzled, and I felt as I did on entering St Peter's.

One of the distinguished visitors to the Exhibition, however, was not quite so enthusiastic. This was Jane Welsh Carlyle, fault-finder supreme:

. . . Oh how tired I was! Not that it was not really a very beautiful sight – especially at the entrance; the three large trees built in because the people objected to their being cut down, a crystal fountain, and a large blue canopy gives one a momentary impression of a Bazaar in the Arabian Nights Entertainments; and such a lot of things of different kinds and of well dressed people – for the tickets were still 5/– – was rather imposing for a few minutes; but when you come to look at the wares in detail there was nothing really worth looking at – at least that one could not have seen samples of in the shops. . . . And the fatigue of even the most cursory survey was indescribable, and to tell you the God's truth I would not have given the pleasure of reading a good Fairy Tale for all the pleasure to be got from that 'Fairy Scene'. . . .

Despite Mrs Carlyle's strictures, Prince Albert's Great Exhibition was, right from the start, outstandingly successful. Over six million people paid to see it, some of them travelling specially from quite distant parts of the world. The profit made was £165,000, and this helped to pay for the construction of several museums, colleges, schools and other useful buildings. But the crowds had to be fed. During the first six months of the exhibition, according to a book called *Fireside Facts from the Great Exhibition*, published in 1851, a total of 311,731 lb of Bath buns were eaten in the Park

Just six weeks after the Great Exhibition opened, the visitors drawn to Hyde Park were given an extra, and quite gratuitous, thrill when Mrs Graham, the intrepid lady balloonist of the monkey-parachutes, passed over the Crystal Palace with her husband. The good lady's balloon had risen into the air, on this occasion, from Batty's Hippodrome in the Kensington Road. As the balloon had left the Hippodrome, however, the envelope had struck a pole on the top of the building and a tear had been made in its fabric. So, as the balloon passed over Paxton's great glass-house, all the ballast had to be thrown out. The grappling iron, which did considerable damage while the balloon drifted just above the neighbouring houses, caught, eventually, in a coping stone at the top of a mansion belonging to a Colonel North, in Arlington Street, St James's. Both the Grahams were flung out on to the roof, from where they were rescued, in an insensible condition, by the police. Mr Graham was seriously injured, and this may have led to the termination of his ballooning career. Mrs Graham, however, recovered quite quickly, and continued her roof-skimming exploits for at least another two years.

In the year of the Great Exhibition, the arch of Seravezza marble that John Nash had designed as the grand entrance for the front of Buckingham Palace was taken down. Nash had modelled it on the Great Arch of the Emperor Constantine at Rome, but when it had been set in place, nobody liked it, least of all the Members of Parliament who had been tricked by Nash's master into providing the money for a new grand palace when they thought they were voting sufficient only for the refurbishing of the old Buckingham House. Suggestions were made that the arch should be removed from its position in front of the Palace and placed instead on an extension of Pall Mall so that it would serve as a grand entrance to the Green Park; but when the change was finally made the arch was re-erected, instead, near the spot on which the gallows had stood in the old days at Tyburn. (The reliefs to be seen today on the south side of the Marble Arch are by E. H. Baily, who was responsible for the statue of Admiral Lord Nelson which stands on the column in Trafalgar Square. Those on the north side are by Sir Richard Westmacott, who produced the statue of the Grand Old Duke of York which is mounted on the column in Waterloo Place.)[4]

By the early 1850s, Rotten Row had become the regular rendezvous of the fashionable world, as the Ring had been nearly two centuries before. On 7 June 1854 – to give only one example of the kind of royal but intimate spectacle that had become increasingly frequent there – His Majesty the King of Portugal was seen out riding in the Row with His Royal Highness Prince Albert. But the members of the upper and middle classes were not alone in thinking that they had a right to enjoy the amenities of Her Majesty's London Parks and Gardens – the workers of the metropolis also were starting, inconveniently, to intrude where they were not really wanted, and His Royal Highness the Second Duke of Cambridge found that his early years as Ranger of the Central Parks were rendered increasingly uncomfortable by this unprecedented break-up of the good old social barriers.

The first major row to break upon the poor Duke's head involved the right of bands, military or non-military, to play in the Parks on Sundays. The matter was brought to a head by a letter written on 10 May 1856 to the Prime Minister, Lord Palmerston, by the Archbishop of Canterbury, Primate of the Established Church. In this letter, the Archbishop claimed that it was 'a vital question as regards the national religion'. The letters and petitions which reached him daily convinced him, the Archbishop went on, that Lord Palmerston's Administration might be seriously affected if the proceedings were persisted in, which had been so unhappily begun.[5] Lord Palmerston, threatened in this way with the downfall of his Government, replied within a few hours from Broadlands, his country home:

My dear Lord

I received your letter of today just as I was leaving London for this place. I concurred in the arrangements for performances by Military Bands in Kensington Gardens and in the Parks for a couple of hours on Sunday afternoons, after Divine Service, because I thought that those arrangements would afford the inhabitants of the Metropolis innocent intellectual recreation, combined with fresh air, and healthy exercises, and such recreation did not seem to me to be at variance with the soundest and purest sentiments of Religion, which was my opinion, and such is my opinion still; for I have heard nothing on the part of those who object to these arrangements which has altered my view of the matter.

But I find from Your Lordship's letter and from representations which have reached me from other quarters that a great number of persons whose opinions are entitled to respect look upon the matter from a different point of view, and entertain, in regard to it, strong opinions differing from my own.

In this state of things, I am naturally led to ask myself whether the advantage to be gained by a continuance of these musical performances is sufficiently great to compensate for the evil of running counter to the religions of a large body of the community, and to that question there can be but one answer, namely that it is not.

I shall therefore in deference to the sentiments expressed by Your Grace, on your own part, and on that of others, take steps for discontinuing the Band-playing in Kensington Gardens, and in the Parks on Sundays. . . .[6]

Lord Palmerston's decision, apparently dragged from him against his own personal inclinations by the Archbishop of Canterbury, roused the more active members of London's working classes to fury. These worthy people felt, in the words of Sir Benjamin Hall, Her Majesty's Commissioner of Works, that they were being deprived, 'by some natural influence', of a most natural source of enjoyment,[7] and they held a great protest meeting at St Pancras in a room which normally held two thousand people. The room became so crowded, reported Sir Benjamin, that whenever anyone in it moved, everyone else had to sway from side to side. Outside, there was a crowd larger even than the crowd within. On the following morning, a deputation of ten persons 'who might fairly be said to represent the working classes, being men of a very inferior stamp'[8] waited upon the Minister for Works and informed him that they would endeavour by all legitimate means to obtain the withdrawal of the Government's prohibition. When the members of another deputation expressed their views with some force to the Prime Minister, Lord Palmerston was adamant:

. . . It was impossible for the Government to be changing its course from week to week according to each different request that might be made to it [he reported to Her Majesty Queen Victoria]. They then asked if private bands were to play in the Parks, the Police would be ordered to turn them out? Viscount

Palmerston told the spokesman who seemed a respectable man to come to the Home Office at Five o'clock and that he would then get an answer from the Home Secretary. . . .[9]

The Home Secretary would inform the Queen that no permission for private bands had been given, went on Lord Palmerston. To give such permission would in truth be doing indirectly that which it had been determined not to do directly. At the same time, he continued, the matter was a difficult one to deal with:

> . . . The Parks are undoubtedly under your Majesty's Control; that is to say those which are properly speaking Royal Parks, such as Hyde Park, the Green Park, and St James's Park and Kensington Gardens and Victoria Park and Regent's Park which have been formed for Public Use by Parliamentary Grants are under the Control of the Board of Works and therefore indirectly under Your Majesty's Control . . . Private bands would be excluded on Sunday just as on any other day by a rightful exercise of Royal Authority. But beyond the question of Right there is one of Prudence. If a few persons intrude into the Parks improperly they can easily be removed by the Police, but if Bands accompanied by Many thousand persons come in removal by force might lead to disturbance, and it would be preferable to have recourse to other means such as Remonstrance and Persuasion. . . . The Park Gates might on the next Sunday be shut, but that would be attended with inconvenience to the Public, and the Gates might be forced open, if there were persons intent upon mischief. . . .[10]

Sir Charles Phipps, Keeper of the Privy Purse, wrote from Osborne on 22 May 1856 to thank Sir Benjamin Hall for news of the great Bands-in-the-Parks controversy:

> . . . I have always been in favour of any recreation and amusement upon the Sunday that does not entail the labour of those who have a right to, and require the rest of, the seventh day, and I was very sorry when the measure was taken of forbidding the

bands to play in the different Parks, but I cannot but think that more importance has been attached to it than it deserves, that as a privation to the working classes it has been much over-rated, and that it has been made a vehicle for agitation by persons who equally take advantage of any other circumstances that may possibly excite the passions of the multitude. It must be remembered that the practice of the band playing in Kensington Gardens only began a year ago, that no great desire had been previously expressed for such entertainment, and that as far as those gardens are concerned, very few *working men* ever availed themselves of the opportunity offered them. . . . The innocent recreation and amusement of the class who are confined during the week is of great importance and most desirable, but I do not think military music a necessary ingredient of it. It is a new want, which has been hardly known to the working classes. . . .[11]

Two days later, a letter appeared in the *Daily News* announcing that a private band would play in Hyde Park on the following day 'by permission of the Ranger'. This caused the authorities some very real anxiety, since His Royal Highness had given no such sanction, nor had the First Commissioner of Works. It would be unwise, 'in view of the excited state of feeling about the Sunday bands to risk any collision between the Police and the people which was not absolutely necessary', decreed Sir George Grey, the Home Secretary. So he asked that the number of police on duty at the gates of the Park should not be increased on this occasion, and he said that he did not think it would be prudent to interfere by force to prevent a band entering and playing in the Park on that Sunday, if one should appear.[12] As it happened, it rained, and the danger was averted. Steps were taken after that to bring up to London, on an official basis, the band from the Brighton Pavilion.

A later First Commissioner of Works, the Honourable William Cowper, wrote in September 1865 to the Keeper of the Privy Purse, Sir Charles Phipps, to tell him that a 'Mr Jullier' had offered to arrange afternoon concerts in Kensington Gardens, as long as a suitable platform were erected. Mr Jullier would be content with the remuneration provided by the hire of chairs, the First Commissioner added – he had a disinterested desire to raise the taste of music among the public and would undertake that only a high class of music should be performed.[13] Sir Charles put this up to the Queen, but Her Majesty directed him to say

> . . . That she could not approve of Kensington Gardens being thus handed over to Mr Jullier to make a promenade Concert of them. Her Majesty thinks that such a plan would be open to the gravest objections, and would wish that the proposal should not be entertained. . . .[14]

But the Queen did think that if a proper application were made there would be no difficulty in obtaining the occasional attendance, upon stated days, of the Cavalry band stationed at Knightsbridge.

Though Prince Albert's Crystal Palace has vanished – it was taken down after its primary purpose was fulfilled and removed to Sydenham, where it was almost entirely destroyed by fire in 1926 – there are today several visible reminders, in Kensington Gardens and Hyde Park, of the instigator of the Great Exhibition of 1851. At the head of the Serpentine, for instance, there is a formal Italianate Pavilion, with a loggia, that is said to have been designed by Prince Albert himself – he clearly based his design on that of the much admired 'Petit Trianon' of Versailles. Two springs flowed here in ancient days – one, which gave out medicinal waters which were supposed to be useful for curing sore eyes; the other ('St Agnes' Well') which was merely used for ordinary drinking. Seated on a bronze throne near Prince Albert's tumbling waters there is a statue, executed by Calder Marshall in 1858, of Doctor Jenner of Berkeley, in Gloucestershire, who first discovered that smallpox might be effectively combated by vaccination.

Most striking of all the Parks' reminders of the Prince Consort is, of course, the fantastically ornate Memorial that was put up in Kensington Gardens after the Prince's tragic death from typhoid fever in 1861. The impetus for this great London landmark came, in the first place, from the Prince's grievously sorrowing widow.

The Albert Memorial was designed by Sir Giles Gilbert Scott, the energetic restorer – much too energetic, in many people's opinion – of so many of Britain's medieval cathedrals and churches. Sir Giles's project was chosen by the widowed Queen with the help of a committee that included the Earls of Clarendon and Derby, the President of the Royal Academy (Sir Charles Eastlake), and William Cubitt, the Lord Mayor, from among the designs submitted by six prominent architects. Her Majesty thought that the neo-Gothic ciborium or shrine, envisaged by Sir Giles ('My idea was to realise one of these imaginary structures with its precious metals, its inlayings, its enamels, etc., etc. . . .') and containing a statue of the late Prince, would be wholly appropriate, and the members of her advisory committee entirely agreed. Some modern critics may have suggested unkindly that the over-all aesthetic effect of the Albert Memorial is a little overpowering, but this view was not shared by Sir Giles, who always regarded it as the very greatest of all his works.

Sir Giles's Memorial took at least nine years (1863–72) to build and cost £120,000: then a colossal sum. The fifteen-foot high statue of the Prince Consort, wearing the collar of the Knight of the Garter, the Garter itself above the muscular calf of his left leg, and holding one volume of the catalogue of the Great Exhibition of 1851 – not, as many people believe, a Bible – was executed by John Henry Foley, R.A., cast in gun-metal provided by the Government stores at Woolwich, and overlaid 'with gold of triple thickness'.

Round the figure of the Prince, shown seated, at the designer's suggestion – 'I have chosen the sitting position as best conveying the idea of dignity befitting a royal personage', said Sir Giles – there were arranged further figures and groups of figures that were intended to record for public survey for all time the late Prince's main interests and subjects of study.

On the first rising of the steps above the quasi-classical base (two hundred feet long, made from granite brought from Penryn, in Cornwall) Sir Giles placed four great marble groups representing the continents – Europe, symbolized by a bull, and carved by Patrick Macdowell; Asia, by an elephant, carved by J. H. Foley; Africa, by a camel, carved by William Theed; and America, by a bison, carved by John Bell. These were intended to allude to the international character of the Prince Consort's work. Above them,

Sir Giles put groups that symbolized Agriculture (W. Calder Marshall), Manufacturing (Henry Weekes), Commerce (Thomas Thornycroft) and Engineering (John Lawlor). For the podium, Sir Giles commissioned a series of 169 sculptures, executed by H. H. Armstead and J. B. Philip, in which a keen-sighted observer who knows something about architecture, music, painting, poetry and sculpture can spot portraits, real or imagined, of geniuses as varied as Cheops (of Great Pyramid fame), Thomas Flaxman, Felix Mendelssohn, Palestrina, Phidias, Pugin, Schiller, Van Eyck, Virgil and David Wilkie. Allegorical figures of the Fine Arts can be seen in the mosaic tympana (they were executed by Messrs Salviati of Murano, in Italy, to the designs of the Englishmen Clayton and Bell, and they loom now in the most surprising fashion, above columns of granite quarried in the Ross of Mull). Aloft, in the spire, tremendous bronze-gilt figures represent the Christian virtues of Faith, Hope, Charity and Humility, while another set of earnest and most competently executed Victorian sculptures bring to the attention of all viewers the moral virtues of Fortitude, Justice, Prudence and Temperance. Eight bronzes, at the corners, record the Prince Consort's intense and constant interest in astronomy, chemistry, geology, geometry, rhetoric, medicine, philosophy and physiology. Even in their smallest and most intimate details these nineteenth-century sculptures are to modern eyes somewhat daunting. 'Physiology', for instance, carries on her left arm an infant who represents 'the highest and most perfect of physiological forms', while her finger points to a microscope which 'lends its assistance for the investigation of the minuter forms of animal and vegetable organisms'. There could hardly have been a more appropriate tribute to the Prince Consort's own earnest and industrious nature.

The actual construction of the Albert Memorial was carried out by Messrs Lucas Brothers, who had already shown by their work at the Royal Albert Docks and at Liverpool Street Station that they were capable of a bold and imaginative use of cast iron. During the building, several dinners were given for the workmen, and at these eighty or more men sat at the 'tables', which were improvised from scaffolding planks. Beef, mutton, plum-pudding and cheese were served at the meals, and ale was also handed round, though a large proportion of the guests were teetotallers who preferred to drink lemonade or ginger beer. The architect responsible for the Memorial described, in this way, one of these dinners: 'Several toasts were given and many of the workmen spoke, almost all of them commencing by "Thanking God that they enjoyed good health" and alluding to the temperance that prevailed among them and "how little swearing was heard".'

While the memorial to Prince Albert was being constructed, a tall granite obelisk was put up in the Gardens, a few hundred yards to the north. The obelisk commemorates the celebrated explorer John Hanning Speke, who died tragically on the eve of a meeting to be held at Bath at which his rival, Sir Richard Burton, was to challenge Speke's claim that he had discovered the source of the Nile. Although the official verdict at the time was that Speke had accidentally shot himself while partridge-shooting, there is some likelihood at least that the harassed explorer committed suicide. The inscription on the obelisk remains judiciously neutral about the success – or otherwise – of Speke's explorations. It says simply:

In memory of SPEKE:
Victoria, Nyanza and the Nile. 1864.

Although the Bayswater Sewer had been stopped in 1834 from discharging itself into the Serpentine, the loss of water being made good by the Chelsea Waterworks Company which pumped in slightly fresher water from the Thames, the accumulated putrid matter had ever since remained on the bed of the lake, and the stench that rose from it in hot weather became at last absolutely intolerable. (Sir Benjamin Hall, writing from Stanhope Gate on 26 July 1858 to Sir Charles Phipps, complained that the state of the Serpentine during the hot weather had been so offensive that he had been compelled, even at that distance, to keep his windows closed at night on account of the abominable smell. There had been an article in *The Times* about it on the previous Monday, he reported, but the statement made there that people drank the Serpentine's

water must, he felt, have been a hoax.)[15] In 1866 or shortly afterwards, official steps were therefore taken to remove the noxious
mud and deposits, and to provide a constant stream of more or
less pure water that would pass through the Serpentine at all
times of the year.

It was clear that before this operation could be properly begun,
all the fish would have to be removed from the Serpentine. A
professional fisherman from Hammersmith was therefore engaged,
and from a rowing boat he attempted to make his initial haul.
As so often happens in London when anything of especial interest
occurs, a crowd formed. There were a few hoots, a little slow
hand-clapping, and a certain amount of good-humoured booing.
Only the little fishing boys, with their empty pickle jars, reserved
judgment. Then, 'Jimmy!' shouted one of them, 'We'd better go
home! The gent is killing all the tiddlers!'

The 'gent' from Hammersmith was not killing all the 'tiddlers';
he was trying to save them. He had three water carts at his disposal,
and as soon as any one of these carts was judged to be full of fish,
it would be trundled off to the Round Pond, by Kensington Palace,
to deposit its load. The carts, made eleven journeys in all, taking to
their temporary asylum more than five thousand fish. Most of the
carts' involuntary passengers were bream, carp of the Crucian or
Prussian varieties, roach or tench. One eel, one trout and one
perch were also netted, but the perch was almost a cripple. It had,
according to a contemporary observer, an upper jaw rounded
into a knob like an apple, so that its deformed face looked like a
pantomime mask.

More or less at the same time as the Serpentine was being made
a little more savoury, the whole question of the use of Hyde Park
for controversial gatherings was being thrashed out.

Back in July 1855, a number of shopkeepers had proposed to
hold an open-air meeting in the Park to protest against a Sunday
Trading Bill. The Commissioner of Police of the Metropolis, the
experienced Sir Richard Mayne, had not allowed them to hold
their meeting. Three months later, a loquacious carpenter had
ventured to collect an audience in the Park to hear his views, and
as he encountered no opposition he repeated the performance on

the following Sunday, congratulating his supporters on their good sense in meeting 'in their own park'. In the next month, three more public meetings of the kind were held, but as they all turned, almost imperceptibly, into riotous gatherings, the police had to be called in on each occasion to restore order.

Then, in 1859, a big crowd assembled in the Park to present an address of sympathy to the Emperor Napoleon III, and to congratulate him on the policies he had pursued in Italy. Three years later, another big crowd gathered in the Park to pledge their support for Garibaldi. But on the latter occasion the meeting ended in bloodshed. So, when the leaders of the Reform League approached Sir Richard in 1866 and said that they wanted to hold a mass rally in the Park, the Commissioner refused to grant them the necessary permission. Undeterred, the demonstrators marched to the Park, and there they found the gates shut and the police guarding the entrances. This made the Reformers extremely angry. They tore down hundreds of yards of the iron railings on the Park Lane side of the Park and swarmed on to the forbidden ground. The rioting and bloodshed that followed are believed to have persuaded the authorities that they ought perhaps to adopt a slightly more conciliatory attitude.

When, therefore, the next Commissioner of Police was approached with a similar request in 1872, he arranged with the Duke of Cambridge and with the First Commissioner of Works for a place to be specially designated for meetings. This area was 150 yards from the 'Reformers' Tree' where the last riotous meeting had been held, and it is now universally known as 'Speakers' Corner'. A visit to the Corner on a Sunday is regarded as a more or less essential engagement for all those visiting London to see the sights for the first time.

By 1879, Her Majesty Queen Victoria was becoming increasingly concerned with the condition of the Royal Parks of London, especially Hyde Park and Kensington Gardens:

. . . The Queen is sorry to hear of the dangerous state of the Parks at night in consequence of Gas being put out earlier. Is this so? Can the evil be remedied? . . .[16]

A memorandum was prepared by Sir Edmund Henderson, Commissioner of Police of the Metropolis, for the Secretary of State for Home Affairs so that he might reassure Her Majesty:

> . . . There are no grounds for alarm. . . . An immense number of persons have visited Hyde Park since the waters have been frozen, sometimes as many as 20,000 at one time and many have remained till the Park was closed at 12 midnight, but there has been no disorder.
>
> No doubt the Parks are resorted to after nightfall by a class of persons who cannot be called unobjectionable, but so long as they are not disorderly and conduct themselves with propriety there are no grounds for interfering with them.
>
> A good deal of perfectly legitimate courtship is also carried on by persons of a rank of life who have no other opportunity or place and this has often given rise to matters which are not justified by the facts . . .[17]

In the following year, a dogs' cemetery was opened behind the Lodge at the Victoria Gate on the Bayswater Road side of Hyde Park. (The need for such a place is believed to have been first expressed by the Ranger, His Royal Highness the Duke of Cambridge, just after one of his wife's favourite pets had died.) From then until World War I, pet dogs – and cats and cage birds – were interred in this sad little plot, many of the three hundred gravestones being engraved with epitaphs as poignant as this:

IN LOVING MEMORY OF

PUSKIN

MY GENTLE FRIEND

AND COMPANION FOR ELEVEN YEARS

SO SADLY MISSED

. . . . .

SLEEP LITTLE ONE SLEEP

REST GENTLY THY HEAD

AS EVER THOU DIDST AT MY FEET

AND DREAM THAT I AM ANEAR

> I FAITHFULLY LOVED AND CARED
> FOR YOU LIVING. I THINK WE
> SHALL SURELY MEET AGAIN

– or as deftly composed as another:

> AFTER LIFE'S FITFUL SLUMBER, HE SLEEPS WELL

In the same year as the pets' cemetery was opened, a statue of Lord Byron, modelled by R. C. Belt and cast in bronze, was put up at the southern end of the Wellington Drive, quite near the Ladies' Achilles. This work, which shows the poet seated on a rock accompanied by his collie dog, was dismissed by Augustus Hare as 'inadequate', while Trelawney is said to have found that it bore no resemblance whatsoever to his celebrated friend.

During 1883, the Duke of Cambridge, still Ranger of the Central London Royal Parks, was faced with a demand that was quite as difficult to ignore as the popular clamour for military bands had been: the masses seemed to want physical refreshment when they went into the Parks as well as intellectual enjoyment. And there were various commercial enterprises which were ready to supply the masses with nourishment of different kinds, if this were allowed. But the Duke resolutely refused to consider the erection of any places of refreshment in the Parks. He wrote to Sir Henry Ponsonby, Queen Victoria's Private Secretary:

> . . . I have invariably, as Ranger, set my face against the erection of any places for *Refreshment* in the Royal Parks, as I consider that these Parks are for the enjoyment of *fresh air*, and are not to be turned into Tea Gardens. If we ever allow one or more stands to be erected, depend upon it we shall have many more, and the Parks, already over-crowded in the summer, will become quite intolerable. . . .[18]

Sir Henry submitted the Ranger's letter to Queen Victoria, pointing out that

. . . The Duke of Westminster asks leave to erect two kiosks in Hyde Park where coffee and refreshments may be sold. The Duke of Cambridge strongly objects.

Sir Henry Ponsonby does not think that it would be advisable for Your Majesty to ask the Duke of Westminster to withdraw his request, as the Duke of Cambridge suggests.

If the Duke of Westminster stood alone in this matter he would, of course, obey Your Majesty's wish.

But he is only the head of a Company which will raise a clamour if they think their request has not received a fair hearing. . . .[19]

The Queen said that she was as strongly opposed to the proposal as the Duke of Cambridge had been, but she gave Sir Henry Ponsonby no instructions to write to the Duke of Westminster. The Duke of Cambridge therefore suggested that 'agitation' for the construction of refreshment kiosks might be avoided if it were publicly known that the project was distasteful to Her Majesty, but Sir Henry disagreed[20] – such a proceeding, he suggested, would arouse the very agitation that it was desirable to avoid. In the end, the First Commissioner of Works, foreseeing almost unending trouble if kiosks 'for the sale of non-intoxicant refreshments' were not provided 'for the poorer visitors to the Park', and realizing that further applications might have a 'less reliable guarantee for respectability than those at present put forward',[21] managed to persuade the Royal Ranger to climb down from the lofty stand he had taken. The Queen, approached again, intimated that she would offer no further opposition to the proposal.[22]

Thus, 1883 was a bad year for the Duke of Cambridge, and his embarrassments were increased during the autumn, when proposals were made that the new Underground Railways should pass under the Central London Royal Parks. The Duke, deeply concerned about this, was at least partly reassured by a letter he received from Sir Henry Ponsonby, writing from Windsor on 27 November:

. . . Sir
The Queen commands me to let Your Royal Highness know

that Her Majesty gave her approval to the Parks Underground
Railway Scheme on the express condition that there were to
be no blow holes or other disfigurements in the Parks – If the
Line cannot be made without blow holes, it must not be made
at all. . . .[23]

A tangible reminder of the quiet and glorious years of Queen
Victoria's reign, when the peace of the Central London Royal
Parks was still not being destroyed by the noise of petrol-driven
cars (or by the worse noise of aircraft overhead) can today be seen
by the Broad Walk near Kensington Palace. This is Her Royal
Highness Princess Louise's generally admired likeness of Queen
Victoria, her mother. The Queen, carved from Carrara marble,
is shown as she would have been at the time of her accession. She
is wearing a crown and holding a sceptre. An inscription on the
base of the statue recalls that it was the loyal gift of the Queen's
Kensington subjects 'to commemorate fifty years of her reign'.
It stands, fittingly, in front of the handsome building in which
the Princess Victoria was born, and where she was woken, at the
age of eighteen, in the early hours of a cold June morning, to hear
that she had come to the throne. By the time her reign was over,
Hyde Park and Kensington Gardens had become, under the
Queen's eternally watchful eye, places of great dignity and elegance.

Chapter 7

Hyde Park and Kensington Gardens in the twentieth century

When His Royal Highness the Duke of Cambridge, Ranger of St James's, the Green and Hyde Parks, and Ranger of Richmond Park, died on 17 March 1904, His Majesty King Edward VII decided not to appoint anyone to replace him. Instead, the King – painfully conscious, it may be, of all those long years that had ended so very recently during which he, under his mother's strict and vigilant eye, had hardly been allowed to do anything whatever of real importance – announced his intention of retaining both those offices in his own hands. It was seen, then, that the administrative work of the Parks in question would fall to the Office of Works, under the Sovereign's personal supervision, to a far greater degree than in previous reigns.

Next, King Edward announced that the offices of Deputy Ranger of Richmond Park and of the Deputy under the Ranger of St James's, the Green and Hyde Parks should be held during the rest of their lives by the men holding those offices at the time, but that when those men died, no further appointments to those positions should be made. Meanwhile, he wanted the two Deputy Rangers to understand quite clearly that they could give no orders without his permission, and that any suggestions they might care to make for the well-being of the Parks should be submitted to him through the First Commissioner of His Majesty's Works. Although this move would have seemed to bring the Monarch within range of the bitter criticisms that were being so often levelled against those who carried out the day-to-day supervision of the Royal Parks, the King's decision was at least temporarily justified. For the first time for several decades, it was found, the Office of Works was freed from the evils of divided and subdivided control and its supervisors were able, in consequence, to create an efficient system for the management of the Parks.[1]

It was not long before the new, self-appointed Ranger had to make some really important decisions. In one of the first of these testing experiences, a memorandum suggesting that some alterations should be made in the Rules of the Royal Parks was submitted to the King, for his approval or otherwise, by the officials of the Office of Works. For the first time in history, the problems posed by the development of the internal combustion engine had to be seriously considered, and the Treasury Solicitor, in consultation with the police, had recommended that powers should be taken to prevent, by legal means, motor omnibuses and cycles carrying goods for shops from making use of the Parks. Complaints had also been made that the makers of the new automobiles were bringing their unfinished cars into the Parks in order to try their speeds and in the process were behaving generally in a thoroughly objectionable manner. To the relief of his officials, the King sanctioned the new regulations without demur.[2] (One wonders, however, what King Edward would have thought of the vast subterranean car store that has been constructed, in more recent years, in the north-east corner of Hyde Park!)

In the following year, 1908, a man living near Bishop's Stortford, in Hertfordshire, wrote to Sir Dighton Probyn, Bt, who was then Keeper of the Privy Purse:

Sir

I had the honour of meeting you when you favoured my late father . . . with a visit to look at his Hackneys.

It is reported in our local paper (the *Herts and Essex Observer*) that His Majesty the King has forbidden any girls over the age of 12 years to ride astride in the Park.

I am taking the liberty of asking you if this is correct, as

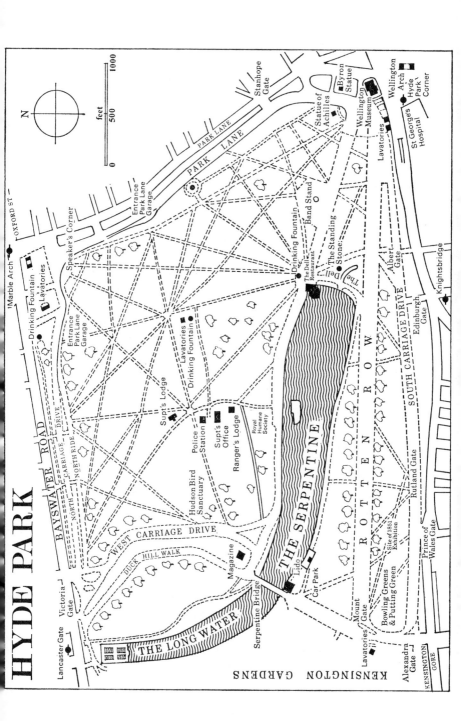

Sir Thomas Barlow[3] *strongly recommended* my daughter to *continue* to ride astride, when she was 15 years of age.

I remain, Sir

Your Obedient Servant

Frank Flinn[4]

Three days later, Sir Dighton replied to this, on paper headed 'Buckingham Palace':

Dear Sir

I am in receipt of your letter of the 30th ult. . . .

With reference to the report which you say has appeared in your local paper that "The King has forbidden any girls over the age of 12 years to ride astride in the Park," I do not think that is quite correct.

I believe, in fact I know, that His Majesty disapproves, like most English Gentlemen do, of ladies riding strideways, but I am not aware, nor do I believe, that His Majesty has issued any command "forbidding" ladies to do so . . .[5]

Three days after that, His Majesty's First Commissioner of Works, Sir Schomberg McDonnell, wrote to the King's Secretary, the Lord Knollys, G.C.V.O.:

My dear Francis,

Since you spoke to me some days ago I have been going at great lengths into the Rules and Regulations of the Parks in order to discover what means can be devised to prevent women riding astride.

I have also consulted the Police and the Treasury Solicitor.

They are both strongly of opinion that no legal power exists by which these women can be excluded from the Park. I am sorry to say that I have been forced to the same conclusion.

If the Circus woman who rode in Directoire costume, and nearly caused an accident to Winston Churchill, was to reappear I think we could get rid of her by sending the mounted Policeman to tell her that she must remove herself.

Being a foreigner, with a wholesome fear of the police, this would probably be sufficient; also it is arguable that she is there for the purposes of advertisement which is forbidden. But if she was to defy us and decline to go I doubt if we could expel her. If we did so an action would lie against us: at least that is the opinion of the Police and the Solicitor: and I have no doubt that they are right.

As regards the other women and children who ride astride I am convinced that it would be extremely dangerous to attempt to exclude or to remove them.

Of course I could argue that it is the order of the Ranger: and the King having reserved to himself the powers of the Ranger they could not bring an action against His Majesty. But they certainly could and probably would bring an action against the First Commissioner, and I think they would be successful: for under the Parks Regulation Act we have no power to deal with them.

So as you will see the situation is a difficult one.

It is hardly perhaps for me to make the suggestion; but I cannot help thinking that if it was known that ladies who adopt this mode of riding will not be received at Court it would have a salutary effect, though it would have little effect upon children except through their parents.

I am sorry that I cannot suggest any more drastic method but I feel sure that in the present state of the law it is a dangerous matter to handle.

Ever Yours
Schomberg K. McDonnell[6]

This letter was accompanied by a note written by the Monarch himself, and headed H. M. YACHT VICTORIA & ALBERT:

I quite agree that nothing can be done but do let it be known that ladies who ride astride in the Park will not be allowed to to come to Court but Circus Riders who do it for advertisement could I dare say be got rid of.

ER[7]

And the First Commissioner replied to the King's Private Secretary:

> . . . I return H.M.'s note and I suppose that the Lord Chamberlain will deal with the offending Ladies.
>
> Meanwhile we will tell the Police that if the Circus Lady reappears she is to be requested to leave the Row . . .[8]

And there the matter appears to have died.

The addition of sculptural works of various kinds to Hyde Park and Kensington Gardens has gone on during the present century at irregular but not infrequent intervals.

In 1903, the authorities agreed that a cast of G. F. Watts's large equestrian figure that represents 'Physical Energy' should be placed in Kensington Gardens, the site selected, a few hundred yards only from the Albert Memorial, being a particularly important one, as this large piece of sculpture catches the eye, now, at the vanishing point of perspective of no less than eight of the Gardens' principal tree-lined avenues. As far back as 1870, Watts had been working on a huge equestrian monument – it was to be sold, when finished, to the immensely rich Duke of Westminster, and it was intended to act as a memorial to the Duke's distinguished ancestor Hugh Lupus, who in the time of King William I had been Warden of the Marches. In 1902, the year in which Watts had been asked by King Edward VII to accept the newly-founded Order of Merit, the artist had agreed to a suggestion that the statue should be cast in bronze and that the cast should be set up at Groote Schuur, near Cape Town, as a memorial to Cecil Rhodes and to Rhodes's achievements as an Empire builder. The further cast set up in Kensington Gardens after Watts's death can be better understood, perhaps, if the artist's own words about it are recalled. It was, he said,

> . . . A symbol of that restless physical impulse to seek the still un-achieved in the domain of material things. . . . The idea is symbolically to suggest that activity which (after something has been achieved) is compelling man to undertake a new enterprise. The horse is restrained by the hand which, as if on the

tiller of a rudder, is not reigning [*sic*] it back. This is a symbol of something done for the time, while the rider looks out for the next thing to do. . . .

Four years after 'Physical Energy' was set up in Kensington Gardens, a double-life-size portrait of King William III, with long hair, plumed hat and knee boots, was presented to King Edward VII by Kaiser William II 'for the British nation'. This statue, the work of a sculptor named Bauche, was set up in the Gardens on the south side of Kensington Palace, and now looks down at those approaching the Palace from Kensington High Street.

Most beautiful of all London statues (according to a survey carried out among its readers in 1912 by a periodical called *John O'London's Weekly*) is Sir George Frampton's 'Peter Pan', which was put up in Kensington Gardens in that year. This sentimental representation of Sir James Barrie's never-ageing little paragon (based, it is now known, on a series of photographs of young Michael Llewelyn Davies, in fancy costume, taken by Barrie himself) stands on an *art nouveau* base that is liberally supplied with bronze bunnies and fairies and other endearing small creatures. Wendy, with a puzzled expression on her face, is also included. Percy Wyndham Lewis, the author and painter, was openly critical of the Barrie cult when he wrote: 'The sickly and dismal spirit of that terrible key-book *Peter Pan* has sunk into every tissue of the social life of England'; but when some vandals ventured to tar and feather the statue the uproar in the papers lasted for over a week.

The memorial for the Cavalrymen killed in the 1914–18 War, carried out by Captain Adrian Jones and put up by the Stanhope Gate, is accomplished and uncontroversial, but the same cannot be said of the notorious carving commissioned by the Royal Society for the Protection of Birds and carried out by Jacob (later, Sir Jacob) Epstein as a memorial to W. H. Hudson. This was placed in 1925 inside a small bird sanctuary a little to the north and east of the Rennies' bridge over the Serpentine. In his writings, Hudson often described with great feeling the birds he had studied

in the London parks, recalling in one particularly memorable passage
the severe winter of 1892–3 when 'hundreds of working men and
boys would take advantage of their free hour at dinner time to . . .
give the scraps left over from their meals to the birds'. Public
feeling was offended by the heavy and apparently insensitive forms
of Epstein's 'Rima' – Rima being, as readers of Hudson's works
may remember, a semi-human embodiment of the spirit of the
forest in his *Green Mansions*. H. J. Massingham, in *London Scene*,
criticized Epstein's memorial at some length, saying:

> . . . The large eagle-like bird in the sculpture must be a portrait
> statue of old Hudson himself. When I used to go and see him at
> St Luke's Road, Bayswater, and go out to lunch with him at
> Whiteley's, it was like taking one of the hunched eagles at the
> Zoo out of his cage for an airing. . . .

'Take this horror out of the Park!' screamed the headlines of
the *Daily Mail* after the relief had been unveiled, with obvious
distaste, by the Prime Minister, Mr Stanley Baldwin. A letter
demanding that 'Rima' should be removed from the park was
published in the *Morning Post* – it bore the signatures of Hilaire
Belloc, Conan Doyle and several other writers. Some of the more
affronted – and less literary – critics managed to demonstrate
their disapproval by daubing the work with green paint.

But Epstein had his champions, too. 'It cannot be in the public
interest to humiliate a well-known and experienced sculptor who
has done his best with a public commission', wrote the eminent
artist Muirhead Bone to Lord Peel, who was His Majesty's Commissioner of Works. The precedent would be established, Bone
went on, that no sculpture of a bold or unconventional kind could
ever hope to secure official permission. 'Rima', then, was allowed
to remain in the park.

There are two other rather odd features – one in Hyde Park,
one in Kensington Gardens – whose origins ought to be explained.

In the Dell – the attractive glade through which the outgoing
waters of the Serpentine appear to flow – there is a large stone
that could well have been taken there from some ancient druidic

or Gorsedd circle. (Some people have mistakenly said that it was brought to London from Stonehenge by King Charles I.) The stone came, in fact, from Cornwall and was incorporated in a drinking fountain put up in the Dell in 1861. When the fountain was demolished some years later, the stone, weighing about seven tons, was allowed to remain where it was.

The other mystifying object is the 'Elfin Oak', a half tree-trunk which was set up in Kensington Gardens, a little to the north and east of the Round Pond, in 1928. Fashioned by Ivor Innes in the quaint style of the period, with gnomes, elves, goblins and other fantastical small creatures, the oak has since been moved to the Children's Playground at the north-west corner of the Park and it has been refurbished recently by Spike Milligan, the comedian.

The question of what is, and what is not, acceptable behaviour in a Royal Park has been for a long time warmly debated. (As early as 1787 the 'Proclamation Society' for the suppression of vice, founded by William Wilberforce, was campaigning against 'the lungs of London' being turned into 'the lusts of London'. And, in the 1970s, the holding of 'Pop Festivals' in Hyde Park has aroused storms of controversy.) The matter caused a national sensation in April 1926 when two constables of 'A' Division of the Metropolitan Police, patrolling a footpath in Hyde Park, saw a man and a young woman sitting on two chairs about ten yards from the path. The man appeared to the constables to have his right hand under the young woman's dress, and her left hand was, as the constables discreetly described it, 'on his person'. One of the policemen wrote down what happened as they approached the intimate pair:

> . . . When we arrived close up to them I said 'We are Police Officers in Plain Clothes, we shall take you into custody for behaving in a manner reasonably likely to offend against public decency.' Both immediately stood up, the man pulled his overcoat across his front with his right hand and commenced to fasten up the front of his trousers with his left and said, 'I am not the usual Riff Raff I am a man of substance, for God's sake let me go.' The woman made no reply. . . .[9]

Unfortunately for the policemen, the 'man of substance' happened to be Sir Leo Chiozza Money, author of several advanced books on economics, ex-Cabinet Minister, and a friend of many important people. After Sir Leo, struggling violently, had been taken with the young woman to the Police Station in Hyde Park, he insisted that he should be allowed to speak by telephone to the Secretary of State for Home Affairs, with whom, he claimed, he was on very close terms. In fact, Sir Leo's attempts to get in touch with the Home Secretary considerably delayed the couple's temporary release.

The two appeared at Marlborough Street Police Court on the following morning, and were remanded until 1 May in their own recognizances. Inquiries made during the remand established that nothing was known that might be detrimental to the young woman's character. She and her family were apparently 'quite respectable'.

At the remand hearing, Counsel appeared for both sides. Sir Leo, having a very deep pocket, had been able to call on the services of the brilliant (and expensive) man of law, Sir Henry Curtis Bennett. Sir Henry, with his legendary acumen, seized on the fact that the two police witnesses had failed to take the name and address of a man who happened to have picked up and handed in Sir Leo's umbrella, and who might conceivably have acted as an independent witness of the affair. Before he had finished his cross examination, the crafty barrister, by drawing this red herring across the trail, had somehow made it appear as if it was the two policemen who were on trial and not Sir Leo and his lady friend. Without waiting for the young woman to be called to give evidence, the Learned Magistrate, H. L. Cancellor Esquire, found the defendants Not Guilty, and awarded costs against the police.

Any ordinary man might well have been satisfied with such an outcome to a case like this, but Sir Leo was not content to let matters rest, and he fussed around so busily in the very highest circles that on 7 May 1928 Sir William Davison, M.P., rose in the House of Commons to ask Sir William Joynson-Hicks, the Secretary of State for Home Affairs, whether his attention had been called to the recent case before Mr Cancellor, at the Marlborough Street Police Court, where two persons of good repute and position had been arrested and charged by policemen in plain clothes for an alleged offence against public decency in Hyde Park. Sir William asked, further, if the Home Secretary was aware that the charge had been dismissed, with costs against the police, and he wanted to know what action was being taken. The Home Secretary promised to make a statement at the earliest possible moment.

Very soon after that, the matter became more involved. The Home Secretary asked the Director of Public Prosecutions to look into the affair, in case the two police officers concerned had committed perjury. The Director of Public Prosecutions sought the help of the Commissioner of Police of the Metropolis. The Commisioner of Police of the Metropolis appointed one of his Chief Inspectors, a Mr Collins, to make the necessary inquiries. In the course of his inquiries, Mr Collins invited the lady in the case to visit him at the Metropolitan Police Headquarters, and he sent a police car to fetch her to New Scotland Yard.

The young woman stayed with Chief Inspector Collins for some four hours, and after the interview was over she told Sir Leo about it. Sir Leo, reacting hysterically, made so much fuss in his elevated circles that a Parliamentary Tribunal had to be set up, under the chairmanship of Sir John Eldon Bankes, K.C., 'To enquire into the matter of the interrogation of Miss Marjorie Irene Savidge by Chief Inspector Collins at New Scotland Yard on 15th May'. A blaze of publicity followed at once. 'Savagery at Scotland Yard!' screamed the headline to an article in *The Outlook*, a Magazine for Men and Women price twopence, and other and more reputable papers reacted in a similar manner. Chief Inspector Collins was allowed to take legal action against the editor and publisher of *The Outlook*, the two policemen originally involved were permitted to commence proceedings for libel against the editor and publisher of *The Observer* for an article that had appeared in that paper, and a number of similar cases followed.

The outcome of the inquiry was almost entirely satisfactory to the police. On 16 July 1928 the Secretary of State for Home Affairs stated in the House of Commons that he had informed the Commissioner of Police for the Metropolis that in his opinion the action of the officers in question should not be regarded as in any way reflecting to their discredit. Far from being 'savage', Chief Inspector Collins had treated Miss Savidge with fatherly consideration. He had even, it was stated in the report on the inquiry, called her by her Christian name. This caused a certain amount of genteel leg-pulling when the report was debated in the House of Lords. As the Earl of Birkenhead told Lord Arnold, who had spoken with some indignation of the familiarity,

> I can assure the noble Lord, if he will take it from me who have no small experience in this matter, that the practice of calling young ladies by their Christian names has, since the War, become very common in all sections of society. There is nothing alarming about it. The noble Lord's morality need not be in any sense disturbed by it. On the other hand, I should have supposed these police officers were putting the young lady at her ease, and I would suggest to the noble Lord that he might attempt that method himself some other time in a similar difficulty.

Sir Leo Money was taken to court again, five years afterwards, for kissing a thirty-year-old shop assistant in a Southern Railway train against her will. On this later occasion, his friends in high places refused to support him. They had had enough. He was fined Two Pounds, and the affair went off without a parliamentary tribunal being set up.

The year 1929 was an historically difficult one in the Western world. In the early part of the year in Great Britain (as this country was then called) unprecedented numbers of men were unemployed, and protest meetings of equally unprecedented vehemence were held in Hyde Park. In May, there was a General Election. During the run-up to the election the Liberal Party promised to cure unemployment by building a national system of trunk roads at a cost of £42 m. The Conservatives promised to clear the slums. The Labour Party, promising quite a lot of things, won 287 seats and became for the first time the largest party in the Commons. The new Government was able to do little of lasting benefit, however, because on 29 October 1929 the Stock Market in New York fell through the floor. Within just one week after that never-to-be-forgotten day, while ruined financiers flung themselves to death from the high floors of sky-scrapers, 240 leading securities declined in market value by $15,984m. The Wall Street crash immediately affected investment and trade throughout the world, and the almost simultaneous collapse, in Britain, of Clarence Hatry's commercial empire helped to intensify the abysmal gloom. In spite of the disastrous circumstances prevailing at the time, however, this Labour Government, inspired by the compassionate Minister George Lansbury, did manage to bring off *one* successful and lasting achievement – they established a Blackpool-type 'Lido' on the banks of the Hyde Park Serpentine. (His Majesty King George V insisted on looking at samples of the water under a microscope before he would agree to the idea, in case the Lido should be a hazard to his subjects' health.) This amenity has since been enjoyed, in hot summer weather, by innumerable bathers of most ages and all shades of political opinion. (Some hardy people even appear to relish a swim in the lake in the middle of winter. They are 'City gents, about thirty altogether, who do it to keep their systems toned up', explained the Head Attendant recently. 'Brisk dip first thing in the morning – in winter we open at 6 a.m., close at 8.30 – does you the world of good.' Occasionally, the 'gents' have to break the ice with sledgehammers so that they can get their daily plunge.)

Just as during the 1930s and 1940s London itself changed perceptibly – some people would put it even more strongly than that – so, too, in true microcosmic fashion, did Hyde Park. Of course, the Park's basic landscape remained, in geographical terms, more or less the same – neither Her Majesty Queen Mary, Consort of King George V, nor the much-loved lady who was the next Queen of England were great lake-diggers or great mound-raisers, as King George II's Queen Caroline had been – but in at least one other respect during those decades Hyde Park improved (as Mr Samuel Goldwyn might have said) for the worse.

The thin end of the wedge of this paradoxical deterioration may have started, it could be argued, when King Edward VII and his advisers let pass a great opportunity – the last, surely, any

5

Sovereign of England would ever have – to exclude all petrol-driven automobiles from his Central London territories. A Monarch who in 1908 had said firmly that the Royal Parks were his, and that he would not allow them to become places to be passed through as quickly as possible by people in fast noisy vehicles who were eager only to be somewhere else, might have lost his Crown and possibly even his head, but his memory would have been idolized for ever by all appreciative loiterers and enjoyers – people, in short, of the kind who had stood on chairs by Rotten Row only a few years before so that they could catch a glimpse of the lovely Mrs Langtry or some other fashionable beauty as she was driven past in her elegant carriage. By 1930, alas! parts of Hyde Park resembled the Brooklands racetrack, and they have got no better since.

During World War II, large tracts of Hyde Park were occupied most effectively by anti-aircraft gunners who sent up from them into London's upper air levels some lethal 'firework displays'. After the War was over, the Park was used for assembling those members of the Armed Forces, and others who had been ordered or invited, to take part in the memorable Victory Parade. Shortly after that, Hyde Park was allowed to relapse once more into its normal and comparatively somnolent peacetime condition, with equestrians, footballers, oarsmen and oarswomen, dinghy sailors, canoeists, putters, bowlers, kite fliers and dog exercisers providing the principal diversions, but one is still apt to see teams of artillery-men speeding across the upper levels of the Park as they race with their guns to the place from which they are to fire off a ceremonial salute in honour of a Royal Birthday, or of some other joyful occasion.

In spite of such man-made disturbances, Hyde Park and Kensington Gardens manage to seem refreshingly natural today, for all that they are so close to the crowded streets and squares of Permissive London. There are not many wild animals now to be seen in these two Parks – rabbits and hedgehogs occasionally, greedy grey squirrels always, and in the late evening perhaps a bat – but their well-wooded expanses are understandably attractive to wild birds: representatives of ninety-four different species were seen by, or reported to, the members of the Committee on Bird Sanctuaries in the Royal Parks during 1970. Of this remarkable total the adults of about thirty different species are known to have built nests and reared their young in the Parks. Most, if not all, of the wild birds seen in St James's Park can also be observed in Hyde Park and Kensington Gardens, but there are, in addition, a small number of truly woodland birds that prefer the leafier groves to the north of Knightsbridge – the blackcap, which sings so beautifully, is heard there every summer, and the willow warbler is known to have nested recently in the Bird Sanctuary by the Long Water. In 1972 two pairs of long-tailed tits brought up their families successfully in Hyde Park. Visitors of even greater rarity that have been seen on or near the Serpentine include the little auk, the avocet, the hoopoe, the osprey, the black tern and an Iceland gull.[10]

The majority of the trees in Hyde Park today are fine specimens of species that are fairly well known – there is a handsome walnut tree (*Juglans Regia*) opposite the Lido, for instance, and a particularly good example of *Quercus Robur* (the 'Common' or 'English' oak) a little to the south of the reservoir public conveniences. But the Park has its rarities too, and a few trees of which the staff are particularly proud.[11]

Near Hyde Park Corner, for instance, a tree-lover can see the relatively scarce yellow wood (*Cladastris Lutea*) – a tree introduced originally from the eastern states of America. There is a Caucasian elm (*Zelkova Carpinifolia*) in the Enclosure at Hyde Park Corner. And in the same Enclosure one can see the beautiful cut silver leaf maple (*Acer Saccharinum Laciniatum*) which has leaves that shimmer unforgettably when moved by the lightest of breezes.

Near the monument to W. H. Hudson, a little to the north-east of the bridge over the Serpentine, there are specimens of *Magnolia Delavayi* (this has leaves that are among the largest found on any evergreen tree or shrub grown out of doors in the British Isles) and of the Chinese varnish tree (*Rhus Potaninii*), a lovely tree first brought from the Far East in 1902 by E. H. Wilson (its leaves turn, in autumn, from pink to the richest crimson). And, near the Lower Dell Path, one can see the relatively scarce *Pterocarya Fraxinifolia*, or Caucasian wing-nut tree. The leaves of this tree, turning bright yellow in October, make a magnificent show.

Several of the most noteworthy trees now in Kensington Gardens are to be found by, or near, the famous Flower Walk.

At the west end of the Flower Walk one can see the Chinese persimmon (*Diospyros Kaki*) – a small tree that has been cultivated for centuries in the Far East for its edible fruits and is cherished here for the spectacular orange and plum-purple colours displayed in autumn by its large lustrous leaves. Not far away are fine specimens of the cork oak (*Quercus Suber*) and of the strange tree which is known by arboriculturists as *Umbellularia Californica* and variously, by lesser men and women, as the 'Californian bay', the 'Californian laurel', the 'Oregon myrtle' and the 'Headache Tree'. The tree was given this last and oddest name because its leaves, if crushed, give off a rich fruity aroma which is liable to cause a sharp headache some time after it has been inhaled. (Veteran gardeners used to tell hair-raising stories of finding their elderly employers prostrate and unconscious after they had been overcome by the powerful fumes.)

But not all the unusual trees in Kensington Gardens are concentrated by the Flower Walk. Near the Art Gallery that has been opened by the Serpentine there is a particularly fine golden-leaved Indian bean tree (*Catalpa Bignonioides Aurea*) which is usually the last of all the trees in the Park to come into leaf; between the Round Pond and the Bayswater Road can be seen the very scarce 'true service tree' (*Sorbus Domestica*); by the North Walk the *Zelkova Sinica* or 'Chinese zelkova', the young growths of which are most attractively pink-tinted in Spring; by the water's edge, near the Peter Pan statue, the deciduous swamp cypress (*Taxodium Distichum*), a strikingly beautiful tree introduced into this country by John Tradescant from America about 1640; and, by Kensington Palace itself, the *Paulownia Lilacina*, which is closely related to the Chinese foxglove tree, introduced via Japan in 1834. The *Paulownia* gives a wonderful display in June with its lilac-coloured flowers which are, like the flowers of our native foxglove, pale yellow in the throat.

In the opinion of many perceptive people, Hyde Park and Kensington Gardens – beautiful, still, at almost any hour of daylight in any month of the year – are at their very best in the very early morning in the late Spring and early Summer, when the azaleas and similar sugary plants are in full bloom. Then, before motor traffic has had a chance to become heavy in the roads fringing the Parks, and while the sun is still low enough over the horizon to provide some spectacularly dramatic lighting effects, the sleek black horses of the Sovereign's Household Brigade with their gorgeously caparisoned riders at exercise in the Park, and the elegant, gleaming carriages and brakes from the Royal Mews being driven there may seem to the bemused onlooker to be taking part in one of the most sumptuous theatrical productions ever to be staged or put on the screen. No commercial undertaking could, indeed, ever afford to mount such a magnificent pageant – or, even if the necessary funds were available, would have the technical resources to do so. Fortunately for the citizens of London who pass Hyde Park and Kensington Gardens while all this is going on, this feast for the eyes is perennial, and is offered to the early-rising spectator without any immediate charge.

Chapter 8

Greenwich Park – the Stuarts, and after

Between Greenwich Park and the River Thames stand, now, some of the most magnificent buildings in the world.

The earliest of these buildings – the superbly proportioned Queen's House – was a gift from King James I to his wife, Anne of Denmark. Relations between the two had become a little strained – possibly, on account of James's liking for handsome and lively young men – so Inigo Jones, as architect to the Queen, was invited in 1616 to build a new home for her near, but not actually adjoining, the old Palace of Placentia, which was piled up, in a truly jumbled medieval fashion, on the bank of the river.

At that time, the main road from Deptford to Woolwich ran right across the royal grounds, neatly dividing those parts of the manor that were closest to the riverside palace and were largely laid out as private gardens from the wilder and more heavily wooded deer park to the south. The surface of this road was poor – the wheels of the heavy carts that passed along it used to churn the Greenwich soil into mud in wet weather – and it was separated from the royal lands on either side by a high brick wall.

Surveying the ground for possible sites for a house for the Queen, Inigo Jones saw that about half-way along the wall on the south side of the road, there was a small structure known as the 'Lodge Gate', through which members of the Royal Family and their courtiers would pass when they wished to enter the more distant parts of the Palace precincts. The building was used, too, as an elevated grandstand from which privileged spectators could

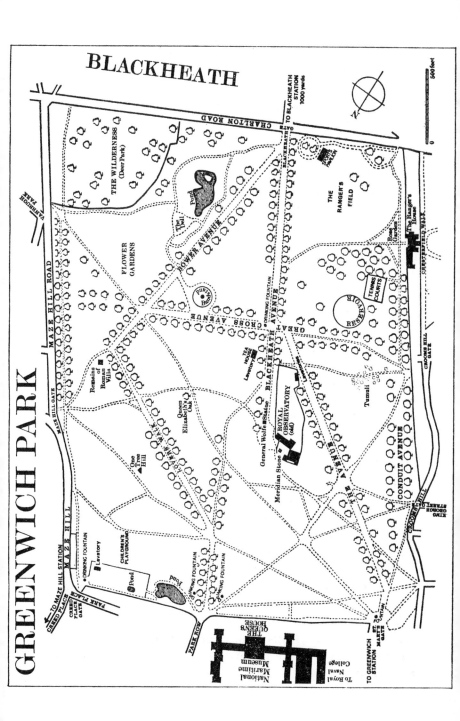

GREENWICH PARK

BLACKHEATH

watch hunting and other sports that took place in the Park. Inigo
Jones examined this old building and saw that the ground where
it stood would make the best possible site for the proposed Queen's
House. He decided that the house should form, by its basic shape,
a bridge over the public highway.

The Queen's House that went up on this spot was then, and
still is today, one of England's greatest architectural masterpieces.
While he had been touring in Italy in the years 1601 and 1613,
Inigo Jones had carefully made measured drawings of the elegant
villas which Andrea Palladio had been designing in that country for
the landed gentlefolk. In a restrained and elegant fashion, the great
Welsh architect made use of his newly-acquired knowledge, according to this admirable principle, as expressed in his own words:

> ... For as outwardly every wyse man carrieth a graviti in
> Publicke Places ... so in architecture ye outward ornaments
> ought to be sollid, proportionable according to the rulles, mascu-
> line and unaffected. ...

As it was first envisaged, the house was to consist of two rectangular
blocks, one on each side of the public road, with a raised, canti-
levered and very grand passage-chamber (known as 'The Bridge
Room') between them. Before it had risen above ground floor
level, however, the Queen died, and work on the building was
discontinued.

During the 1630s, Inigo Jones worked on the Queen's House
again – for Henrietta Maria, wife of King Charles I, on this later
occasion. Allowed to keep the house as her home after the Restoration, the King's mother found it, in the new expansive age, too
small for her needs, and she asked Inigo Jones's pupil John Webb
to enlarge it. Webb added two further bridges over the public
road – one on each side of the original Bridge Room – and so gave
the house the almost perfect square form that is so much admired
today by observant visitors to Greenwich Park.

Soon after King Charles II was restored to the throne in 1660,
the royal palace at Greenwich and its park were given a thorough
and realistic survey.

The old Tudor and pre-Tudor buildings huddled by the river, which had been sadly neglected during the Commonwealth and were probably riddled with woodworm, dry rot and other horrors, were hopelessly out of date and were promptly pulled down. The materials of which the old building had been made were tipped into the Thames – a solitary crypt, to which visitors are rarely admitted, is all that remains of Placentia – and on the flattened and extended site King Charles set out to have a new and very grand palace built, as grand as any that he had seen over in Europe. He asked John Webb to act as the architect, and Webb proposed to the King that he should put up an elegant three-sided court overlooking the Thames. Charles agreed, and in 1664 Webb started work on his great enterprise. He began by putting up a long range of buildings on one side of the projected court – the 'King's House', which is still in existence.

King Charles had decided, meanwhile, to have the old deer park to the south of the Queen's House completely re-landscaped so that it would provide a civilized pleasure ground for his splendid new Greenwich Palace. He invited André Le Nôtre, the celebrated French master of garden design, to plan this great undertaking, and to supervise the actual planting he appointed Sir William Boreman as Keeper of the Park. Le Nôtre produced a semi-formal layout in the French style, that was criss-crossed with more or less straight avenues and paths. For several years, during the 1660s, Sir William Boreman's gardeners worked their way round the Park, constructing terraces, which have by now practically disappeared, on the north-facing slopes of the high escarpment which divides the Park into an upper and a lower half, and planting, according to Le Nôtre's instructions, hundreds of Spanish chestnuts, elms, limes, London planes and other trees, some of which have survived to the present day.

It would be impossible to pretend, though, that Le Nôtre's scheme, which looked so well on paper, worked out as satisfactorily in practice. If the great Frenchman had journeyed to England to study at first hand the ground he had been commissioned to re-landscape, he would surely have taken into account the inevitable effect of the great central slopes, which may not have been shown clearly on the maps and charts he was studying. As it was, Le Nôtre failed to cross the Channel, and his grand central avenue of trees that was intended to lead from Black Heath towards the Queen's House leads, instead, towards a skyline, beyond which the ground drops away sharply for more than a hundred feet. To see the Queen's House in all its splendour, now, from the upper levels of Greenwich Park, one has to reach that skyline, and then look down.

By 1669, the funds that King Charles had available for the building of his great Greenwich Palace were rapidly running out, and the King, who had become very fond of Hampton Court, was equally rapidly losing interest in his alternative home so far away downstream. Work stopped on the unfinished palace at Greenwich, then, and the place stood empty for the next twenty years.

In 1675, however, some building took place in the neighbourhood that was to make a great difference to Greenwich Park. By then, the King had become seriously concerned with the difficulties that his seamen were having in navigation, and with their need for greater certainty. But his attention had been drawn to a Reverend John Flamsteed, who had declared that no person could ever discover longitude exactly until some really accurate celestial observations had been made. So, King Charles appointed Flamsteed as his first 'Observator' or Astronomer Royal, and he commissioned Sir Christopher Wren, by Royal Warrant, to design a suitable building 'for the Observator's habitation and a little for Pompe', as Wren drily described it.

The building had to be put up very cheaply, for there was at the time a serious shortage of royal money. So it was decided that Wren should use the site and foundations of Duke Humphrey's old Watch Tower in which, in 1579, the Earl of Leicester had been locked up after Queen Elizabeth had become angry with her one-time favourite for marrying the Countess of Essex. To cover the cost of the necessary materials, £520 was raised from the sale of old spoiled gunpowder.

The imposing front elevation of Flamsteed House – as Wren's building is now called – is like a piece of stage scenery made from rose-coloured bricks with stone dressings, flanked by a pair of decorous summerhouses. Behind this grand Renaissance façade Wren contrived, for the Reverend Mr Flamsteed, the famous 'Octagon Room', designing the high eight-sided working place especially so that it would accommodate the extra-large clocks which the first Astronomer Royal had ordered from Thomas Tompion. These giant timepieces, invented only a few years before, were fitted with thirteen-foot long pendulums that were suspended above the clock faces. The extreme length of the pendulums was thought at the time to shorten the relative length of the swing, thus minimizing air resistance and causing less friction, but this refinement was afterwards found to be unnecessary. In spite of their superfluous height, Flamsteed's great clocks were used for the first really accurate measurement of Mean (or Average) Time – a remarkable feat with which the name of Greenwich will always be associated.

Below the Octagon Room, one can now see the rooms in which Flamsteed lived during the three decades he devoted to his historic researches. They were by no means happy years for the great astronomer. He was troubled, from the very start, by poverty, since the King failed to keep his promise to provide instruments for his first 'Observator' and Flamsteed had to obtain, and pay for, his own. Then the King failed to give Flamsteed the sufficient annuity he had undertaken to pay – the Astronomer Royal found that he was expected to live on a meagre £100 a year, which was scarcely enough to allow him to employ any competent assistants, and he had to eke out his stipend by giving private tuition to the sons of the rich. As a result, possibly, of his incessant labours under these pitiful conditions, Flamsteed's health broke down.

To add a last straw to his troubles, Flamsteed fell out with the eminent scientist Sir Isaac Newton. Newton, who was working at the time on his entirely new and immensely important theory of gravity, badly needed to make use of the exact astronomical data that he knew Flamsteed was amassing. Unwilling to publish any part of his observations until he could be certain of the accuracy of them all, Flamsteed was (from Newton's point of view) unnecessarily obstructive. Determined not to be balked, Newton published, with his friends, a pirated version of Flamsteed's masterwork, the *Historia Celestis*. The book was so 'mangled and garbled', in Flamsteed's view, that when after three years he was given the three hundred copies that had not so far been issued, the old man made a great bonfire of them 'as a sacrifice to Heavenly Truth'.

Although the buildings at the old Royal Observatory now contain some splendid collections of early astronomical and other instruments, to many people the most compelling exhibit of all is a narrow straight strip of metal that is set in a cobbled courtyard outside the South Block. This line of demarcation has been internationally recognized, since 1884, as the Prime Meridian or longitudinal zero of the world, and visitors queue up to be photographed with a foot on each side of the line – that is, with one foot in the Eastern Hemisphere and the other in the Western.

Shortly after they were invited to the English throne King William of Orange and Mary his Queen decided to build a Naval Hospital for disabled and superannuated seamen. It was to be put up on the lines of Les Invalides, and of the Hospital for Army Pensioners which had only recently been opened at Chelsea. As the royal couple preferred to live at Kensington and at Hampton Court, Greenwich would make a very good place for it, they thought. There, the elderly and disabled seamen for whom the Hospital was intended would get constant entertainment from watching the great number of ships that passed on their way up and down the river. So they invited Sir Christopher Wren to act as the 'Surveyor' or principal architect of the scheme. Wren was enthusiastic – so enthusiastic, in fact, that he is believed to have worked for twenty years or more on the project without charging any fees.

Aided by Nicholas Hawksmoor, then, Wren planned and drew a superb range of baroque buildings, which would have had as their culminating point a massive central Hall and Chapel topped by a great dome like the one on St Paul's Cathedral that is now so much admired. If Wren's Hospital had been put up as he intended, it would have been one of the most splendid architectural achievements in Europe. Unfortunately, though, the Queen noticed that the masterpiece, if put up according to Wren's plans, would shut off completely any view of the river that might have been enjoyed from the Queen's House, and vice versa. She insisted, therefore, that the strip of land between Inigo Jones's villa and the Thames should be left clear of all buildings and she asked Wren, in effect, to take his plans away and to start thinking all over again.

Wren, in reply, suggested that he should move to one side the whole of the building he had planned, leaving, in that way, a free view of the river from the Queen's House. But that would have meant demolishing the block already built for King Charles II by John Webb, and the Queen would not agree to that plan, either. So Wren had to compromise with his adamant royal patron and the buildings that went up eventually, though very fine and rich, are, as Doctor Johnson observed to James Boswell, 'too much detached to make one great whole'.

Even though it had such a magnificent Painted Hall and so superb a Chapel and so many other architecturally splendid features, no one could claim that Wren's great Hospital ever fulfilled its original purpose successfully. The architect had been, in a sense, much too ambitious – the elderly and disabled sailors who were to be housed in the Hospital would have been much happier in more modest and more homely surroundings. 'Columns, colonnades and friezes ill accord with bull beef and sour beer mixed with water', complained a Captain Baillie, in the late eighteenth century. The old mariners grumbled on – about their food and drink, their boredom, and the senseless humiliations that were imposed on them if they dared to protest, or in any other way misbehaved themselves – until Victorian days.

Wren's work at Greenwich was continued by two other masters of the baroque style – Nicholas Hawksmoor and Sir John Vanbrugh, who were appointed successively Surveyors to the Royal Hospital. Close to the Maze Hill Gate of the Park, one can still see 'Vanbrugh Castle', the mock-medieval turreted mansion which Sir John built in 1719, and in which he lived until 1726. This strange *jeu d'esprit* is often referred to as 'Bastille House', but it is not clear whether this name was given to Sir John's home because it resembled, in some of its details, the French fortress, or because Sir John himself once spent several months in that grim prison, suspected of being an English spy. (At the time of writing,

'Vanbrugh Castle' has ceased to be a boarding school for the orphaned sons of Royal Air Force men and is up for sale.)

On the western fringes of the Park, there are several fine mansions built during the late seventeenth and early eighteenth centuries.

Some of the most elegant of these were constructed illegally, during the reign of King Charles II, on ground known as 'The Waste' which lay between the Park and Black Heath. The man responsible – Andrew Snape, Serjeant-Farrier to the King, and described by John Evelyn as 'a man full of projects' – helped himself to the ground first, and asked permission to do so afterwards. It was only after prolonged litigation that a formal lease was negotiated.

Macartney House – at that time, rather smaller than it is now, for some extensions have since been built on to it – was bought in 1751 by General Edward Wolfe, who paid £3,000 for it. The General's son James, who described his father's home by the side of Greenwich Park as 'the prettiest situated house in England', often stayed there between campaigns (for four years he courted unsuccessfully a girl named Elizabeth Lawson, who lived at The White House next door) and it was from Macartney House that the younger Wolfe left in 1759 for his historic, and more satisfying, adventures at the conquest of Quebec. A statue of James Wolfe – the work of Tait Mackenzie – now stands near the old Observatory in Greenwich Park and provides a focal point, of a sort, for André Le Nôtre's mismanaged Grand Central Avenue, which was intended by the Frenchman to lead from the Black Heath Gate of the Park to the superlatively satisfying climax of a view of the Queen's House. The Wolfe Statue was unveiled shortly before World War II by the Marquis of Montcalm, who was a direct descendant of James Wolfe's principal opponent.

Chesterfield House – now called 'The Ranger's House' – was inherited, on his brother's death in 1748, by Philip Stanhope, Fourth Earl of Chesterfield. Lord Chesterfield improved and enlarged the relatively small brick villa that was standing on Snape's site, adding single-storey wings with semicircular bays. Here he wrote many of his famous *Letters* to his natural son – 'Without the desire of pleasing no man living can please', he exhorted the long-suffering young man. 'Let that desire be the spring of all your words and actions' – and he enriched his acre of ground which, he said, afforded him more pleasure than kingdoms do to Kings, by the successful cultivation on it of pineapples, melons and grapes. In 1815, Chesterfield House became the official residence of the Rangers of Greenwich Park. Nineteenth-century occupants of the house included His Royal Highness Prince Arthur, Duke of Connaught, and Field-Marshal Lord Wolseley.

The Ranger's House, which was acquired by the London County Council in 1902, was damaged during World War II and then restored in 1960. Further restoration was carried out in 1974, and the building is now given immense distinction by being used to house the sumptuous paintings of the Suffolk Collection which show many sixteenth- and early seventeenth-century royal and very grand personages at their finest. Chamber music concerts, art exhibitions and meetings are occasionally held in the Grand Salon in the South Wing, which was almost certainly decorated by Isaac Ware, who built Chesterfield House in Mayfair. (This splendid room has a particularly handsome plaster ceiling which incorporates in its design the badge of the Order of the Garter.) It is an exceptionally rewarding experience on a warm summer afternoon, to be able to walk in Greenwich Park past flower beds filled with herbaceous plants and shrubs which have a slightly old-fashioned flavour such as buddleia, perowskia and rosemary, through a rose garden, up a short flight of stone steps, and through the back door of Lord Chesterfield's house into his beautifully proportioned rooms.

One of the great houses that were put up on Snape's ground has disappeared practically without trace. This was Montagu House, which stood at the corner of Chesterfield Walk, where a Greater London Council Parks Department Depôt stands today. For some years, Montagu House was lived in by Caroline, Princess of Wales, estranged wife of King George III's eldest son, when she had the sinecure job of Ranger of Greenwich Park which brought her a stipend of £500 per year. Here Princess Caroline committed the alleged indiscretions which led to the so-called 'Delicate Investigation' of 1806 into her morals and behaviour. As soon as he could, after his detested wife left the country in 1815, the Prince Regent had Montagu House demolished and the materials sold at auction. Only one sad relic of the house remains – an open-air bath which the Princess had had constructed in the grounds, and which can now be seen inside the Park, midway between The Ranger's House and the Chesterfield Gate. The bath may have been, originally, covered – it was only revealed when a dilapidated summerhouse was demolished in 1890 – and its sides and the steps by which anyone using the bath would descend into the water were formerly covered with small enamelled white tiles, most of which are now missing. A lead pipe, two inches in diameter, carried water to the bath, but apparently there was no outlet, so the water must have been removed by being baled out, or by the use of some kind of pump.

About 1700, passes were issued to people of good reputation who lived in the district and who wanted to enjoy the seclusion of Greenwich Park. The Hanoverian monarchs took little interest in Greenwich, however, and after 1730, for more than a century, the Park was sadly neglected. The public was not freely admitted until the reign of King William IV.

Between 1807 and 1816, East and West Wings were added to the Queen's House. Added also, to link them to the original building, was the Colonnade which follows the line of the old Woolwich road. The extensions, designed by Daniel Asher Alexander, are said by some local historians to have been intended to commemorate Admiral Lord Nelson's great victory at the Battle of Trafalgar; others, lacking firm evidence either way, claim that the new blocks were put up solely to accommodate the nine hundred pupils – the children of seamen – who were to attend the Royal Hospital Schools, and the Colonnade, they say, was meant to provide a playground and assembly area for the scholars in wet weather. Fortunately, the extensions, in spite of their size, harmonize quite pleasantly with the style of the Queen's House, and the Colonnade may even be said to be an improvement, visually, on the old road.

By 1869, the number of old naval pensioners accommodated in the riverside Hospital had dwindled to such an extent that it was rather pointless to keep the Hospital going. The few remaining old men were quietly moved out to cosier quarters and four years later the buildings were used to house the Royal Naval College, which was moved to Greenwich from Portsmouth and has been there ever since.

In 1880, an elegant cast- and wrought-iron bandstand was put up in the Park near the junction of the Blackheath and the Great Cross Avenues. At roughly the same time, on the other side of the junction of the avenues, a Tea House was put up to accommodate the increasing number of visitors. Here, when it was newly opened, dinners with ham were served for 1s. 6d.

At roughly this time, too, one of the most ancient trees in the Park died – the massive oak around which, according to a local tradition, King Henry VIII had danced with Anne Boleyn. It was certainly standing in their day, and would by that time have been noticeably large. In its internal cavity, now six feet in diameter, Queen Elizabeth I is said to have frequently taken refreshments. A door was at one time placed over the entrance to the tree's hollow trunk, a window overlooking the slope known as One Tree Hill was cut in the side, the floor was paved, and a rustic seat, on which up to fifteen people could sit in relative comfort, was put around the interior. At one time, the tree was used as a jail, in which people who offended against the Park regulations could be temporarily secured. It has also been used as an office from which the Park workers were given their wages. Railed off now, the tree's decrepit stump appears to be held up largely by the ivy that swarms over it in profusion.

On 15 February 1894, the peace of Greenwich Park was dramatically disturbed by the sound of an explosion. On the Zig Zag Path below the old Observatory, the park keepers found a twenty-six-year-old Frenchman named Martial Bourdin kneeling in a pool of his own blood. Bourdin – an Anarchist, who had been on his way up to Flamsteed House with a bomb that he intended to plant there – had suffered terrible injuries, including the loss of his left hand, when the bomb had gone off prematurely, but he was still alive and was able to say, in English, 'Take me home'. He succumbed to his wounds shortly afterwards, however – the victim, some say, of a plot intended to discredit the international

Anarchist movement. The incident provided Joseph Conrad with the theme for his dramatic novel *The Secret Agent*.

In 1899, some new additions were made to the Royal Observatory and became known, by reason of their position, as 'The South Block'. The South Block was opened to the public in 1967 and now contains most of the larger and later instruments included in the Greenwich collection. An outstanding feature in this block is a re-creation, by the Victoria and Albert Museum authorities, of the Reverend John Flamsteed's 'Sextant Room', where, it may fairly be claimed, the basic principles of modern astronomy were first defined. The Museum has set up a small planetarium, too, at which public displays are given – usually, during the afternoon.

There have been fallow deer in Greenwich Park for more than 450 years – the first account we have of them dates from January 1510, when £13 6s. 8d. was paid to one Eustace Browne 'for deer to enstock Greenwich Park'. Then, in 1518, twenty 'quick deer' were transferred by Francis Bryan from Eltham to Greenwich. When A. D. Webster was Superintendent of the Park in 1902, he complained that in recent years several bucks and does had died through being fed indiscriminately by visitors to the Park – in one instance, he said, two hatfuls of orange peel had been found in the stomach of the dead beast. By 1927, the deer were suffering sadly from the increased traffic in the Park and from the worrying attentions of dogs, and it was thought advisable to keep them in a confined space during the week-ends when the Park was busiest. Today, a herd of about thirty head live in their own paddock in the Wilderness at the south-east corner of the Park. From time to time, the blood lines of this herd are changed by the transfer to Greenwich of different beasts from the parks at Bushey, or from Richmond.

Today Greenwich Park is one of the best loved (and on warm summer days one of the most thickly populated) of all London's open spaces. The park officials who, being there every day, have a chance to observe so much, have noticed that regular visitors to the Park, of which there are many, tend to prefer either the lower levels, in the near vicinity of The Queen's House, or the higher ground to the south of the old Observatory. It is not exactly a case

of 'And never the twain shall meet', but the distinction between
the two different classes of visitor is so apparent that it might be
studied profitably by a sociologist.

The lower levels of the Park have, distinctly, the atmosphere
of a seaside holiday resort. There are steep, well-grassed slopes
down which the young can run, roll, or (illegally and dangerously)
ride a bicycle. Between the Park Row Gate and Maze Hill is the
largest children's playground in any of London's Royal Parks,
with a sandpit, innumerable swings, see-saws and other amusing
appliances, and a splendid pond, in which no one could possibly
drown, and which in Summer is packed tightly with little boats.
There are plenty of drinking fountains and lavatories within easy
reach of all, even the very youngest. What more could anyone
want, who cannot manage to get to Southend-on-Sea or Bognor
Regis?

The main features of the higher, and southerly, levels of the
Park provide pleasure in a perceptibly less hectic way.

The Wilderness, in the south-east corner, is, as its name implies,
a largely uncultivated enclosure that looks as if it might be part
of a big country estate. It extends over some thirteen acres, and
its more open parts accommodate the fallow deer mentioned above.
The Wilderness is also regarded as the Park's principal bird
sanctuary.

Next to the Wilderness are the Flower Gardens, which have
lawns shaded by ancient cedar and sweet chestnut trees, as well as
a great variety of beds and borders that are filled, through the
successive seasons of the year, with varied and colourful displays –
some of them being fine enough to earn awards from the Royal
Horticultural Society.

From the Flower Gardens one can walk through the Dell to
the Lake – a small one, little more than a pond in fact, but a sanctuary for ducks, and graced with a delightful island, from which
miniature cascades fall into the surrounding water surfaces. The
gardens on the fringes of the Lake have been most imaginatively
planned.

Just to the west of the Blackheath Avenue, and near the Blackheath Gate, is the Ranger's Field, which looks like an English

village green of the most picturesque sort, and on which cricket is played, during the summer months, by the West Kent Wanderers and their chosen opponents.

In these rural surroundings, wild animals thrive, although they may not show themselves often except to the few people who are about in the Park at dusk or in the very early morning. Field voles and house mice scuttle about busily at these times, and there are hedgehogs and foxes in plenty. (The latter are liable to become diseased, though, so that they no longer resemble the handsome, bushy-tailed creatures of the open countryside.) There are no badgers in Greenwich Park at the moment, but grey squirrels abound, and have to be forcibly discouraged from digging up the gardeners' cherished tulip bulbs.[1]

There are many varieties of wild birds to be seen in the Park, too, besides the ducks already mentioned – knowledgeable observers have distinguished as many as sixty different kinds, including such rarities as the hobby. Kestrels and sparrowhawks are regularly sighted, and there is at the time of writing a carrion crow with one white wing. This crow is not the only example of albino colouring to have been observed among the birds of Greenwich Park in recent years. One wholly white 'blackbird' has made its home in the Park, as well as several partly white ones, and a bird thought to be an escaped canary was identified, shortly after, as an albino great tit.

The Park of Greenwich today contains some extraordinarily fine trees, and some rare specimens. Even a relatively unobservant visitor can hardly fail to notice the few contorted Spanish chestnuts that have managed to survive from the plantings of 1663–5 – there is one twisted old monster quite near the Blackheath Gate, for instance – or the swamp cypress near the St Mary's Gate, or the tulip tree (*Liriodendron Tulipifera*) which bears its peculiar tulip-shaped yellow-green flowers each June and July in the southernmost corner of the Park. There are many other trees in the Park, though, that are likely to catch, and hold, the more informed eye.

In the flower gardens between the Bower Avenue and the Wilderness there are some splendid Lebanese and deodar cedars, and good specimens of the *Catalpa Bignonioides* or Indian bean.

Remarkable, too, is the 'paper birch' (*Betula Papyrifera*) just to the east of the Dell – with the white papery bark of trees of this kind the North American Indian is said to have made his canoes. And even a keen student of trees is liable to be puzzled, at first sight, by the 'single-leaved ash' (*Fraxinus Diversifolia*), a strange variant that occurs very occasionally in wilder surroundings than these.

As a visitor to the Park walks from the Blackheath Gate along the Bower Avenue towards the remains of the Roman Villa and the Maze Hill Gate, he or she will pass some quite unusual trees.

Only a stone's throw from the Pond, there is the remarkably beautiful Chinese yellow wood (*Cladastris Sinensis*) which has leaves that are soft green above a delicate blue-grey on the underside, and which is nearly covered in July with white flowers that are subtly tinged with pink. A little farther along the Avenue one comes across the 'pride of India' or 'golden rain tree' (*Koelreuteria*) introduced originally from China or Korea in or about 1763, which has attractive yellow flowers in mid–August, followed soon after by the tree's conspicuous fruits, each of which contains three black seeds. Just before the Bower Avenue meets the Great Cross Avenue the student of trees can find *Kalopanax Pictus* or the 'prickly castor-oil tree'. At first glance, these trees can be taken for maples, but their identity is easily established if one looks for the stout prickles on their branches and sucker growths.

And elsewhere in Greenwich Park there are certain trees that it would be a pity to miss.

Near the fence that separates the enclosed ground from the Charlton Road, for instance, there is one of the largest and finest specimens in Britain of the *Evodia Hupehensis*, a rare tree introduced from China in 1908, which is one of the very latest of any to flower each year. Not far from the *Evodia* is a *Paulownia Tomentosa*, or foxglove tree. And between the Ranger's House and the Ranger's Field there is a splendid specimen of the very rare chestnut-leaved oak (*Quercus Castaneifolia*) which was introduced from the Caucasus in 1846 and has fine tapered leaves edged with sharply pointed teeth. But, it must be emphasized, this is only a short selection from the trees that Greenwich Park has to offer.

In view of their long and eventful histories, are there ghosts, one might wonder, that haunt any of the Royal Parks of London? If there are, Greenwich Park may well be one of the most frequently visited by spirits – wistful reminders, perhaps, of the rough days when Margaret of Anjou wanted to take Duke Humphrey's riverside manor from him, or of the equally ruthless times when Anne Boleyn, attractive mistress of the Palace of Placentia, was fatally unfaithful to her unpitying husband King Henry VIII. Two at least of the officials responsible at the time of writing for the upkeep of Greenwich Park have seen, in the dim half-light of some early summer morning, a shadowy and unexplained figure move silently, like a wraith of mist, across the grassy plains of the Park. But there have been no members of the general public inside the gates when these 'sightings' have occurred. Possibly, the phantom that has been observed is the shade of some really haughty and intolerant courtier of old – the sort who, once commoners had been admitted, would not have been seen dead in the Park.

Chapter 9

Richmond Park

There may have been a manor house at Richmond-upon-Thames as early as 1066, though the name of 'Richmond' would not have been associated with the place until nearly four centuries later.

The first manor on this lovely stretch of the Thames of which there is any positive record belonged to King Henry I (1100–35). It would have been a typical country house of the period, with a large central hall and a few rooms leading from it. To reflect the beauty and brilliance of its site, the royal owner called the manor 'Shene' or 'Schene'.

By the fourteenth century, Shene was a particularly important royal house. King Richard II's first wife Anne, daughter of the Emperor Charles IV, was especially fond of the place and spent nearly all her time there. But then disaster struck. In 1394, when the plague was raging in London, many people moved out to Shene, and Queen Anne, it seems probable, caught the infection from one of these refugees, for at Whitsuntide she started to sicken and died within a matter of hours. Richard, who was genuinely and passionately in love with his wife, at first could not grasp the fact that she would never return to him. When, at last, he realized his loss, he told his workmen to raze the manor building to the ground.

King Henry IV built up Shene again so that it was grander than ever before, but in 1499 the riverside buildings were burned down in a great blaze that lasted for more than three hours, destroying most of their contents and ruining the manor that the Queen – Elizabeth, wife of King Henry VII – and her children dearly loved (it made an excellent change for them from the other royal homes at Eltham and Greenwich, and they much preferred it to Windsor). Like a good husband and father, King Henry undertook to rebuild the house yet once more, and he did this on so handsome a scale that the place really qualified, from then on, to be referred to as a 'Palace', the area in its immediate neighbourhood being called 'Richmond' because the King happened to be the Earl of Richmond (the town in Yorkshire). The name 'Shene' was kept for the east and west parts of the ancient manorial lands.

The complex of brick and timber buildings put up by King Henry VII contained a Great Hall one hundred feet long and forty feet wide, a chapel hung with cloth of gold, and many other expensively furnished apartments, and it covered an expanse of nearly ten acres which commanded the whole of the river front from what is now Old Palace Lane to Water Lane. The royal lodging, a freestone building three storeys high, with fourteen lead-covered turrets, was described at the time as 'a very gracious ornament to the whole house and perspicuous to the country around'. The closeness of Richmond Hill, which is well supplied with natural springs, made the provision of running water for the Palace relatively easy, and there was a sensational stone fountain in one of the courts:

> Ornamented with lions and red dragons and other goodly beasts, and in the midst certain branches of red roses, out of which flowers and roses is evermore running a course of clear and most purest water into the cistern beneath. This conduit profitably serves the chambers with water for the hands, and all other offices as they need to resort.

During the early part of his reign, King Henry VIII was fond of Richmond, but despite all its modern conveniences he soon lost interest in the place when he saw the even grander palace that Cardinal Wolsey was raising for himself upstream at Hampton Court. When Wolsey thought it politic to offer Hampton Court to the King, Henry kindly invited Wolsey to use the Palace at Richmond, but the Cardinal was not to enjoy the place for long,

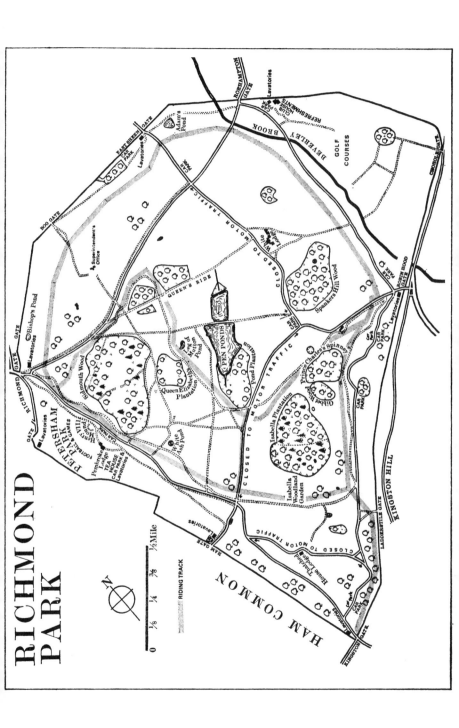

for he soon fell utterly from favour, and had to take refuge in a lodge that was part of the old Monastery of Shene. (There, the senior monks, it is recorded, 'persuaded him from the vain glory of this world and gave him divers shirts of hair, the which he often wore after'.) When Henry took over the Monastery lands he turned them into a royal game preserve (it is now known as 'The Old Deer Park').

The New Park at Richmond – the 'Richmond Park' we know today – was the personal creation of King Charles I, and was brought into being when the King, aware that Hyde Park was too near to the City of London and to Westminster to be really private any longer, decided to enclose some 2,500 acres of unspoiled old English land, a little farther away from the capital, to make a new and very much better hunting preserve. The King's determination to carve out this preserve – even so, not very far away from London – in the teeth of fierce local opposition and at a time of highly charged political feeling added significantly to the growing list of grievances that his subjects were harbouring against him: grievances that were all too soon to find expression in the Civil War and King Charles's execution.

The King's great project failed from the start to appeal to most of the local landowners whose property he needed, though a few agreed to settle without much argument for the very fair prices that were being offered by the Crown.

More influential opposition came from Lord Cottington, who was the King's Chancellor of the Exchequer, and from William Laud, who was Bishop of London. Cottington was against the King's plan because he knew that the enormous cost of purchasing so much land and of building round it so long a brick wall (almost ten miles of it, according to one estimate) would put a well-nigh unbearable strain on the national finances. Laud opposed the scheme because he knew that if the King went ahead with it he would make himself even more unpopular than he was already with the citizens of London, who were appalled by the taxes they were having to pay. Charles, obstinately believing in the Divine Right of Kings to do more or less what they pleased, started to build the enclosing wall round those parts of the land that were already his. As the Park grew in size, the local landowners who had been opposing the King began to change their tune. They saw that if they did not come to terms with the Crown, they risked losing the use of their own properties without managing to obtain any adequate compensation. One after another, they gave in.

The end of the Civil War brought great changes to Richmond and to the recently completed Park. The Royal Palace at the foot of the hill, valued at more than £10,000, was sold by the Parliamentarians to Thomas Rookesby, William Goodwin and Adam Baynes. They re-sold it to Sir Gregory Norton, one of the judges who had signed the death warrant of the King. Norton died little more than a year later, and the palace, sadly neglected, started to deteriorate until it was almost beyond repair.

The New Park at Richmond was chiefly valued at this time as a prime source of venison. (An order dated 13 September 1651 requested that 'Mr Remembrancer doe presently goe from this Court and require the Keepers of the Newe Park to kill in that Parke a brase of Fatt Staggs of this Season. And deliver the same for the use of the Parliament and Councell of State on Munday morning next'.) As a small token of gratitude for the support that they had been given by the citizens of London during the Civil War, the Parliamentarians gave the Park – as if it were their own to give! – to the City, and the citizens of London gladly started to help themselves to the Park's deer.

When England had had enough of the dreary Commonwealthers, and King Charles II had returned amid scenes of joy from his exile, the new King looked at Richmond Palace, but as he did not fancy making a home for himself there he offered the place to his mother, the Dowager Queen. Queen Henrietta Maria, used to the up-to-date luxuries of the Queen's House at Greenwich, thought the old buildings at Richmond bleak and uncomfortable and declined her son's offer. The whole of the Palace was therefore pulled down except the medieval Gate House, in which Queen Elizabeth I is believed to have lain in a sadly stricken state during her last illness, and the Wardrobe, which still stands with the Gate House by Richmond Green.

The citizens of London were meanwhile overjoyed at the downfall

of the inefficient and depressing Puritans, and as a tangible
expression of their pleasure – and in a brave attempt to get on to
the best possible terms with the New Management – they gave
Richmond Park back to the Crown – indeed, they had decided
to do so before King Charles even landed in this country. For a
century and a half after that, the Park was greatly enjoyed by most
members of successive Royal Families; King William III and his
Queen Mary were particularly fond of hunting there.

When King George I died in 1727, while on one of his return
visits to his native Hanover, his son George, Prince of Wales, was
living in a house called Richmond Lodge in the Old Deer Park.
As soon as the news of the King's death reached London, Sir
Robert Walpole, the Chief Minister of State, called for his horse
and galloped down from his Chelsea home along the country roads
to carry the tidings to the new Monarch. Sir Robert at first got
little reward for his trouble, for King George II, who had quarrelled
almost incessantly with his father now deceased, promptly and
contemptuously dismissed his father's principal adviser from
office, appointing in his place Sir Spencer Compton, who was
described as a 'plodding heavy fellow, with great application but
no talents, his only pleasures, eating and drinking'. Within a very
few months, the new Sovereign was to realize that he had made
a great mistake. Sir Robert was reinstated, and – an important
step for Richmond Park – his eldest son Lord Orford was given
the post of Ranger of the Park. Without apparently occupying
any office of profit under the Crown in this respect, Sir Robert
managed to share with his son the pleasures and responsibilities
of this not very onerous job.

Encouraged by the King, who professed to be a great sportsman,
Sir Robert and his co-Ranger at once set about draining the Park,
which, before the Walpoles took an interest in it, had been boggy,
overgrown, and a haunt of deer-poachers and other wild and unscrupulous men. They had soon converted it into a beautiful and
well-stocked hunting ground. To please the King, who was not
perhaps quite so great a sportsman as he thought himself, they
introduced into the Park flocks of wild turkeys – three thousand
of them. (The wretched birds, harried by dogs, would be forced

to take refuge in the trees, where His Majesty could shoot at
them without difficulty or fatigue.) A pleasant picture of the Royal
Family's activities in the Park at this stage of its history was given
in August 1728 in the *Stamford Mercury*:

> On Saturday their Majesties together with their Royal High-
> nesses the Duke [of Cumberland] and the Princesses, came to
> the new park by Richmond from Hampton Court and diverted
> themselves with hunting a stag, which ran from eleven to one,
> when he took to the great pond, where he defended himself
> for half an hour, when he was killed. His Majesty, the Duke,
> and the Princess Royal hunted on horseback, her Majesty and
> the Princess Amelia in a four-wheeled chaise, and the Princesses
> Mary and Louisa in a coach. Her Majesty was pleased to show
> great condescension and complaisance to the country people
> by conversing with them and ordering them money. Several
> of the nobility attended, amongst them Sir Robert Walpole,
> clothed in green as Ranger. When the diversion was over, their
> Majesties, the Duke, and the Princesses refreshed themselves
> on the spot with a cold collation, as did the nobility at some
> distance of time after, and soon after two in the afternoon
> returned to Hampton Court. . . .

It was not long before the King and his family had no cause to
return to Hampton Court or anywhere else after a morning's
hunting, for the sporting Monarch had already commissioned
Lord Pembroke to design for him a 'shooting box' in this quiet
rural retreat, and the construction of the main block of it was already
quite well advanced. (The house, built of Portland stone, was at
first referred to as 'The Stone Lodge'. Then, to distinguish it
from 'The Old Lodge', which was Sir Robert Walpole's house
in the Park, it became known as 'The New Lodge'. Finally, it
was given the name by which we know it today – 'The White
Lodge'. In this house, on each Sunday afternoon during the Summer months, the King and Queen would take tea together in the
gloomy, black-papered drawing-room. The house is used, at the
time of writing, by the Royal Ballet School.)

Sir Robert Walpole spent a lot of his own money improving
The Old Lodge for his own use and enjoyment, and before his
son had been Ranger for long the First Minister of the Crown
had got into the habit of spending most of his week-ends there,
insisting that he could do a great deal more work in the quiet of
the countryside than he could in the rage and bustle of Town.
According to the *Dictionary of National Biography* the closing of
the House of Commons on Saturdays dates from this period
exactly.)

On two occasions at least the Prime Minister had to be hurriedly
fetched from his retreat in Richmond Park when Queen Caroline
wished to see him urgently.

On the first occasion, in 1736, the Queen was on edge because
the King had gone off to visit one of his current mistresses in
Hanover, and Sir Robert had gone off with a Miss Skerrett to
Richmond Park. Unable to do anything constructive about her
husband's philanderings, and obviously resenting Sir Robert's
absence from the capital, the Queen asked Lord Hervey to summon
Walpole at once as she wished to pass on to him the good news
that the King had safely reached Helvoetsluys in Holland. Lord
Hervey, according to his *Memoirs*, promptly dispatched a messenger
to Sir Robert at The Old Lodge, letting him have the good tidings
about the King's safety, but not venturing

> to tell him that he found the Queen looked upon his retirement
> with Miss Skerrett to Richmond Park just at this juncture as
> a piece of gallantry which, considering the anxiety in which
> he left Her Majesty, might have been spared, as well as the
> gallantry of His Majesty's journey to Hanover which had occa-
> sioned that anxiety. . . .

As Sir Robert Walpole aged, and as his time as Ranger, or
co-Ranger, of Richmond Park neared its end, the question of the
general public's access to the Park became more than usually
vexed. Sir Robert felt, not unreasonably, that the amount of
money he had spent on 'improvements' and the extraordinary
burdens of his high public office entitled him to complete privacy

and freedom from casual intruders in his leisure moments. So he had the old 'ladder-stile' gates removed from the walls of the Park, for by these the enclosed land could be entered freely at almost any point on the Park's perimeter. Then, the more effectively to control entry to the Park, he had small lodges built beside the official Park gates, and in these lodges he installed strong and capable Keepers who were given instructions that they should admit only 'respectable persons' in the daytime, and those few carriages to which special passes had been issued. The local people, infuriated by these new restrictions, protested loudly, but the Walpoles, both father and son, stood firmly by their rights, and the outsiders, gentlefolk and bumpkins alike, grumbled in vain.

The troubles became really serious in 1751, when the Princess Amelia, the King's youngest daughter, took over the Rangership of the Park on the unfortunate death of the Earl of Orford. The Princess – more autocratic than any present-day member of a Royal Family would dare to be – moved into The Old Lodge and made it her principal home, treating the Park entirely as if it were her private property, closing it to the public altogether and admitting only her own personal friends and a few other persons to whom she granted special permits. The local inhabitants, seething with rage, tried to remind the Princess that free access to the Park had been traditionally allowed ever since the land had been enclosed by King Charles I. The Princess did not even condescend to reply.

The first open skirmish in the great Who-Owns-Richmond-Park struggle came three years later, when a number of gentlemen led by a Mr Symons tried to enter the Park but were refused permission by one of the gatekeepers, a burly woman whose name was Deborah Burgess. The gentlemen then brought a legal action against the Deputy Ranger, one James Shaw, more than £1,000 being subscribed by the residents of East Sheen to defray the expenses of the case. The trial, conducted by the Lord Chief Justice, lasted two days, but after a number of witnesses called by the defence had testified that anyone prepared to pay 2s. 6d. (quite a large amount, at that time) could enter the Park, the verdict went against the plaintiffs.

But one stubborn Richmond man refused to accept the validity of this judgment. This was a brewer named John Lewis, who was determined to carry on the struggle, if necessary on his own, until the townspeople's ancient rights of access to the Park were freely restored. Gilbert Wakefield, brother of the Vicar of Richmond, recorded the heroic story as he heard it from Lewis:

> . . . Lewis takes a friend with him to the spot [the East Sheen Gate]; waits for the opportunity of a carriage passing through; and when the doorkeeper was shutting the gates, interposed and offered to go in. 'Where's your ticket?' 'What occasion for a ticket: anybody may pass through here.' 'No; not without a ticket.' 'Yes, they may, and I will.' 'You shan't.' 'I will.' The woman pusht, Lewis suffered the door to be shut on him, and brought his action. . . .

Lewis's suit was brought, in the first instance, against the door-keeper, the muscular Deborah Burgess, but it was really aimed at the dictatorial Ranger, the Princess Amelia, and everyone in the district knew it. For three years the Crown managed to prevent the case from being brought into court, but eventually, through Lewis's dogged persistence, it was heard at Kingston Assizes on 3 April 1758.

The trial, held before Sir Michael Foster, of the King's Bench, lasted a day. Lewis did not ask that both vehicles and pedestrians should be given unrestricted entry to the Park, as he had seen from the previous case that this plea would be unlikely to succeed. Instead, he based his case on the rights of way granted by King Charles I to those on foot. When the verdict was given in Lewis's favour, there were loud cheers in court.

The Judge then asked the plaintiff if he would like to have a door made in the wall of the Park, or if he would prefer to have a step-ladder set up by which the wall might be climbed over. Lewis, realizing that a gate would have to be kept shut to prevent the deer escaping from the Park, and that it would probably be kept bolted as well, told the Judge that he would choose the step-ladder.

Within a month of the Assizes at Kingston, ladder-stiles fitted with gates had been built, like bridges, over the Park walls near

(*Above*) London, seen from Greenwich Park (*Below*) The Queen's House, seen from Greenwich Hill

(*Above*) Easter Monday on the River Thames: a jovial party makes for Greenwich in 1847 (*Below*) High jinks in Greenwich Park, as seen by 'Phiz' (Hablot K. Browne)

(*Above*) The storming of Richmond Park: the determined townspeople of Sheen and Mortlake insist on their right of access to the royal pleasure grounds (*Below*) Richmond Park – from a nineteenth century painting

The palace, gardens and park at Hampton Court, as they were in the eighteenth century

(*Above*) Victorian families at their ease in Regent's Park. (From a nineteenth century engraving) (*Below*) The Zoological Society's Gardens in Regent's Park have drawn the public in crowds, ever since the 'Zoo' was opened in 1826

(*Above*) The North Gate Bridge over the canal in Regent's Park shortly before the explosion of 1874 (*Below*) The explosion on the Regent's Canal – the aftermath

(*Above*) The model fishing vessel *Christine Denise* reaches its launching spot by the Round Pond in Kensington Gardens (*Below*) A favourite walk in Regent's Park

The Queen Victoria memorial in front of Buckingham Palace is reflected in the waters of the lake in St James's Park

East Sheen and Ham, and a 'vast concourse of people from all the neighbouring villages' assembled and tried to climb over into the Park.

But they had underestimated the determination of the Royal Park Ranger. Infuriated by the outcome of the court case that had been brought against her, the Princess Amelia had given orders that the rungs on the ladder-stiles should be spaced so far apart that no one but a very athletic mountaineer could hope to use them.

Once again, John Lewis appealed to the Law. When he told Mr Justice Foster that old men and children would be quite incapable of negotiating the Princess's ladders safely, he found the Learned Judge entirely sympathetic to his arguments 'I have observed it myself', said His Worship. 'And I desire, Mr. Lewis, that you would see it so constructed that not only children and old men, but old women, too, may be able to get up.'

John Lewis became a popular hero in the neighbourhood of Richmond Park after that – he was so much admired that when his printing business ran into trouble as a result of a great flood that surged through his premises, the townspeople of Richmond got up a fund and bought him an annuity. The Princess Amelia, on the other hand, who was already most unpopular in the neighbourhood, had lost so much face by the lawsuits and their consequent happenings that she was virtually compelled to give up the Rangership of the Park. She sold it therefore to King George III shortly after his accession, for an annuity secured on Irish lands. Then she went off in high dudgeon to the other side of the Thames, where she settled at Gunnersbury.

To fill his Aunt's place as Ranger, King George III appointed John Stuart, the Third Earl of Bute. The appointment was made on 23 June 1761, and Lord Bute went to live in the New Lodge. King George continued to take a lively interest in the upkeep of the Park, however, and under his personal supervision many repairs and improvements were carried out by the Board of Works. Relations with the general public were at this time wholly cordial, the Earl of Bute issuing cardboard tickets of admission for carriages, one of which, numbered and marked 'Free Ticket', having a picture

6

of the Park and its deer, and bearing an endorsement by the Earl, can now be seen in the Richmond Public Library.

On 10 March 1792, the Earl of Bute died and King George III took the Rangership back into his own keeping. With real enthusiasm for the place, the King announced that he intended to have all the swampy parts of the Park effectually drained, 'the roads turned where beauty and advantage could be gained by so doing', and the open parts ornamented with plantations. The 'eligible and compact farm' that was already operating after a fashion in the confines of the Park was to be given His Majesty's particular attention. Unfortunately, the long-drawn-out wars with France, and His Majesty's mysterious illness, caused the King's optimistic plans to be largely frustrated. Attempts were made to grow cereals in the farm fields, and the land at first yielded fairly good crops, especially of oats, but later the hungry and gravelly nature of the soil and the damage done by the Park deer made it advisable for the ground to be laid down once again as permanent pasture.

From 1801 until 1844, the New Lodge (by now, the 'White Lodge') was occupied by Viscount Sidmouth – better known, perhaps, as 'Henry Addington'. Many distinguished people visited Lord Sidmouth while he was living in the Park, among them Richard Brinsley Sheridan, William Pitt, and Sir Walter Scott, who was to include, later, a fine description of the local landscape in his novel *Heart of Midlothian*. For years, a small table was carefully preserved in the White Lodge because, it was said, Admiral Lord Nelson had sat at it when he went there for dinner on 10 September 1805 – some six weeks before the Battle of Trafalgar. On the table's surface, the story went, the Admiral had sketched out, after dinner, with his finger moistened in wine, the plan by which he proposed to break the enemy's hitherto impregnable line.

In 1813, Lord Sidmouth was made Deputy Ranger of the Park, and a year later the Princess Elizabeth, daughter of King George III, was given the Rangership. As soon, then, as the country had recovered a little from the economic stresses of the Napoleonic Wars, some larger areas of the Park, which already contained a certain amount of older timber, were enclosed and made into the plantations that are so justly celebrated today.

The ground to the south-east of Spankers Hill was planted first, in 1819, with oak, larch, spruce, sweet chestnut and other trees, and the western slopes were similarly treated in 1824. (An extension to the north-east was enclosed and planted in 1877 and still shows its later origin.) No one knows for certain how this hill got its name – probably, like so many of the other features of the Park, it commemorates some individual connected with the place.

In 1823, work started on the largest of the plantations – the 'Sidmouth Plantation' – the area being covered mainly with sweet chestnuts, a smaller number of oaks, and a few fine beeches. There is a pathway through this plantation, running east and west, which is known as 'The Driftway'. The fine rhododendrons in this plantation make the Driftway, early in June, a very popular place with visitors.

The Upper and Lower Pen Ponds, which are situated almost in the centre of Richmond Park, are now among its chief attractions. Only some kind of a stream was flowing across this part of the Park when King Charles I decided to enclose the ground; the ponds were formed and enlarged at various times after that, partly by embankment and partly by excavation. In 1824, the eastern side of the Pond Plantation was planted, principally with oaks, the western and southern areas being planted later in the century. For years, this plantation was the site of the Park's heronry. In 1825, the Hamcross Plantation was added to the Park. This consisted almost entirely of oaks.

Consisting also almost entirely of oaks, with a few sweet chestnuts and beeches, the Conduit Plantation was brought into being in 1829. This plantation was given its name because it stands on the site of one of the three conduits which supplied water to King Henry VII's fabulous palace at Richmond. The position of the conduit is still marked by a low concrete-covered brick structure on the plantation's south-western boundary.

In 1831, work started on the central and north-western areas of the 'Isabella Plantation'. (In eighteenth-century plans, the area now being occupied by this plantation was shown as 'Isabell Slade', the name probably commemorating the wife or daughter of a former Ranger or Deputy Ranger of the Park.) While all these improvements to the Park were being so vigorously carried on, the Keepers at the entrance lodges were said to be 'remarkable for their civility' and freely admitted carriages whose owners had obtained orders from Lord Sidmouth, together with virtually all comers on foot.

Among the less ruly comers were the vandals who streamed out from the City to hunt the Park's attractive red squirrels. According to Edward Jesse, who was Deputy Surveyor of the Royal Parks in 1834, and who published in that year his interesting *Gleanings of Natural History*,   .

Within the memory of some of the old persons residing in Richmond Park, squirrels were in such vast numbers that parties of fifty or sixty persons have come from the metropolis and its neighbourhood for the purpose of killing them. They were furnished with short sticks, with lead at one end, with which they knocked the animals down. These squirrel hunts occasioned many fights with the keepers, in one of which a keeper, of the name of Bishop, was nearly killed. The squirrels were in consequence destroyed by the staff of the park, and it is now but seldom that one is seen.

James Sawyer junior, who was Head Keeper of Richmond Park from 1825 to 1872, recorded some of the troubles he had with unwelcome intruders in the Park. In a report issued in March 1840, Sawyer complained:

In a Park of this magnitude with various public footpaths, and so near to the great metropolis, from which hundreds of persons of all descriptions are flocking in fine weather, it is very necessary to have many lookers-out, in all directions of the Park, and Plantations, for without great attention, particularly in the breeding and game seasons, few nests would escape the professional Egg Stealers or curious Stragglers, besides numerous Wanton Nesters.

Sawyer estimated that there were two hundred brace of pheasant in the Park at the time he made his Report. (The wild turkeys had been allowed to die out a long time before. They had been too much of a temptation to poachers, who too easily became violent when apprehended. And, when the birds had roosted in the ivy that had been allowed to grow thickly over the old Park walls, they had badly scared too many nocturnal travellers, who thought they were ghosts.)

In August 1834 the fifty-nine acres of Petersham Park were bought for £14,500 and added to the larger expanse of Richmond Park. A brick ha-ha about 170 feet long had been made in 1792 along part of the boundary between the two parks so that a truly magnificent vista might be opened up without any of the park deer having a chance to escape. On the amalgamation of the two parks, more high fences and thick trees were taken down and the lovely Terrace Walk was made between the Richmond Gate and the stables of the Pembroke Lodge. Edward Jesse, quoted earlier, was largely responsible for this great improvement. Jesse's love of trees made him deplore the bad habit people had (and still have) of cutting their names on the bark of the fine trees by the Terrace Walk – a practice, he said, 'which was, perhaps, exclusively English'. In 1834, Mr Jesse obtained permission to place a board in a prominent position at the Walk. On this board, visitors could read these lines:

Stranger, from harm protect these trees and seat,
Where young and old for health and rest may meet.
All should unite to guard what all may share,
A general good should be the general care.

Near the Terrace Walk, at the north end of the Pembroke Lodge gardens, there was, and is, a curious earthen hillock, known to this day as 'King Henry the Eighth's Mound'. Authorities agree that this was originally a barrow or ancient burying-place. (Edward Jesse, writing in 1835, said that it had been opened, and that a considerable deposit of ashes had been found in the centre of it.) The Park Keepers through several generations seem to have told

credulous listeners that this was the spot on which King Henry
VIII stood, on 19 May 1536, while he was watching for a rocket
that would be fired, in or near the Tower of London, to tell him
that his unfaithful wife Anne Boleyn had been duly beheaded, and
that he was legally and morally free to marry her successor, the
Lady Jane Seymour. As the King is known from authentic records
to have attended a party at Wolf Hall, Wiltshire, some sixty miles
away, on the evening of the same day, there would appear to be
little or no truth in this story. Probably, the original name of this
mound – 'The King's Standinge' – indicates that this was where
the Sovereign stood during deer drives, before the ground was
enclosed, to take his pot-shots.

At this time, in the north-east corner of the Park, there stood
an ancient ash tree, known as 'The Shrew Ash'. (Part of the tree
was blown down in 1875, and the rest was believed to be almost or
entirely dead. It remained in this state until 1905, when the Commissioner of Works put a prop beneath the old tree's apparently
lifeless main limb, and a fence to protect the dead trunk. Soon
after this, the tree, perversely, threw up from its roots a vigorous
young sapling.)

During the early nineteenth century, people still believed that
if a shrew mouse ran over a horse, a cow or a sheep the poor animal
would become ill, its limbs would stiffen, and it would eventually
be quite paralysed. To counteract the evil effects of the shrew, it
was thought, a hole would have to be bored in an ash tree, a live
shrew inserted and securely plugged in. After that, a twig cut from
the ash tree would cure the sick animal, if it were applied to its
paralysed limbs.

The Shrew Ash was also believed to have some extraordinary
power in the treatment of sick and ailing children. Stacey, the
Keeper of the Sheen Gate in the middle years of the nineteenth
century, used often to see mothers arrive at the Park in the early
hours with their 'bewitched' infants, or with young children
suffering from whooping cough, consumption, or some other
disease. Many of these mothers would have travelled long distances
for the 'cure', and they would invariably bring with them some
old crone who would act as a 'Shrew Mother' or 'Witch Mother'

and would preside over the secret rituals that were to be performed by the old ash exactly as the first ray of sunrise broke over the horizon.

Early in May each year, until quite late in the nineteenth century, the 'Eel Fair' would be enjoyed in Richmond Park. At this annual jollification many people from Richmond, Mortlake, and other towns and villages in the neighbourhood, would gather to catch the prodigious numbers of young eels that had made their way up from the sea and were arriving at the Pen Ponds by way of the stream at the outflow. The Eel Fair stopped only when the River Thames and the Beverley Brook which flows into it became so polluted that the young eels failed to get up to the Park.

After Lord Sidmouth's death in 1844, the White Lodge became again, for more than a century, a Royal Home. Queen Victoria's aunt, the Duchess of Gloucester, lived in it for a time while she was ostensibly acting as Park Ranger. In 1858, Albert, Prince of Wales (later King Edward VII), was installed in the Lodge with his vigilant tutors. Three years later, Queen Victoria herself moved into the place, after her mother had died and she wanted some peace and quiet in which to recover from the shock. When the Queen no longer wanted it, she handed it on to her relations the Duke and Duchess of Teck, who took a great interest in local affairs and were very much liked.

The Tecks' daughter Mary was intended as a bride for the Prince of Wales's eldest son. After the Duke of Clarence died, however, she married his younger brother Prince George (later King George V). Their eldest son, Edward Albert Christian George Andrew Patrick David (later Prince of Wales, and later still King Edward VIII) was born in the White Lodge on 23 June 1894.

The Old Lodge, which had been Sir Robert Walpole's principal country retreat, was found in 1838 to be in a very bad state of repair, and was presently demolished, leaving no trace. Some other buildings in the Park, however, have gained in importance as they have aged.

The Thatched House Lodge is one of these. There seems to have been a building of some kind on the site some years before

1754, when it was shown on a plan of the Park and referred to as 'Aldridge's Lodge'. (Aldridge, one of the Keepers, had been dead by that time for about eighteen years.) By 1771, the house had been given the name by which it is known today – probably, on account of the thatched summerhouse that Sir Robert had had put up in the grounds, the walls and ceilings of which were later covered with paintings, probably by Angelica Kauffmann. From 1963 to the time of writing The Thatched House Lodge has been the home of Her Royal Highness Princess Alexandra and her husband Mr Angus Ogilvy.

Sheen Cottage, on the Park boundary, just a little way to the east of the East Sheen Gate, is another attractive old residence. In plans of the Park drawn in 1754 and 1771, a building is shown on the site with the name 'The Dog Kennel' and it was here, probably, that the hounds were kept. When the Ranger's pack of harriers was given up, the cottage seems to have been occupied for a time by his Bailiff. About 1787, however, a Mr William Adam (later 'Baron Adam') moved into part of it and soon afterwards Mr Adam paid the Bailiff a considerable sum of money to give up the rest and to move out into some of the adjoining outbuildings which were suitably fitted up for him. Members of the Adam family continued to live in Sheen Cottage until 1852 and their long occupancy is commemorated by the name of the small lake, 'Adam's Pond', which is not much more than a stone's throw away.

Pembroke Lodge, near the Richmond Hill entrance to the Park, is a long two-storey house that is now divided into flats for park officials, with, on the ground floor, a well-run cafeteria and restaurant. This Lodge was the boyhood home of Bertrand Russell, and in his autobiography the great philosopher wrote with deep affection of the time he spent there, praising in particular the extraordinary views that extended to Leith Hill, Windsor Castle and even beyond – which, he said, gave him a permanent liking for broad horizons and sunsets.

But buildings, however handsome and wonderfully situated, are not what most people go to Richmond Park today to see. For the Park is essentially a semi-wild place, and being only about six miles from the centre of London is quite unique in that respect. In its 2,500 acres successive Rangers, Keepers and Superintendents have managed to preserve, almost miraculously, the lusty and spacious appearance of an area of England's untamed landscape as it must have been before the farmers and gardeners of the eighteenth century started their emasculating 'improvements'. Once out of sight of the cars streaming along some of the roads in the Park, and momentarily free from the roaring of the noisy aircraft overhead, a visitor can easily believe that he or she has been transported back in time to the rustic and cheerful countryside which, we are told, existed in these overcrowded islands before the Industrial Revolution.

The trees, to begin with, are largely indigenous – there are the ancient hulkers that were standing on the ground when Lord Sidmouth and his associates started to make their plantations just after the Napoleonic Wars; there are the unsensational native timbers that were put in at that time; and there are the 70,000 trees, all of them English hardwoods such as beech, chestnut, hawthorn, hornbeam, oak and rowan, that were planted in less than two decades after Mr G. J. Brown, Chief Forester on the Harewood Estate in Yorkshire, became Superintendent of Richmond Park in 1951. Soft, exotic foreign trees and the blossoming wonders that are quite suitable for the suburban gardens of Surrey are conspicuous here by their absence, though a single Chile Pine managed to get itself planted in the Park, by some oversight, during the 1930s.[1]

Then there are the deer that roam freely in the Park – nearly three hundred red deer and a similar number of fallow deer. Sometimes, the deer can be distinguished only with the greatest difficulty from the bracken in which they are sheltering under the Park's venerable oaks.

The herds of red deer consist of stags, hinds and calves – their coats, which are red or brown in Summer, becoming darker, greyer and thicker in the Winter months. In the late Summer, the stags, some of which are very large, start to become restless as the 'rut' or mating season approaches. The rut itself takes place in the months of September and October, and the Park, at this time, becomes a little noisier than usual as the stags roar out their challenges and, in their more passionate moments, rush aggressively at one another. (All visitors to the Park are advised, in the interest of safety, to give the deer a fairly wide berth at this time of the year.)

The fallow deer in the Park are a little smaller than the red deer, and their herds are said to consist of 'buck' (the males), 'does' (the females) and 'fawns' (the young of either sex). The fallow deer start mating two or three weeks after the red deer, and the bucks' cries of challenge are a little less dramatic than those of the stags, but they too should be left severely alone until they have had time to cool off.

From time to time, the deer in the Park have suffered some extraordinary misfortunes, in spite of the care with which they have been protected. In the year 1825, for instance, not one single calf was dropped by any of the Park's hinds, though they had bred freely, as usual, in the preceding year and resumed their normal breeding habits in the following year. In 1886 and 1887 the herds suffered an even more grievous loss, when the deer were attacked by rabies. Behaving in the abnormal fashion expected from animals suffering from this dreadful disease, the deer bit their own skins and tore out their hair and attacked one another mercilessly. More than two hundred of the animals are said to have died, or to have been shot, before the trouble was eradicated.

The deer in Richmond Park today have to be discreetly culled, annually, to keep the stock in the finest possible condition. A certain proportion of the resulting venison is allocated to the Royal Table, to certain Officers of the Crown, and to some other people entitled by Royal Warrant to a haunch for their own use. (Among these are the Prime Minister, members of the Cabinet, and the Archbishops of Canterbury and York.) The remainder is sold, under contract.

As well as the deer, there are several smaller mammals which, at the time of writing, are known to thrive in the favourable, semi-wild conditions of Richmond Park, the most noteworthy, perhaps, being the fox and the badger. (In former times the Park teemed with rabbits, but when, on the death of His Royal Highness the

Duke of Cambridge in 1904, the estate ceased to be used for private shooting parties, small game were no longer preserved there, and orders were issued that as many as possible of the rabbits should be killed off. Some two thousand four hundred conies were promptly shot or trapped, after which Mr Wells, then Superintendent of the Park, declared that since the rabbits had been destroyed he had never seen the deer look better.)

The Pen Ponds, which are well stocked with fish of various kinds – bream, carp, dace, gudgeon, perch, pike, roach and tench have been taken in them – are of especial interest to ornithologists. The members of the Committee on Bird Sanctuaries in the Royal Parks have recommended for many years that tame waterfowl should not be placed on these ponds, as they are on so many ponds in the other Royal Parks, since there is a strong tendency for the more interesting wild birds to leave when there is too much competition for food and nesting sites. As a result of this enlightened policy, watchers by the Pen Ponds have seen in recent years, among other birds, the coot, cormorant, goosander, great crested grebe, great northern diver, heron, mallard, moorhen, pochard, red-necked grebe and tufted duck, as well as a variety of gulls.[2]

Elsewhere in Richmond Park, many wild birds are to be found that cannot stand the disturbances to which they are apt to be subjected in the more urban parks – there are crows, jackdaws, jays, kestrels, kingfishers, little owls, magpies, nuthatches, tree-creepers, yellowhammers and three different kinds of woodpecker to be seen, or heard, as well as the occasional woodcock. In the more open parts of the Park, meadow pipits, tree pipits, redstarts and skylarks may be encountered. The Park is rich in warblers, too – the blackcap, chiffchaff, garden warbler, whitethroat and willow warbler all nest here regularly and their songs are delightful to hear. There may not now be as many occasional visitors of great rarity as there were when C. L. Collenette completed, in the mid-1930s, his classic study of the birds in Richmond Park – the aircraft and motor traffic in the neighbourhood undoubtedly keep many away – but sufficient still come to the Park to keep keen bird-watchers happily occupied in almost every month of the year.

Two changes that have been made in or near Richmond Park since World War II have caused a certain amount of disquiet to those who have known and loved the area in its truly wild and 'uncivilized' state.

The first was the erection of the high buildings of the Roehampton Housing Estate which glower down on the Park at its north-east corner, where the skyline was formerly composed almost entirely of splendid trees. The view of the Park from these uncompromising slab blocks is said to be exhilarating, but the view of the slab blocks from the Park is rather less satisfactory.

The second change – in some people's opinion, for the better; in others', for the worse – has been the opening of the Isabella Plantation to the public and its subsequent development. Formerly, the Plantation was little more than an overgrown thicket, impenetrable in places, and with little charm or interest. Now a small stream has been diverted so that water flows constantly through it, and its glades have been cleared and planted with a myriad of azaleas, heathers, primulas and other flowering plants, many of them exotic. The wood, which attracts dense crowds of visitors in the Spring and early Summer, is now undoubtedly one of the most spectacular features in any of London's Royal Parks, but its character has entirely changed and is now quite alien to that of the more subdued plantations in its vicinity. If only all this excellent work had been done somewhere else, sigh the conservatives.

Chapter 10

Bushey Park and Hampton Court Park

Of all the Royal Parks of London, Bushey Park and Hampton Court Park lie farthest from the centre of government – they are more distant from Westminster, even, than Greenwich. They may have more ancient royal connections than Greenwich, too, for Kingston, or 'King's Town', was one of the few places at which the Lower Thames could be crossed, before bridges were built, and in the town at least seven Saxon sovereigns are believed to have been crowned.

The Manor of Hampton, from which the two parks were created, consisted originally of about 3,000 acres. The whole domain has been divided – probably, ever since Saxon times – by the highway that leads from Kingston and Hampton Wick to Hampton. This road passes now in front of the garden gates of Hampton Court and within 250 yards of the Palace. To the north of this road lies Bushey Park which, with its wild extremities, is fringed on its western, northern and eastern sides by the districts of Hampton, Teddington and Hampton Wick. To the south of the Kingston Road lies the Park called variously the House or Home Park, bounded on its three other sides by the Thames, and by the Palace and its grounds.

The natural features of the country in which Hampton Court is situated are not particularly striking. The ground is flat – so flat that it has hardly any undulation that rises more than twenty feet above dead level, and the soil, though light and gravelly, was not originally very well suited for growing timber. In primeval times, in fact, the whole area appears to have been a tawdry extension of the famous Hounslow Heath, which it immediately adjoined. The river, however, which is particularly clear and swift at this point, is a priceless natural amenity. And the very flatness of the ground makes the parks' long avenues of trees particularly impressive.

By the middle of the thirteenth century, the Knights Hospitallers of St John of Jerusalem were in possession of the whole Manor of Hampton. Somewhere – probably at Hampton – they had a 'preceptory', and there was a small mansion or manor house, probably on the site of the present Palace. The house was still inhabited by the Order in 1503 when Elizabeth of York, who was pregnant, went there for eight days from Richmond Palace to 'make a retreat' and to pray for a happy delivery. That was just a month before she died in childbirth.

The next important date in the history of Hampton Court is 1514, for Henry VIII visited the Manor in that year, with Katherine of Aragon – the King and Queen had probably been invited to inspect the property which his Chief Minister, Thomas Wolsey, was about to acquire. Wolsey wanted a secluded country place within easy travelling distance of London where he could withdraw occasionally for rest and quiet without being too far from the centre of affairs. The great statesman took the Manor from the Knights Hospitallers, 'with all its appurtenances', for a term of ninety-nine years, agreeing among other conditions that he and his assignees should, at the expiration of the lease, leave to the Prior and his successors 'a thousand couple of conies in the warren of the said manor, or else for every couple that shall want, 4d.'

Busy as he was with affairs of state and with his various bishoprics, Wolsey set out at once with characteristic energy to plan the construction of a palace that would be worthy of the many and assorted dignities which he had attained and the enormous wealth he had acquired. The old manor house already stood in the middle of some two thousand acres of pasture land. Wolsey proceeded to convert all this into two parks, partly fencing them with paling, and partly enclosing them with a stout red-brick buttressed wall, sections of which survive to this day.

By May 1516, the building of the new Palace was so far advanced

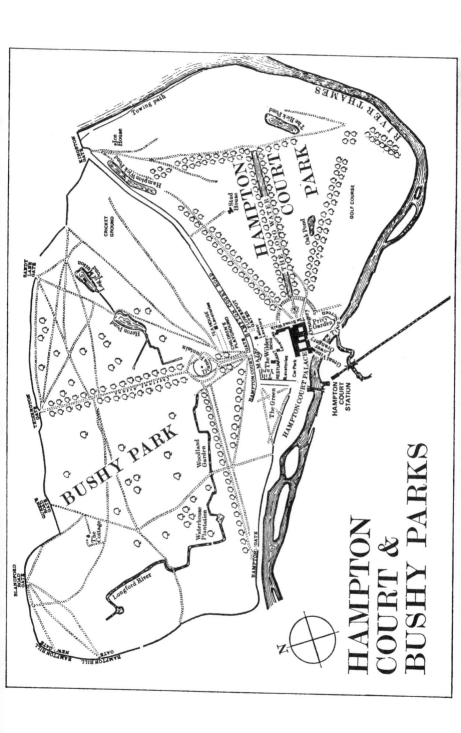

HAMPTON COURT & BUSHY PARKS

that Wolsey was able to entertain the King and Queen to dinner in his new seat. From then until 1520, the Cardinal was in the habit of travelling down from London to Hampton Court whenever he could, giving orders that he was not to be troubled with business until he returned to town. 'When he walks in the Park he will suffer no suitor to come nigh unto him, but commands him away as far as a man will shoot an arrow', reported a certain Allen, confidential agent of the Earl of Shrewsbury, Lord Steward of the Royal Household, who had rushed down from London to see Wolsey about his master's duties, but had been coldly rebuffed. The mysterious disease known as the 'sweating sickness' was then raging in London, and Wolsey, no doubt, was seeking to avoid infection.

The magnificence with which Wolsey surrounded himself at Hampton Court soon aroused the envy of his royal master, and by 1525 the Cardinal had found it advisable to make the whole place over to Henry, with its valuable contents. (For some years, nevertheless, he continued to write, as he had previously done, in letters not addressed to the King: 'From *my* manor of Hampton Court'. He also continued to use Hampton Court as if it were his own, entertaining there, for example, in October 1527 the French Ambassadors and one hundred of the 'noblest and wealthiest gentlemen in all the Court of France'[1] for three days' hunting.)

In 1529, Wolsey was flung from his high estate and banished from the King's presence, and Henry entered into absolute possession of Hampton Court and all its treasures. From that time on, while waiting for his divorce from Katherine of Aragon, Henry spent much of his time riding out with Anne Boleyn, or walking in the Parks with her,[2] and he was shooting at the 'rounds', or butts, in the Park when the news of Cardinal Wolsey's death was brought to him. He subdivided, with brick walls, Bushey Park into three smaller enclosures – the Hare Warren to the east, the Middle Park, and the Upper Park, to make it more convenient for coursing and shooting, and for the same purpose, he divided the House Park, south of the Kingston Road, into two – the 'Course', next to the road, and the House Park proper. He had both parks well stocked with deer and other game, his enthusiasm for the chase being so insatiable that he would never go hunting 'without tiring eight or ten horses, which he caused to be stationed beforehand along the line of country he meant to take'.[3] To hunt on this scale, however, Henry would usually have to travel as far as Windsor Forest.

As he grew older, and fatter, and less able to tire out eight or ten horses without suffering, himself, a little bodily discomfort, King Henry wanted to hunt the stag without all the preliminary fatigues of getting to Windsor. He therefore started to acquire by purchase or exchange all the manors that lay near Hampton Court, on both sides of the river, and his overbearing methods and the damage done by his deer caused much local resentment.

As soon as Henry was dead, the people who lived in the vicinity of Hampton Court petitioned the Council for redress. Their commons, meadows and pastures were overrun with deer, they said, and the whole country around was made desolate. The members of the Council listened sympathetically and gave orders that the deer should be removed. Royal hunts had to take place, after that, within the confines of the parks. In one of the most notable of these, King Philip of Spain, on his brief second and last visit to England, came down to Hampton Court for a couple of days 'for to hunt and to kyll a grett hart'[4] in the Park.

Queen Elizabeth I inherited from her father an ardent love of stag-hunting and often shared in the sport provided in her Parks for the entertainment of her guests. When she was present the proceedings had usually to be staged with a little, at least, of the romantic pageantry with which she loved to invest every action of her life. An account exists, for instance, of 'a delicate bower being prepared, under the which were her Highness' musicians placed, and a cross-bow by a nymph, with a sweet song, delivered to her hands to shoot at the deer'.[5] On another occasion when she went out 'to hunt the hart', dressed in the brightest green, she was met on entering the chase, by fifty archers, also in green, with scarlet boots and yellow caps, with gilded bows, who presented her with a silver-headed arrow, winged with peacocks' feathers.[6]

Queen Elizabeth's elegant hunting parties at Hampton Court may have been abnormally balletic, but at least they could be enjoyed by those living in the neighbourhood. The sporting activities of her immediate successor, King James I, were not intended to have any public appeal, for James, fresh from Scotland, felt that it was essential to his royal dignity to revive something of the severity of much earlier monarchs who, with their harsh Game Laws, had made indulgence in any field sports the exclusive prerogative of the Crown and the aristocracy. On 9 September 1609, then, he issued from Hampton Court a proclamation 'against Hunters, Stealers and Killers of Deare, within any of the King's Majesties Forests, Chases or Parks', in which he said that unless there were some change in his subjects' conduct, he would have to bring back into force the ancient forest laws in all their pristine stringency. He followed this with a further proclamation in which he expressed his 'high displeasure and offence' at the great number of 'vulgar people' who, with 'bold and barbarous insolency', not only flocked to the Royal Meets to see the fun and stare at His Majesty, but who sometimes even ventured, without special permission, to join the sport and follow the hounds. The King's will and pleasure was that these 'vulgar people' who 'rode over his dogs and broke their backs and spoiled his game by their heedless riding and galoping'[7] should be immediately apprehended, and conveyed to the nearest jail, and kept there during his royal pleasure.

In spite of his professed keenness for 'the sport', James I could hardly have been called, by modern standards, a sportsman, for he was quite prepared to go out quietly into one or other of his parks and take pot-shots from behind a tree at the tame deer as they browsed in the shade. His most desperate runs, too, were usually strictly confined within the fences or walls of a quiet small enclosure. 'The huntsmen remain on the spot where the game is to be found with twenty or thirty hounds', reported the author of *The Travels of John Ernest, Duke of Saxe-Weimar*, who came to England in 1613 and was entertained by the King with a great hunt at Hampton Court.

If the King fancies any in particular among the herd, he causes his pleasure to be signified to the huntsmen, who forthwith proceed to mark the place where the animal stood; they then lead the hounds thither, which are taught to follow this one animal only, and accordingly away they run straight upon his track; and even should there be forty or fifty deer together, they do nothing to them, but chase only the one, and never give up until they have overtaken and brought it down. Meanwhile the King hurries incessantly after the hounds until they have caught the game. There is therefore [added the foreigner] no particular enjoyment in this sport.

The foreigner was not expressing a universally popular view – the the King stocked the parks at Hampton Court so amply with game, and the place consequently became so renowned, that to have had a day's hunting in James's preserves was definitely considered by most foreigners of distinction an experience to boast about.

King Charles I was as fond of Hampton Court Palace and its Parks as his father had been, and the place owes one of its chief amenities, to this day, to his enterprise and care-free investment – to give the Parks a ready supply of running water he had a long watercourse (the 'Longford River') cut all the way from the River Colne. This was a remarkable, and very expensive, piece of civil engineering, for the river has a completely natural appearance, and has allowed the landscape gardeners who have worked in the Parks from time to time to incorporate streams, waterfalls, ponds and fountains in their more ambitious schemes, contributing greatly to their success. After its work in Bushey Park has been completed, the Colne water flows through a culvert underneath the main Hampton Court Road and supplies the canal in Hampton Court Gardens and the Long Water in Hampton Court Park before it is allowed to run away into the Thames.

During the quarrels between King Charles I and his Parliament, and during the Civil War that followed, the peace of Hampton Court was much affected by the tribulations of its owner. In 1642, for a start, six days after he had made his abortive attempt to arrest the intransigent Five Members in the House of Commons, King Charles withdrew to the Palace from Whitehall, with his wife and children and all his household. Five years later, after a series of military defeats, and after the King had put himself, in the vain hope of advantage, into the hands of the Scottish Covenanters, he was brought back by the Army to Hampton Court and reunited there with two of his children, Prince Henry and Princess Elizabeth. Though kept in a state of semi-captivity in the Palace, the King was allowed to hunt in its Parks. Eventually, as every schoolchild used to know, he managed to escape from Hampton Court and, failing to reach safety in France, was taken to Carisbrooke Castle in the Isle of Wight.

When the struggle between King and the Parliamentarians was finally resolved, and, as we have seen, the impoverished victors decided that they would have to raise some money by selling off the Crown Lands, the Council of State recommended that Hampton Court, together with Whitehall, Westminster and a few other palaces, should be excepted from the sale and 'be kept for the public use of the Commonwealth'. The parks at Bushey and Hampton Court were accordingly put up at auction and sold to the highest bidders, but after Oliver Cromwell, who had been proclaimed Lord Protector, decided that he would like to make Hampton Court Palace a family home, they were quickly bought back again.

Richard Cromwell, who for a few months succeeded his father as Lord Protector, was reluctant to leave the State Apartments at Whitehall, and his visits to Hampton Court were brief. On one occasion, though, when he had travelled to the Palace to shoot deer in the Park, and had just shot one, a messenger arrived from the Commons ordering that 'none were to be killed', and he had to leave off his sport, not daring to shoot any more.[8]

With the Restoration, Hampton Court and its Parks moved into their fullest glory. King Charles II, who spent his honeymoon in the Palace, acted swiftly to have the gardens put in order again, after a long period of strict economy that had just passed, and to him we owe the first laying out of the Home Park in its present form – the planting of the great avenues of lime trees that radiate from the centre of the east front of the Palace was clearly inspired by the planning of the great estates he had seen on his travels abroad, while the canal or 'Long Water' which extends from the same front towards the river for a distance of three-quarters of a mile is equally clearly a reminiscence of the Dutch scenery with which he had become familiar while living in Holland.

King Charles II also had the Parks liberally re-stocked with game. Not everyone today, however, would approve of the way stags were hunted during his reign at Hampton Court. When Cosimo III, Duke of Tuscany, was travelling in England, he was entertained by Prince Rupert and shown some stag-hunting in the Park. His secretary Magalotti left a description of the 'sport':

> . . . When the huntsmen had stretched out the nets after the German manner, inclosing with them a considerable space of land, they let the dogs loose upon four deer which were confined there, who as soon as they saw them took to flight, but as they had not the power of going which way they pleased, they ran round the net, endeavouring by various cunning leaps to save themselves from being stopped by the dogs, and continued to run in this manner for some time *to the great diversion of the spectators*! till at last the huntsmen, that they might not harass the animals superfluously, drawing a certain cord, opened the nets in one part, which was prepared for that purpose, and left the deer at liberty to escape . . .

Among King Charles II's more endearing characteristics, we know, was his open-handedness – he was always ready to distribute sinecure posts to his favourites and to people to whom he had some cause to be grateful. He gave the Keepership of all the parks at Hampton Court to General George Monck, Duke of Albemarle, and appointed further Under Keepers for each park or part-park separately. (Bushey Park was still loosely subdivided into three – the Upper Park, on the Hampton Hill side; the Middle Park; and the Hare Warren, nearest to Kingston – but the fences between them were not being kept up and were shortly to be removed.) Under the Duke of Albemarle, during the first few years of the new King's reign, the Middle Park had several Keepers. In November 1665, however, one of King Charles's especial cronies, Edward Proger, was appointed to the post. He was to keep it for forty-eight years.

Proger was a most interesting and colourful man. The son of a Welsh courtier, he had been born at Westminster in 1621. He had been made a Page of Honour to King Charles I and had so distinguished himself during the Civil War that the King made him a Groom of the Bedchamber to the Prince of Wales. When the King was executed, Proger had followed Prince Charles into exile, although the Scottish Covenanters had tried to insist that he should be banished from the Royal Presence 'as an evil instrument and bad counsellor of the King'. What his offence was, they had not made clear. Proger is usually described in shocked tones by Victorian writers because of Andrew Marvell's suggestion in his satires on the Court that he was, if not actually a procurer for King Charles II, at any rate a go-between in the King's relations with his many mistresses. It is known that Proger's wife, Elizabeth Wells, had a brief *affaire* with Charles before her marriage to Proger – this liaison is commemorated in some mildly bawdy verse written by the Duke of Buckingham – and it was said that Mrs Proger's eldest daughter bore a strong resemblance to the King. Such situations were not, however, rare at that time.

Proger was no stranger to the Middle Park at Hampton even before he was appointed to the Keepership of it. A memorandum signed by the King on 30 December 1663 recorded that:

> ... We have commanded Our Servt Edward Proger Esq One of Ye Grooms of Our Bedchamber to build a Lodge for Our Service in one of Our Parks att Hampton Court called North Parke, And to make a faire walke or laine there in such a manner as Wee have directed ...

Proger spent four thousand pounds on building this lodge and laying out its surroundings – a very large sum of money, compared to similar places that were being put up in and around the Royal Parks at the same time – and he did not hesitate to petition the King that he should be fully reimbursed, even though the Lodge was not, as it turned out, to be lived in by the King, but was to serve instead as one of Proger's private residences. (He is said to have had others, in London.)

The arrival of the Prince and Princess of Orange in England after the abrupt departure of King James II, and their accession to the throne as King William III and Queen Mary, meant more changes for the Palace and the Parks at Hampton Court. Ten days after they had been proclaimed, the new Rulers travelled down to have a look at the place and William was at once delighted with the situation of the Palace and the aspect of the surrounding country-side – its flatness reminding him so poignantly of his own well-loved home in Holland, a similarity which was stressed by the long straight canal, fringed with avenues of lime trees, that he could see from the Palace windows, and which was so very like those that he was used to in Haarlem and The Hague. Neither the King nor the Queen cared very much for the inconvenient old buildings of which the Palace was formed – 'so irregular', they found them – and therefore, undeterred by the historical associations of the place, they decided to have some of the less convenient parts of the old palace pulled down and a new and extensive range of State Apartments put up in their stead. The architect entrusted with the designing of the new apartments was Sir Christopher Wren.

The King and Queen's urge to renovate and improve soon led them to make some radical changes in the gardens of the Palace and in the Parks. Although, according to Daniel Defoe, most of the planning was done by the King himself, the royal couple relied on the advice and help of George London, the Brompton nursery-man, who had learned his craft from Rose, the famous gardener of King Charles II's time, who, in his turn, had studied under Le Nôtre. Helping, too, was London's pupil and working partner Henry Wise. Sir Christopher Wren kept a masterly eye on the whole grand design.

Bushey Park, which, up to that time, had been not much more than a flat and rather bare piece of ground, was completely trans-formed by the work done by King William and Queen Mary and their men. Their most ambitious change involved the construction of a great drive through the Park, sixty feet in width and about a mile in length, which was intended to form a grand approach to the reconstituted Palace and should have led in a straight line from the North (or Teddington) Park Gate to a new and stately Entrance Court (which, after all, never got built).

Near the Hampton Court end of this Great Avenue, William

and Mary decided to have a circle, in the centre of which would be dug a Great Basin, four hundred feet in diameter and five feet in depth. On both sides of the road and parallel to it and also round the Circle they planted four rows of lime trees, with a row of horse-chestnut trees nearest to the road. Then, from the Circle and at right angles to the great avenue, they threw out two further great avenues, each originally about three-quarters of a mile in length, of which one led to the Paddocks and the other towards the village of Hampton. To realize this scheme, 732 lime trees and 274 chestnut trees were planted, in all, at a total cost of £4,300.

Into the centre of the big Basin, the happy planners decided to move the large fountain which had been standing till then in the Privy Garden of the Palace. The Duc de Monconys, who had driven down to Hampton Court in 1663 with M. de la Molière, had seen it there:

> . . . Composed of four syrens in bronze, seated astride on dolphins, between which was a shell, supported on the foot of a goat. Above the syrens, in a second tier, were four little children, each seated, holding a fish, and surmounting all a large figure of a lady – all the figures being of bronze, but the fountain itself and the basin of marble . . .

According to an inventory made in 1659, the figure at the summit was meant to represent Arethusa, though, as she holds a golden apple in her hand, it seems more likely that the sculptor was thinking of Venus. Shortly after she was moved to her new home in Bushey Park, people started to refer to her as 'Diana', and that is what she has been called ever since.

After the death of Queen Mary from smallpox, at Kensington Palace, the works being carried out at Hampton Court were brought more or less to a standstill as the King had little heart for continuing with projects that he and his wife had conceived and were so busily superintending up to the very moment when she was taken ill, and nothing much more was done for several years. Early in January 1698, however, the famous old Palace of Whitehall, which had already been partly consumed by fire in 1691, was reduced, through the carelessness of a Dutch washerwoman, to a heap of smoking ruins, and King William was induced to turn his attention once more to Hampton Court. In his declining years the Palace became again one of William's principal homes.

Suffering possibly from dropsy – his legs were most painfully swollen – and dosed by his bemused and contentious physicians with an abominable and probably harmful mixture of medicines, which included ale impregnated with the leaves of ground ivy, gentian, centaury, chalybeate pills, vitriolated tartar, salt of worm-wood, salt of steel, steel prepared with sulphur, Epsom salts, crabs' eyes and the juice of thirty hog-lice, the King absolutely refused to give up his favourite exercises and occasionally, in the Bushey and House Parks, 'took the divertisement of hunting, attended by a great number of the nobility', though when he returned he 'had to be carried up the steps of the palace'.[9]

Obliged to return to London to open his Parliament, William resolved to return to Hampton Court at least once a week to continue his hunting in the Parks. In accordance with this plan, he went out hunting on Saturday, 21 February 1702, though he had suffered from a serious attack of giddiness that very morning, and his legs were even more swollen than usual. 'I was riding in the park at noon', he is quoted as having said later, 'and while I endeavoured to make the horse change his walking into a gallop, he fell upon his knees. Upon that I meant to raise him with the bridle, but he fell forward to one side, and so I fell with my right shoulder upon the ground. 'Tis a strange thing, for it happened upon a smooth level ground.' According to most modern history books, the King's horse had stumbled on a mole-hill, but this fact is only mentioned in one contemporary account.[10]

The fall was so violent that the King's right collar-bone was broken, and he had to be carried into the Palace. Though it seemed at first as if the accident would not be followed by any unduly serious results, the King was soon seized with shivering fits and other alarming symptoms, and after two weeks' further suffering, he died on the morning of Sunday, 8 March 1702.

During the early part of her reign, Queen Anne, who succeeded King William, took little interest in Hampton Court and its parks, though she did see that certain of the schemes undertaken by her predecessor and left unfinished at his death were completed – grumbling, invariably, at the expense and postponing payment for as long as she could manage – and she did make the gardeners take up most of her predecessors' dearly loved box hedges. After she had spent a fortnight at Hampton Court in 1710, however, she suddenly took a fancy to the place and gave orders that some 'Chaise-ridings' twenty miles long should be laid out in her parks so that she could pass through them with more ease and safety:

> . . . By taking off the hills, filling in ye holes, digging ditches and watercourses to carry off ye water, where wanted, digging and getting out of ye Fern, Nettles and other weeds that annoy them, making all passable and sowing with Hay-seed where wanted . . .[11]

The 'ridings' planned by the Queen were to be partly in the shady avenues and partly in the open, and Swift in his *Journal to Stella*[12] indicated exactly what she wanted them for:

> . . . She hunts in a chaise with one horse, which she drives herself, and drives furiously like Jehu, and is a mighty hunter like Nimrod . . .

A few days later, Swift told his Stella that the Queen had hunted the stag until four in the afternoon and had driven her chaise no less than forty miles – no mean accomplishment for a woman who was both fat and gouty.

The death of Edward Proger was by this time being eagerly awaited – the poor old chap, aged over ninety, had outlived the Duke of Albemarle, who had been Keeper over him; he had outlived the Duchess of Cleveland, who had succeeded to Monck's post as Keeper of all the Hampton Court Parks as a reward for her many and devoted services to the Crown; and now there was another person, Charles Montagu, First Baron Halifax, who coveted Proger's Keeperships of the Middle Park and the Hare Warren.

Montagu had been born in 1661 and had become Member of the House of Commons for Maldon in 1689. His rise, after that, had been rapid – he had been a Treasury Lord by 1692, in which year he had proposed that he should raise a million pounds for the nation by way of a loan (the loan is now called 'The National Debt', and is considerably larger!); he had raised more money two years later by establishing the Bank of England, which led to his being appointed Chancellor of the Exchequer; and he had been made Premier in 1697. When the Tories had come to power in 1699, however, he had been persuaded to leave the Commons. In February 1708 he had petitioned the Treasury asking that he might be granted a lease of the Upper Lodge in Bushey Park, so that he might repair and live in it. Since then he had been watching old Proger carefully for signs of a decline. Proger managed obstinately to survive until the last day of December 1713, when he was aged 96. Then, according to a memorial tablet in Hampton Church, he was overcome by 'the anguish of cutting teeth, having cut four new teeth, and had several ready to cut, which so inflamed his gums he died'. Halifax then succeeded to the Keeperships of the Middle Park and the Hare Warren, and to Proger's rights in the old Lodge in the Middle Warren.

The Hanoverian monarchs King George I and King George II took their households to Hampton Court with dull regularity, George II enjoying stag-hunting, and coursing so heartily that he was unwilling to leave off even in the close season. 'We hunt with great noise and violence', wrote the King's mistress, Mrs Howard, from Hampton Court on 31 July 1730, 'and have every day a very tolerable chance to have a neck broke.' Mrs Howard's fears were anything but groundless, as this extract from a newspaper of the time will show:

. . . August 25th, 1731. The royal family were a-hunting, and in the chase a stag started upon the Princess Amelia's horse, which being frightened threw her. The Hon. Mr. Fitzwilliam, page of honour to his Majesty, fell with his horse among the coney-burrows, as also [did] a servant to the Queen's coachmaker . . .

Watching all this were a succession of Montagus. The first of them
– the First Baron, and, later, the First Earl of Halifax – had lasted,
to enjoy his enlarged Keeperships (or 'Rangerships', as they were
coming to be called), only until 1715. He had been followed as
Keeper of the three Parks by his nephew George Montagu, Earl
of Halifax of the second creation. (As this Montagu could not
succeed directly to the Earldom, a new one had been brought
into being for him.) That Earl of Halifax died in 1737. (He was
described by the Earl of Egmont, in his diary, as 'a squanderer of
his money so that it is said his daughters will have very small
fortune. He was a great improver of ground, a good companion,
loved horse racing and kept a Mistress'.)

The 'good companion' was succeeded in turn as Ranger of the
Parks by his son George Montagu, who later adopted the name
'Montagu Dunk', following his marriage to a fifteen-year-old
heiress whose parents wanted their name preserved. George, like
his father, enjoyed getting through fortunes. Like his great-uncle,
he became a successful politician. (He was, at various times, First
Lord of the Admiralty, Head of the Board of Trade and Lieutenant
General of Ireland.) With so much to do, this Montagu was not
able to spend as much time as he would have liked at Bushey Park,
but while he was there he managed to become involved in a notable
conflict.

Although the parks at Hampton Court had been reserved, for
some two centuries, mainly for the pleasure of the ruling monarch,
local people had not been completely excluded – as early as 1563,
the men of the neighbourhood had been allowed to practise archery
in the park, and there were a number of footpaths that had been
used, almost from time immemorial, by the villagers.

One of these paths, which led through the Hare Warren from
Hampton Wick to the Hampton Court Gate, had been arbitrarily
closed by Oliver Cromwell when he made the Palace a family home,
and then it had been generously re-opened by King Charles II.
George Montagu Dunk, who seemed bent on turning Bushey
Park as far as possible into his own private preserve, tried, predict-
ably, to close it again. The local people were shocked, and one of
them, Timothy Bennet, a shoemaker of Hampton Wick, braved

Lord Halifax's displeasure and appealed to the law. In this, Bennet was entirely successful, and the villagers' right of free passage through Bushey Park was vindicated for ever. A mezzotint portrait of the heroic Timothy published shortly afterwards bears this inscription:

> ... This true Briton (unwilling to leave the world worse than he found it) by a vigorous application of the laws of his country in the cause of liberty, obtained a free passage through Bushey Park, which had many years been withheld from the people ...

King George III had no use at all for Hampton Court as a royal residence – his aversion to the place began (it was alleged by his son, the Duke of Sussex) when he had his ears boxed there by his crusty and intolerant grandfather. The whole range of buildings, with the exception of the State Rooms, was gradually subdivided, then, into suites of apartments that were allotted, by the grace and favour of the Sovereign, to deserving persons or families. (Before long, the Palace was being referred to by the irreverent as 'The Quality Poor House'.) There are a few people living in the Palace today by courtesy of the Crown.

When George Montagu Dunk died in 1771, the right of bestowal of the Rangership, which had been granted by Queen Anne 'for three lives', became vested once again in the Monarch. The next person to be offered the post was Frederick North, Earl of Guilford and King George III's Prime Minister. (The Rangership would remain by this, roughly speaking, in the holding of the Montagu family, for Lord North's maternal grandfather had been the original George Montagu.) As there was, and is, a law that prohibits a Member of Parliament from holding an office of profit under the Crown, however, Lord North had to be granted the Rangership in the name of his wife, Lady Anne North. The Norths used to live at Bushey House only during the summer months until his political commitments were over. After his final resignation, they lived there almost continuously. After His Lordship had died, practically blind, in 1792, his widow continued to live at the old Lodge – very much grander it was, by that time, than it had been in the Progers' days – until she herself died, five years later.

The Lodge – known by then as 'Bushey House' – became a very lively home after that, for the next Ranger-in-Residence was one of the more fruitful members of the Royal Family.

It was a firmly established principle at that time, and for some time after, that members of the Royal Family could only marry others who were themselves members of a Royal Family. King George III, who had eventually fifteen children, saw, as his family grew, that this would present some almost insurmountable problems, for eligible mates for them would not be exactly over-numerous. He attempted to solve those problems by having a Royal Marriage Bill passed in 1772 'for the better regulating the future marriages of the Royal Family'. By this Bill, descendants of His Majesty King George II were to be debarred from marrying without the previous consent of the Sovereign, his heirs, or his successors. After the age of 25, they could marry against the wishes of their Sovereign, as long as they had the consent of Parliament. These provisions were to have a profoundly disturbing effect on the love life of Prince William Henry, King George III's third son.

Allowed, in his early life, to serve as a midshipman in the Royal Navy, the Prince then began a series of more or less wild *affaires* that brought him inevitably into conflict with his father. The most important (for the Prince) of all these *affaires* started when the Prince of Wales and his uncle the Duke of Cumberland drew his attention to the charms of a Mrs Dorothy Jordan who was appearing at the Drury Lane Theatre, and was regarded by many as one of the most successful comedy actresses of the time. The pair – Prince and comedienne – met and were mutually attracted and by 1791 were to all intents and purposes living together as man and wife.

On the death of Lady North in 1797, then, the Prince (known, by that time, as 'The Duke of Clarence') was appointed to the vacant Rangership of Bushey Park and he and Dorothy Jordan made their home in Bushey House. The couple had had three children already, and in the following years another seven were born to them at Bushey. All the children took the name 'Fitz-

Clarence'. The Duke, meanwhile, lived the life of a typical country squire of the period, farming the land round Bushey House, raising and training a local yeomanry, and carrying out various other pastoral duties. The liaison was tacitly accepted by the King and Queen, and the Duke's brother frequently dined with him at Bushey, but the crueller cartoonists such as James Gillray did not hesitate to scourge quite mercilessly the unorthodox *ménage*.

The Duke and Dorothy Jordan continued to live with their family at Bushey House, then, until 1811. During most of that time, the Duke was kept short of money by Parliament and the occasional earnings that 'Mrs Jordan' brought home from the stage must have been helpful to both of them. It is not clear, even today, why this happy partnership finally broke up, but it is believed that when Dorothy Jordan's earning powers started to decline the Duke may have realized that he would have to start looking round for an heiress who would bring him the money of which he was so perennially in need. Whatever the reason, she left him suddenly after twenty years of their life together, dying in poverty, five years later, in France.

Horses of the highest quality have been bred in the Parks at Hampton Court for a considerable time, and still are. There was a stud of some kind at Hampton Court during the reign of King William III, and it was increased in size and importance by Queen Anne, who ran horses in her own name. It was King George IV, however, who must be considered as the real founder of the Hampton Court stud as it at present exists, since when he was Prince of Wales the First Gentleman of Europe used frequently to visit the royal enclosures in Bushey Park and the Home Park and then in 1812, when he became Prince Regent, he established a stud in the paddocks. The Prince's aim was to breed riding-horses of pure blood, all of which, as far as practicable, he intended to be grey. King William IV, his successor, kept the stud going, but after King William's death the fine collection of beasts was dispersed, forty-three brood mares, five stallions and thirty-one foals being sold by auction for 15,692 guineas. The stables and the paddocks were lent for a time to private users, after that.

Soon after Hampton Court Palace ceased to be used as a principal royal residence, the lady housekeepers and their assistants started discreetly to admit select visitors to the historic and State Apartments and to guide them round, regarding the fees they equally discreetly accepted for their unofficial services as pleasant personal perquisites that went with their jobs. (They were prepared to do this, it seems, on all seven days of the week, thereby provoking complaints that they were instituting, in Britain, the 'Continental Sunday'). One of the first acts of Queen Victoria, after she came to the throne in 1837, was to throw open the Palace to all her subjects without fee and without restriction. It followed that many of the visitors who intended to see the Palace also discovered in the process some of the delights of the neighbouring parks, and gradually during the rest of the nineteenth century the place became increasingly associated with public recreation and pleasure.

For those travelling out from London to Hampton Court, until quite recently, one of the greatest attractions was the annual display of blossom on the chestnut trees in Bushey Park. As early as 1847, horse omnibuses were taking special excursions out to Bushey for 'Chestnut Sunday', and when, in the same year, the railway was extended to Surbiton from Hampton Court the number of visitors increased. 'Chestnut Sunday' was still being celebrated after motor cars were streaming in their hundreds along the Kingston-to-Hampton Court road, but today this great free floral show appears to have lost much of its popular appeal.

In 1851, the Royal Hampton Court Stud was re-formed by Her Majesty Queen Victoria – on the advice, it is believed, of Prince Albert. For many years after this regeneration, the yearlings of which Her Majesty wished to dispose would be sold on the Saturday in the week after Ascot races, in one of the paddocks in Bushey Park. Most of the celebrities of the racing world would assemble in front of Mr Tattersall's rostrum on these scintillating occasions, and the stock sold would invariably fetch very high prices.

Among the other spectacular events to take place in Bushey Park during the nineteenth century were the great Bicycle Meets at which the very latest models were put on display. Until the early 1870s, the discomforts of the early wooden 'bone-shakers' with their iron-rimmed wheels had discouraged all but the most heroic experimenters. Then came the development of the 'Ordinary' or 'Penny Farthing' bicycle, with its steel wheels and solid rubber tyres, which represented such an improvement that bicycling immediately became a craze – not only as a way of travelling, but also as a recreation. The idea of a monster meet of bicyclists was first suggested in 1874, and a few enthusiasts turned up at the rendezvous – the Lion Gates at Hampton Court. In the following year, the meet drew 204 bicyclists, and the year after that between five and six hundred attended.

The rally, on this occasion, started with an undignified dispute as to the route that should be taken and, more particularly, which club should lead the procession. As a result of the argument the members of the Pickwick Club rode off on their own, in a fit of pique, before the procession started. The remainder, led by the London Club which had nearly a hundred members present, moved off at about 6 p.m. and went for a 'spin' through Hampton, New Hampton and Teddington, returning to Hampton Court by way of the Chestnut Avenue in Bushey Park. The bicyclists rode down the great avenue in double file. At the Diana Pond the files parted, one file taking the left track and the other file taking the right. As the riders met on the far side of the Basin they joined hands – a courageous manoeuvre which drew much applause from the spectators.

The meets, after that, continued to increase in popularity until 1882, when the total number of riders who took part was 2,360. The procession – with club members in their smart and neatly fitting uniforms, 'unattached' members, who were accorded a slightly inferior status, and tricyclists, who were condemned to bring up the rear – was on this occasion so long that the leading riders had arrived back at the assembly area before the last ones had left. After that, the rallies became less and less popular until, after 1883, they ceased to be held.

The Royal Parks at Hampton Court contain, and have on their fringes, some really splendid mansions and smaller homes of the good old 'English country house' type which give them additional grace.

The most handsome, possibly, of these mansions – the Montagus'

7

Bushey House – was granted, after the death of His Majesty King William IV in 1837, to his widow Queen Adelaide, and she lived there until her own death in 1849. Subsequently, it was lent by Her Majesty Queen Victoria to Louis, Duc de Nemours, son of King Louis-Philippe of the French, and he lived there intermittently until 1896. Four years after that, with the aged Queen's full approval, the Government took over the site, which is near the Teddington end of the great Chestnut Avenue, for a new and pressing scientific venture. The country badly needed a National Physical Laboratory, at which research could be carried out (particularly research into the accurate determination of physical constants), precise standards of measurement could be established and maintained, and instruments and materials tested, and the old house at Bushey seemed as if it would make an excellent place. A portion of the old mansion became the residence of the first Director of the Laboratory, Sir Richard Glazebrook. The growth and development of the Laboratory since those early days reflect the rapid progress that science and technology have made during the twentieth century.

One other handsome and historic house in Bushey Park is now enclosed and is generally inaccessible to the public – South Lodge, built by King Charles II, which is now occupied by the Admiralty Research Laboratory.

Hampton Court Palace is today one of the principal attractions offered to tourists from abroad – one of the officials principally responsible for the supervision of the grounds has estimated recently that each foreign visitor spends approximately twenty minutes in the place between being set down from car or coach and being required to set off for the next historic destination. Whether or not that is true or just a semi-humorous observation, it is clear that the sights to be seen in the immediate vicinity of the Palace – the old Tilt Yard; King Henry VIII's Close Tennis Court; the Maze, with its high clipped hedges that were planned originally in the reign of Queen Anne; the Great Vine (a *Black Hamburgh*, planted in 1769); and so on – will attract more viewers than the Parks, which are after all to the hurried passer-by merely expanses of more or less open country.

For more leisurely visitors, the Parks can offer some very special delights.

For the sportsman, there are cricket grounds and football pitches in Bushey Park and a fine golf course in the Hampton Court Park, and fishing is allowed in the Diana Basin and in certain of the ponds. (Younger visitors in search of recreation are catered for with a well-equipped playground in Bushey Park, not far from the Hampton Court Gate.)

For garden-lovers who can bear to leave the immediate surroundings of the Palace, there is the superb Waterhouse Plantation in Bushey Park, which is larger and wilder than the Isabella Plantation in Richmond Park but which seems, in consequence, to be less disturbed by the intrusion of humans. The glades in the Waterhouse Plantation, formed chiefly of mature timber with shrubs and plants of more recent introduction and centred on a contrived 'natural' stream, lead one on from vista to splendid vista, so that it is easy to understand why the place earned, with the Isabella Plantation, the verdict from Richard Church: 'Two of the most beautiful man-made scenes that I have found anywhere in Europe'.

People who enjoy studying rare trees and especially fine specimens of commoner trees can spend many days wandering happily round the gardens of Hampton Court Palace and the neighbouring Royal Parks. There is room here only for a brief list of some of the more remarkable treasures in this widely assorted collection.

Within easy walking distance of the Palace buildings, for a start, one can see, in the Tilt Yard, a grafted specimen of the rare Erman's birch (*Betula Ermanii*), introduced from North-East Asia nearly a century ago and noted especially for the striking whiteness of its bark, which peels away as the tree ages, leaving horizontal pink strips of great decorative value. In the Privy Garden, there are remarkable specimens of the judas tree (*Cercis Siliquastrum*), the cow's-tail pine (*Cephalotaxus Harringtonia Drupacea*), the yellow wood (*Cladastris Lutea*) and the Kentucky coffee tree (*Gymnocladus Dioicus*). The Wilderness contains, among many other noteworthy trees, a particularly fine *Catalpa Bignonioides Aurea* – the golden-leaved variety of the Indian bean – and a weeping silver lime

(*Tilia Petiolaris*). There is a very good specimen of the stone pine
(*Pinus Pinea*) on the Terrace.

A little farther afield, one can see in the Home Park a turkey oak
(*Quercus Cerris*) which is, at the time of writing, more than 132
feet high, being one of the tallest trees at Hampton Court. The
100-foot high 'ton' is broken in this Park, too, by a crack willow
(*Salis Fragilis*) and a Lombardy poplar (*Populus Nigra Italica*),
both of which are near the Cypress Pond, while several of the limes
in the avenue by the Long Water are more than one hundred
feet high.

Most, but not all, of the really remarkable trees to be seen in
Bushey Park are located in the Woodland Gardens. In the Wood-
land Garden (North) one can see a London plane (*Platanus X
Hispanica*) which is, at the time of writing, 138 feet high. Here,
too, is an exceptionally fine swamp cypress (*Taxodium Distichum*).
In the Woodland Garden (South) is the tallest specimen in these
Parks of the dawn redwood or 'water fir' (*Metasequoia Glyptostro-
boides*) – a tree discovered in East Szechwan and North-East
Hupeh in South-West China in 1941, described in 1944, and
introduced into this country in 1948. Already, twenty-seven years
later, the specimen in Bushey Park, marked 1949, is 63 feet high.

The least frequented parts of Bushey Park, which lie mainly to
the west of the Teddington Gate, are well populated today with wild
animals and birds, beside the fallow and red deer that are, like
those in Richmond Park, carefully preserved, The badger, though,
a cherished inhabitant of Richmond Park, is rarely if ever seen in
the plantations in Bushey Park, or at Hampton Court. Perhaps there
is some compensation in the number of hedgehogs and voles that
spend their self-absorbed lives in the Parks' more mysterious
places. There are plenty of grey squirrels, too, but these, with
their greedy and destructive ways, should perhaps be regarded as
a bane, rather than as a compensation.

The Waterhouse Plantation in Spring and early Summer resounds
from first light with birdsong (though the public are not admitted
until a little later in the day). Birds frequently heard in small
London gardens such as the blackbird, chaffinch, hedge sparrow,
robin, song thrush and wren arc to be expected there, but it is a

little more surprising to hear blackcaps, garden warblers, willow warblers and whitethroats contributing, on occasions, to the generally stunning effect. The bright-coloured feathers of the bullfinch, cock chaffinch, greenfinch, goldfinch and jay add cheer, if this is needed, to the Plantation's shady places, and one of the most beautiful birds ever seen in Britain, the kingfisher,[13] has nested here. Other well-tree'd parts of Bushey Park are almost as rewarding to the bird-watcher.

Chapter 11

Regent's Park

In his book *Georgian London*, Sir John Summerson has pointed out that the Regent's Park area is unique. 'Once and only once', he has written, 'has a great plan for London, affecting the capital as a whole, been projected and carried to completion.' By sponsoring this grand scheme, and seeing it through until it was quite realized, the eldest son of King George III – Prince of Wales; then Prince Regent; finally King George IV – created his own most lasting memorial. Regent's Park is still one of the finest urban open spaces in the whole world.

The Marylebone Park Crown Estate, from which Regent's Park was developed, was originally part of the Great Forest of Middlesex – a region replete with 'wooded glades and lairs of wild beasts, deer both red and fallow, wild bulls and boars', according to William FitzStephen who, in the twelfth century, wrote his *Description of the Most Noble City of London*. Most of the land lay in the Manor of Tyburn which, during the Middle Ages, the Abbess of Barking held directly from the Crown. When King Henry VIII dissolved the monasteries in 1536, he took over the Manor of Tyburn, and seeing that part of it would make an excellent extension to the game preserves over which he already hunted, near his Palace of St James, he enclosed a roughly circular area on the north-east and he called this 'Marylebone Park'. Round his new Park, King Henry got his men to dig a deep ditch and to throw up a steep embankment, and he had lodges constructed in the Park in which his gamekeepers could live.

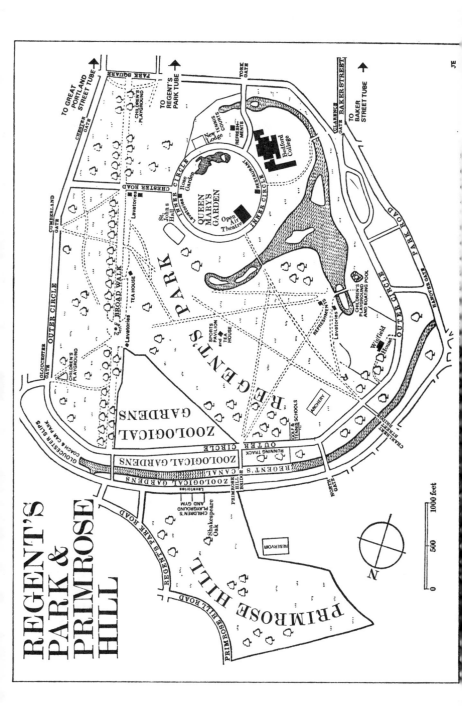

REGENT'S PARK & PRIMROSE HILL

Henry's son, King Edward VI, was also fond of the chase, and he had a fence put up on his father's earthworks to make the Park a better preserve. (The fence took thirteen loads of railing and paling, conveyed specially for the purpose from Westminster, and a carpenter and his assistant worked for eighteen days on its construction.) But Edward died before he could enjoy much hunting at Marylebone.

Mary Tudor, who succeeded to the throne after the death of her brother Edward, decided, with her Privy Council, to save money by breaking up the Parks of Marylebone and Hyde and selling the land to people living around. Fortunately for us, Queen Mary's intended economies were never put into effect. Her sister Queen Elizabeth I was much more appreciative of the Parks that their father had brought into being, and during her reign the enclosed land at Marylebone was well kept up, anyone found trespassing on it, or poaching, being severely punished.

During the war between King Charles I and his Parliament, Marylebone Park underwent some radical changes, being partly cleared of trees and brushwood, by order of the House of Commons, to provide fuel for the poor citizens of London, and then being pledged by the King to his Ordnance Commissioners as security for supplies of gunpowder 'at twelve pence the pound'. After the war was over, Cromwell found himself as short of ready money as Charles had been, and within a few days of the King's execution an Act of Parliament was passed that authorized the sale of the royal estates. Marylebone Park was sold by tender to three cavalry officers in Cromwell's army, who paid a little more than £13,000 for it. The purchasers of the Park went on cutting down its ancient trees, or as many of the ancient trees as were left standing, in an attempt to recover as quickly as possible the money they had paid for the land and to show, if they could, some kind of a profit. By the time King Charles II returned to London from his enforced stay abroad, few of the thousands of splendid oaks, elms and limes that had graced Marylebone Park when he left England were still to be seen. (Most of the oaks had gone to build ships for the Navy.) The sadly denuded Park was promptly taken back into royal ownership; the Parliamentary officers who had misguidedly 'purchased' it were told to go away without compensation, and the new tenants proceeded to plough up most of the ground so that it could be used for dairy farming. Hedges were then planted, so that the land was divided into fields.

By 1745, when Prince Charles James Stuart made his abortive foray into England, the fields at Marylebone and in its neighbourhood were providing the horse-owners of the metropolis with a fair part of the hay that they needed for their mews and stables, and the herds of cows that had displaced the royal deer were supplying many of London's rapidly increasing households with their daily quotas of milk. The fences that had enclosed the old royal hunting ground had almost entirely disappeared. (When the estate was due to be 'improved', in fact, towards the end of the eighteenth century, the surveyors employed were often unable to establish the exact boundaries of the royal lands, and they had to dig around, like present-day archaeologists, in their attempts to find out where the posts of the vanished fences had originally stood.)

The idea that countrified Marylebone Park should be 'improved' appears to have been put forward, in the first place, by John Fordyce, a civil servant from Scotland, who was appointed Surveyor General of the Crown Lands in 1793. (He himself owned extensive estates in North Berwickshire.)

When Fordyce took up his post, the Park was still a charmingly pastoral area, though it did contain a few interesting buildings, including the 'Jew's Harp' tavern, which is said to have been one of the most picturesque inns near London; the 'Queen's Head and Artichoke', a public house that may have belonged originally to the Cook of Queen Elizabeth I; and a number of cottages, most of which were lived in by agricultural labourers. (A few were rented by wealthy Londoners who wanted quiet country retreats to which they could retire from the hurry and scurry of the City. These more genteel tenants guarded their privacy with zeal, one elderly gentleman even venturing to exhibit a notice which threatened: 'Steel Traps and Spring Guns ALL OVER these grounds. N.B. Dogs trespassing will be shot'.)[1] Along the southern boundary of the Park ran the New Road, which had been laid down in 1757

7*

to connect Islington and Paddington, and acted as London's first by-pass.

Fordyce's first important task, after he took up his new appointment, was to consider a request made by the Duke of Portland that he should be allowed to lay down a new turnpike road through Marylebone Park. The Duke's intentions were, no doubt, purely altruistic – a new church was needed for the people of Marylebone, and the Duke had offered to give some of his land for it, provided that an access road could be made over the royal ground. (The proposed road would provide, incidentally, an invaluable link between the two separate portions of the Duke's North London estates.) Fordyce considered the Duke's proposals carefully. He knew, as well as anyone, what five hundred acres of good agricultural land on the margins of a rapidly expanding metropolis might be worth, if those acres were guided firmly but discreetly into the capable hands of modern and enterprising developers. He was well aware of the enormous fortunes that the Bedfords, the Grosvenors, the Portlands and other noble families had made by exploiting the land they had been fortunate enough to own in the immediate vicinity of the capital, and he saw, with characteristic Scottish acumen, that the Crown, by owning the freehold of Marylebone Park, was sitting, metaphorically, on a gold mine. The road that the Duke wanted to lay down would cut obliquely across the land that the Crown, if Fordyce had his way, would wish to exploit, reducing its potential value a thousandfold. Fordyce therefore recommended to the Lords of the Treasury that they should turn the Duke's proposals down flat.

Fordyce next asked that the Park at Marylebone should be freshly and more accurately surveyed, and he suggested that a public competition should be held, so that the very best ideas might be brought forward for its development. His proposals met with the approval of the Lords of the Treasury. Plans of the Park were then engraved and sent to several of the country's most prominent architects, and £1,000 – at that time a reasonably tempting sum – was offered to the person who should come up with the most satisfactory solution to the problem. The architects' response was disappointing. One only – John White, Surveyor to the Duke of Portland – showed any real interest in the matter, and as he lived in the Park and did not wish it to lose its pleasant rural character when the existing leases fell in, he did not produce and enter for the competition the kind of plan, replete with streets and squares, that Fordyce had expected. Instead, White proposed that a roughly circular ring of villas, each standing in its own grounds, should be built on the perimeter of the Park, the centre being kept as a pastoral pleasure ground, complete with a Serpentine Lake. Where the Park neared the New Road, at its southernmost end, White proposed that a splendid crescent should be erected. (This idea, with some of White's other proposals, was to be borrowed by later planners without any proper acknowledgement being made to the originator of the scheme.)

Five years after John Fordyce launched the competition which had had such a disappointing outcome, the middle-aged architect John Nash, who had a 'thick, squat, dwarf figure, with round head, snub nose and little eyes',[2] married a handsome young woman named Mary Anne Bradley who was, it was alleged, the mistress of the Prince of Wales. (She had adopted, or so she said, the five children of 'a distant relative', but malicious people close to the Court circles claimed that the infants had royal blood.) Whether these allegations were true or not, the Prince and Nash were, after that, very closely associated, and as architecture was one of the Prince's chief interests, the two men spent much of their time happily planning, building or altering palaces and grand houses for the Prince's use, or for the use of his wealthiest friends.

Between 1795 and 1802, Nash was working in partnership with the great landscape gardener Humphry Repton, who was an adept at laying out the grounds of large country houses so that they would enhance, in a totally charming way, the buildings they happened to surround. It followed, therefore, that Nash, who had learned a lot from Repton, took a particular interest in the unprecedented and unrepeatable opportunities offered by the proposed redevelopment of Marylebone Park. With the Prince, he studied Fordyce's recommendation, made in his fourth triennial report of April 1809:

. . . Distance is best computed by time; and if means could be found to lessen the time of going from Marylebone to the Houses of Parliament, the value of the ground for building would be thereby proportionately increased. The best, and probably upon the whole, the most advantageous way of doing that, would be by opening a great street from Charing-Cross towards a central part of Marylebone Park . . .

Two months after that report was published, Fordyce died at his home in Whitehall. Nash had by then been for nearly three years one of the Joint Architects to the Department of Woods and Forests. In the following year, the Commissioners who had been appointed after Fordyce's death to look after the Departments of Woods and Forests and of Land Revenues formally gave up the idea of a public competition for the re-designing of Marylebone Park and instead they instructed their surveyors, Thomas Chawner and Thomas Leverton, and their architects, John Nash and James Morgan, to go ahead and get out some plans.

Left to their own devices, Chawner and Leverton would certainly have divided up Marylebone Park with a stark network of straight streets and rectangular squares, practically unrelieved by any curve; so developed, the Park would have acted merely as a con-tinuation of the Portland Estate that lay immediately to the south, and would have provided no relief of any kind from the monotony of the Portman and Southampton Estates, to west and east, which were laid out with middle-class and artisan dwellings of a pleasant but fairly uniform type.

The Commissioners were saved from this limited and depressing expedient, however, by the romantic genius of John Nash. Nash, who had worked in Wales and the Border Counties for such great believers in the 'picturesque' as Richard Payne Knight and Sir Uvedale Price, was determined that the Park, in its next phase of existence, should be anything but dull. In this he was undoubtedly encouraged by the Prince of Wales, who, on being sworn in as Prince Regent, was ready to indulge in some *folie de grandeur.*

First, the two men took John Fordyce's idea that a new road

should be provided, down which people living in the Park could drive easily to the centre of the town, and on this basis they made plans for a grand processional route, a *Via Triumphalis*, that would lead from the Prince's sumptuous London home at Carlton House to a superb country villa, somewhere near the middle of the Park, which would provide the Prince with an appropriately majestic setting for his leisure moments. Besides rivalling the arcaded Rue de Rivoli that Napoleon Bonaparte was creating in Paris, the new road would conveniently divide the poor and run-down district of Soho on the east from the newer and more fashionable building developments of Mayfair. As a start for the road, Nash could take Portland Place, which had been laid out by the Adam brothers, and which he regarded, understandably, as 'the most magnificent street in London'.

The two men must have then discussed, with mounting enthusiasm, Nash's ambitious plans for the Park itself. The ground, regrettably flat and featureless when compared to Wales and the Border Counties, had become, in Nash's excitable mind, a well-wooded region of hills and valleys, watered by wide rivers (or at least a curving canal), and graced by an ornamental lake, the extended arms of which would embrace a most decorative garden. In a rural paradise of this kind, declared Nash, the right sort of people would wish to live.

> . . . The attraction of open Space, free air and the scenery of Nature, with the means and invitation of exercise on horseback, on foot and in Carriages, shall be preserved or created in Mary-le-bone Park, as allurements or motives for the wealthy part of the Public to establish themselves there . . .

The Park was to become, in short, an exclusive and self-contained residential area, in which a relatively small number of delightful villas would be built. These would provide the same kind of accommodation as the large country houses to which the gentry were used, though they might not bear any exact resemblance to those dull rural mansions. They would be cunningly placed in such a way that each would have open views over the Park, but would still be invisible from the others. There would be shops, markets and other conveniences in the Park, too, that were 'essential for the comforts of Life', and tradesmen would be induced to settle there in small houses, though not, of course, where they could be seen from the more desirable residences. Members of the poorer classes who lived in the new housing estates to the east and west would be discouraged from entering the Park if no gates of any kind were provided on those sides. The land to the north as far as Hampstead and Highgate had not yet been built on, and there was no reason for Nash, or the Prince Regent, to foresee that it ever would be.

Nash's plans for Marylebone Park may have seemed revolutionary to the Commissioners – there was no residential area anywhere in London, or indeed in the whole world, quite like the one he proposed to bring into being – but they did not dare to oppose a scheme which, they knew, had the personal backing of the Prince Regent and to which, it appeared, the Prince would be willing to lend his name. They did, however, suggest several modifications. Summoned to the presence of the Lord Chancellor on 29 August 1811, Nash was told that he would have to reduce the number of villas that he proposed to build on the ground from fifty-six to twenty-six; the architect grumbled, but he was forced to agree. Thereupon he had to submit to some other restrictions – the canal that he had proposed to carry across the Park would have to run just inside the perimeter, he was told. (The Commissioners could not chance the rude barge people landing and making nuisances of themselves on the Crown's very select Estate.) Again the architect grumbled – his scheme would lose some of its most picturesque effects by this alteration in his plans, he claimed – but again he was made to give way. He was then asked to move the broad drive or exercise road that he had planned for the Park so that it would run, like the canal, just inside the outer boundary. He had no option but to concur.

Given the necessary authorization to go ahead with his great scheme, Nash set to work with his usual energy. He began by laying down the roads to which the Commissioners had agreed, and by making a few plantations ('which no one was permitted to approach', complained Mr Creevey in the House of Commons). He then ran into serious trouble; the construction of the Regent's Canal was bitterly opposed by the other landowners of the locality, who thought that the stagnant waters it would contain would be a constant danger to health. Next, Charles Mayor, a business associate of Nash's, who had taken the lease of the ground at the north end of Portland Place and intended to put up a grand circus on it to Nash's designs, went bankrupt, owing £22,000, when he had put up only six of the houses, and before he had managed to put roofs on them. For years, during which England was desperately engaged in the war against France and in the war's immediate aftermath, Nash struggled against rising prices, shortage of money, the unreliability of prospective clients, and all the other hazards that can beset the brave man who embarks privately on a vast and expensive enterprise. Harassed by misfortunes as he was, the great architect never lost courage, writing reassuringly to the Commissioners:

. . . It cannot be expected I should have foreseen the interruptions which the Circus and Canal have met with, nor the Causes which have induced those Gentlemen who had put down their names for Villas to decline following up their first intentions. The failure of Mr. Mayor in the middle of his progress was certainly owing solely to the sudden stoppage of those resources of credit which Builders look up to for the success of their speculations . . . Before the Roads were completed and the Park inclosed, the disposition to building became paralysed . . . The main object of the Crown, I conceive to be, the Improvement of their own Estate, to augment and not diminish it, and not to sell any part of it; a magnificent and convenient Street for the Public will be the result, not the cause. The Crown property in Mary-le-bone Park, in extent of ground, is greater than all their London Property beside; and to make it more productive in proportion as it is more extensive, only requires the Street in question; time will do the rest, and Mary-le-bone Park one day become a very prominent feature in the list of Crown Revenue . . .[3]

The Prince Regent, despite all the setbacks, never lost confidence in Nash; and then, in the years between 1819 and 1826, the tide of Nash's fortunes flowed strongly the other way. During those years, the elderly architect managed to ring the Park with ten great stucco terraces, seven smaller terraces or 'places', the handsome crescent that superseded Mayor's uncompleted circus, a square, a barracks, a church, and two residential estates. Though Nash did not make all the working drawings that were necessary for these substantial projects, he designed or approved every façade, and in that important respect, if in no other, the majority of the early nineteenth-century buildings that surround the Regent's Park can fairly be regarded as his handiwork.

It would not be appropriate to describe in detail here each of Nash's great terraces that today provide such an extraordinary architectural background to the southern and eastern expanses of Regent's Park, but the observant visitor to the Park can hardly fail to be fascinated by the similarities (and differences) between York Terrace, completed in 1822, which with the buildings of York Gate to the south was intended by Nash to provide through its central gap a Grand Entrance to the Park; Sussex Place, completed in the same year, with oriental cupolas that remind one of the Prince Regent's Pavilion at Brighton ('A curious group of buildings in the Chinese Taste', commented Slidell Mackenzie, an American visitor, in the 1840s); Hanover Terrace, designed in detail by John Nash himself, and completed in 1823, which has numbered among its most famous residents Charles Dickens, Edmund Gosse, and H. G. Wells; Chester Terrace on the east, completed in 1825; and its near neighbour Cumberland Terrace, finished in the following year. Of all the Regent's Park terraces, the last may be considered, perhaps, as Nash's masterpiece. Resembling a series of small palaces linked by triumphal arches, this was the range of buildings that was to have had the honour of facing the Prince Regent's own pavilion, had that ever been built. But before the Park's principal *raison d'être* had a chance to come into existence, the Prince – by that time, King George IV – had become obsessed with the extensions and improvements that he and Nash were making at Buckingham Palace, and the idea that he should have a residence of any kind in Regent's Park, even a mere *guinguette*, was quietly forgotten.

Of the twenty-six 'country house'-type villas that the Commissioners allowed Nash to build in the Park, only a few actually appeared.

St John's Lodge, the first of these villas to be constructed, still stands by the Inner Circle. It was designed by John Raffield for Charles Augustus Tulk, who was Member of Parliament for Sudbury. From 1829 to 1833 it was the home of the Marquis of Wellesley, who was the elder brother of the Duke of Wellington, hero of Waterloo. The house now belongs to Bedford College, which is part of the University of London, and is used as a hostel for members of the staff and senior students. Its charming and peaceful gardens have recently been opened to the public.

The second of the villas to be put up, The Holme, stands on the western side of the Inner Circle. The house, a beautifully proportioned and delightfully elegant building, almost surrounded by well-tree'd lawns that slope down to the lake, was constructed specially for James Burton, the wealthy builder, who had come to Nash's aid when he was in serious financial difficulties. The job of designing the building was given to Burton's tenth child Decimus, who was only a lad of eighteen at the time. The young man executed this important commission so successfully that he was given a proper professional training in Nash's office, and he went on to design, as we have seen, many of the neatest and most gracious buildings in London's Royal Parks.

One of Decimus Burton's other early exercises, the villa known later as St Dunstan's, was built in 1825 for the Marquis of Hertford, and it stood in the westernmost corner of Regent's Park, approximately where Winfield House, the United States Ambassador's residence, stands now. The villa was given its name after its noble occupant purchased, and put up in its garden in 1830, the famous clock from St Dunstan's Church in Fleet Street, a timepiece which has the hours struck by two grotesque carved and painted figures. During World War I, and for a few years afterwards, the villa was used as a training centre for those who had lost their sight during the hostilities, and the church's name was 'borrowed', once more, for the Association which was doing this splendid work. In 1934, Lord Rothermere, who was at that time occupying Burton's villa, restored the old clock to its original home in Fleet Street, where it can be seen and admired to this day.

In the south-west part of the Park, three villas were built and quickly became well-known. Hanover Lodge, which survives, has been the home of several notable (or notorious) persons, including Joseph Bonaparte, Lord Cochrane (who tried in 1814 to rig the Stock Exchange by spreading a rumour that Napoleon Bonaparte had fallen from power, and was the last man in Britain to be sentenced to stand in the pillory) and Admiral Lord Beatty. Sussex Lodge, which also stood here, was demolished in 1957 to make way for the Royal College of Obstetricians, and Albany Cottage disappeared to make room for the Islamic Cultural Centre, which was the creation of the rich American woman called Lady Ribblesdale.

South Villa was built in 1827 on the south-west side of the Inner Circle. (It stood more or less exactly on the site of Marylebone Park Farm, the largest of the three farms into which the area was divided before Nash started work on it.) For some years, before and after the end of the nineteenth century, this villa was the home of two old ladies, Mrs Abbot and her sister Miss Adamson. When they died, the remaining sixteen years of the lease were bought by the governing body of Bedford College, the oldest college for the higher education of women, which had been founded in Bedford Square in 1849 by a Mrs Elizabeth Jesser Reid, and had survived indifference and censure so successfully that it was in a very good position to expand. With the lease, the Governors of the College obtained permission to pull down South Villa and to replace it with a building that would be much more suitable for academic studies, and fully equipped for them. The residents in and around the Park did not take at all kindly to this idea, and demonstrations were staged. In spite of all the opposition, the College authorities went ahead with their plans, and by 1913 the functional but uninspiring new building, designed by a Mr Basil Champneys, was ready to be declared open by Her Majesty Queen Mary. The Crown had reserved part of the grounds of South Villa to make a public walk by the lake, but this was generally regarded as a poor compensation for the damage that had been done to the genteel, residential 'atmosphere' of the Park. The only remaining feature of the original South Villa is the charming little octagonal gate lodge that stands by the York Bridge.

Another incongruous note is struck on the east side of the Park by the buildings put up, at approximately the same time as the original South Villa, to house the members of the community centred on the Royal Hospital of St Katharine. Ever since 1147, in the reign of King Stephen, this royal hospital had been standing on the riverbank immediately downstream from the Tower of London. (In recent years, it had been used principally to provide homes for poor clergymen and their widows.) Then, in 1825, the Thames-side land was needed so that a big dock, convenient to the City, could be made. The Hospital authorities did not want to shift from their historic buildings, but when, in an attempt to persuade them to do so, the Dock Company directors offered them a site in the new Regent's Park and a grant of £36,000 towards the cost of removal they were virtually compelled to agree. Ambrose Poynter, a pupil of Nash, was given the job of designing the new hospice. The two men were not, by that time, on friendly terms, and Nash let it be known that he was 'astounded' at the phenomenon of Poynter being entrusted with such an important commission. Poynter, in his turn, decided to ignore all the buildings around, which had been so carefully supervised by Nash, and instead, in an attempt to be a little more up-to-date than his master, he elected to work in the newly fashionable and serious Neo-Gothic style which, he felt, would be more suitable for the buildings of an ancient ecclesiastical institution than Nash's playful classical manner. (The critics decided that Poynter had been right, hailing his finished complex, which consisted of a church, two ranges of living quarters, and a Master's House, as 'delightfully monastic'.) The Hospital was disbanded in 1914 since it had ceased by then to serve any purpose that would be fully compatible with a Major War Effort. The buildings, however, remain and are used today by members of the Danish community in London.

Even while they were happening, the changes made in Marylebone

Park under the aegis of the Prince Regent, or King as he became, and John Nash aroused violent criticism and extravagant praise. In 1818, Henry Crabb Robinson was writing in his *Diary*:

> . . . This enclosure [Regent's Park] with the new street leading to it from Carlton House will give a sort of glory to the Regent's government, which will be more felt by remote posterity than the victories of Trafalgar and Waterloo, glorious as these are. . . .

Prince Pückler-Muskau described Nash's architecture, however, as 'monstrous', and Maria Edgeworth, the popular novelist, declared that she was 'properly surprised by the new town that has been built in Regent's Park – and indignant at [the] plaister statues and horrid useless *domes* and pediments crowned with mock sculpture figures which damp and smoke must destroy in a season or two'. Leigh Hunt, while claiming that Mr Nash was 'a better layer-out of grounds than architect', admitted that the public had reason to be grateful to him for what he had done:

> The Regent's Park has saved us from worse places in the same quarter; for it is at all events a park, and has trees and grass, and is a breathing-space between town and country. It has prevented Harley and Wimpole-streets from going further; has checked, in that quarter at least, the monstrous brick cancer that was extending its arms in every direction.

Nash's Park had not only trees and grass to delight the public; it had, and has, a very attractive artificial lake extending over twenty-two acres. (Much of the earth which had to be excavated when the bed of the lake was dug out was used to make the high mound which still stands near the rose garden in the Inner Circle.) And after 1826, the Park was used to accommodate the collections of the Zoological Society of London.

The Society, with which Regent's Park will be for ever associated, was founded in July 1824 at the suggestion of the famous explorer Sir Stamford Raffles, who was elected, with Sir Humphry Davy, the Society's first Joint President. The Society had, at its inception, 151 members, several of whom happened to have their homes in or near the new Regent's Park. It was natural, then, that when the Society's Lords and Masters decided that an open-air menagerie was needed, in which wild animals and other undomesticated creatures could be kept and studied, they should think of the Regent's Park as being the place that would be most likely to provide the most desirable site. The members of the Society's committee approached the Commissioners and asked them for some ground:

> . . . Our first plan would be to have a garden laid out in aviaries, paddocks for deer, antelopes, etc., stabularies for such animals as may require them, lodges, and perhaps suitable apartments for the Society to meet in; and, if possible, pieces of water for fish and aquatic birds. Our buildings would for the most part be low, and in no case offensive, and the plans would be readily submitted to you . . .

The Commissioners, in their reply, offered the Society a five-acre patch on the north-east boundary of the Park. Sir Stamford Raffles, accompanied by a Lord Auckland, went up to look at the land they had been allotted, and the two men did not like it much. So they wrote next day a letter to the Commissioners in which they said that the Society should be offered, instead, some of the highly desirable land in the Inner Circle. The Commissioners had already promised the highly desirable land in the inner Circle to a nursery gardener called Jenkins, of Lisson Grove, and they were unwilling to go back on their word. Sir Stamford and his friends had therefore to be content with the outlying patch they had been originally offered. (They were granted a few extra acres, adjoining this patch, later in the same year.) Someone writing in the *Literary Gazette* said that they did not know how the inhabitants of the Regent's Park would like having lions, leopards and hyaenas so near their neighbourhood. The Commissioners were probably thinking along the same lines when they sent Sir Stamford to such a remote corner of the Park.

The Society wisely chose Decimus Burton to act as its architect, and he designed, as they expected, some very elegant buildings, pens, cages and aviaries to house the beasts and birds donated from the Royal Menagerie at the Tower, and other collections. Members of the public were admitted on weekdays, on payment of a shilling, and the production of a letter of introduction from a Fellow of the Society. (Until quite recently, entry to the Zoo on Sundays was strictly reserved for Fellows and their families.) 'The Ark in the Park', as the new Zoological Gardens were called, quickly became one of London's most popular places of instruction or amusement, the number of visitors rising rapidly whenever some new addition to the Society's stock caught the public fancy, or was given an unusual amount of publicity. Among the most magnetic attractions to be exhibited in the Zoological Gardens during the nineteenth century were the first elephant to be acquired by the Society (in 1828); the first rhinoceros to be seen in Britain for several thousands of years (in 1834); and the Zoo's first giraffes (imported from the Sudan in 1836). When, in 1882, the Society sold a testy old African elephant called 'Jumbo' to Barnum's Circus, and Jumbo was shipped off to America, some enterprising but not strictly truthful journalists tried to pretend that poor Jumbo was being torn ruthlessly away from his loving consort called Alice. Alice, the newspapermen trumpeted, would pine away and die without her 'husband': it was cruelty to animals of the very grossest sort. There was even a popular song on the subject:

> Jumbo said to Alice: 'I love you!'
> Alice said to Jumbo: 'I don't believe you do!
>   If you really loved me
>   As you say you do
> You wouldn't go to Yankee land and leave me in the Zoo!'

Alice, actually, could not have cared less about Jumbo (their 'marriage' had never been consummated, anyway); but the extraordinary publicity given to this sale brought crowds flocking to the Zoo, and with the extra admission fees and the proceeds of the sale the Society was able to have a splendid new Reptile House built.

Archery, as we have seen, has always been thought an appropriate sport for London's Royal Parks. So, in 1832, the members of the Toxophilite Society were allotted a five-acre plot in Regent's Park,

close to York Terrace, at a rent of £125 per annum for thirty-one
years. A small rustic lodge was put up to serve as a pavilion for
the archers. The residents in the Park bitterly resented this,
complaining loudly about its red-tiled roof. The Commissioners
inspected the building, found nothing too awful about it, and
insisted on their right to let the land as a site for a new villa if they
chose, which immediately shut up the complainers. The Society
prospered during the rest of the nineteenth century – so much so
that the archers were able to turn down an approach from some
sportsmen who wished to play croquet on part of their grounds.
Disappointed, the croquet players went off to Wimbledon, where
they formed the Club that now holds the world-famous annual
Tennis Tournaments. The Toxophilite Society declined in member-
ship in the present century until, by 1922, when the lease of their
ground came up for renewal, there were not sufficient members
to keep the Society going. So the ground was once again taken over
by the Commissioners, who pulled the building down, admitted
the general public, and in 1930 made a children's paddling and
canoeing pool near the western boundary. (Once more the residents
in and near the Park protested vociferously; once more they were
overruled.)

Gardeners and gardening have been closely associated with
Regent's Park ever since the Royal Botanical Society of London
was founded in the second year of Queen Victoria's reign, largely
as a result of the activities of James de Carle Sowerby, who was
made the Society's first Secretary. (His son followed him in that
office, and his grandson followed his son.) The Society was allowed
to rent eighteen acres of land in the Inner Circle region of the Park,
and Decimus Burton was invited to lay this ground out as gardens
and to design the necessary buildings. For nearly a century after
that, the Society's Summer Flower Shows were among the most
popular events of the London Season. When the original lease ran
out in 1932, however, the members of the Society were unable to
afford the vastly increased rent which they would have to pay if
they wanted to go on using their gardens, so they decided to dis-
continue their activities. The Royal Parks Department took over
the maintenance of the gardens, which were re-named in honour

of Queen Mary, wife of King George V, who had taken a great interest in their upkeep. (Queen Mary's Garden is now one of the most admired in any part of London.)

In 1842, the Crown acquired Primrose Hill from the trustees of the Eton College estates. This semi-wild elevation to the north-west of the Zoological Gardens had had an eventful history – Sir Edmund Berry Godfrey, Justice of the Peace for Westminster, to whom Titus Oates of 'Popish Plot' fame made his first depositions on oath, was subsequently found dead in a ditch there, face down, transfixed with his own sword; and many other violent deeds that had been done on the Hill were recorded in ancient chronicles. It had tempted Mother Shipton, too, to prophesy in the eighteenth century that 'when London surrounds Primrose Hill the streets of the Metropolis will run with blood'. In an attempt to make the new extension to Regent's Park a little more civilized, the new owners made footpaths up and down the Hill and lighted them with gas lamps. The fine views of London and of the Surrey and Kentish hills to the south that could, and can, be obtained from the summit of Primrose Hill soon made the place popular with walkers and picnic parties.

There were two remarkable tragedies in Regent's Park during the nineteenth century. The first happened in January 1867, when there was a heavy frost, and a great crowd of people was skating on the ice that had formed on the lake. Unfortunately, the ice was not thick enough to bear such a number of skaters. Suddenly, there was a noise which sounded to somebody there 'as though someone had walked on a bed of dry leaves',[4] and scores of people fell through into the very cold and deep water. There was no rescue apparatus around, and there were all too few park attendants within reach (though the gardeners from South Villa rushed down to the lake and did what they could to pull out the drowning victims). Despite their efforts, and those of the appalled bystanders, forty men and boys were drowned or died from exposure, the youngest victim being a child of nine. Princess Feodora of Hohen-lohe-Langenburg, hearing, at Geneva, the distressing news, wrote at once to her 'Dearest Victoria' (Queen Victoria was the Princess Feodora's half-sister):

... It has been very cold in some parts of England I saw in the papers – and how dreadful is the accident on the ice in the Regent's Park! People are so independent in England, such things hardly ever happen in Germany! . . .[5]

Appalled by the awful accident that had taken place on an estate for which they were technically responsible, the Commissioners who had the responsibility under the Crown for Regent's Park at once decided that the depth of the lake should be considerably reduced, and skating in the Park was after that strictly forbidden.

The second tragedy – a strange one – occurred nearly eight years later, when a chain of five barges, carrying gunpowder, was being towed along the Regent's Canal. As the third barge approached the Macclesfield Bridge – one of the bridges built near the north and west boundaries of the Park to span the Canal, and named after the Earl of Macclesfield, who was the first Chairman of the Canal Company – it blew up, severely damaging the bridge and the banks of the Canal, and shattering several of the near-by trees. All three of the men who had been on the barge were killed instantly – one of them, it is thought, having inadvertently caused the explosion by knocking some glowing ashes of tobacco out of his pipe into the cargo.

Once Regent's Park had been opened freely to the public, it attracted the attention of several of the nineteenth-century philanthropists who thought that no open space was really complete unless it was well supplied with statues and fountains. One of the earliest of these gifts – a fountain designed by R. Kevile and presented in 1865 by the Indian potentate Sir Cowasji Jehangir Readymoney is still in position by the lake. Six years later, one of England's richest women, the Baroness Burdett-Coutts, bestowed on the Park the immense drinking fountain, made of bronze, granite and marble, adorned with sculptural reliefs and crowned with a cluster of lamps, that stands, more than a little battered and vandalized, at the northern end of the Broad Walk, near the entrance to the Zoo.

The urge to decorate the Park continued into the twentieth century. In 1909, the year after the scholastic ladies from Bedford

Square got their hands on South Villa, a German painter called Sigismund Goetze took a lease of Grove House (now known as 'Nuffield House'), a villa that had been designed by Decimus Burton, in the Greek Revival style, for George Greenough, the geographer and geologist. Goetze, who was immensely rich, specialized in the production of huge mural paintings; he decorated, with his brushes, almost the whole of the first floor of the Foreign Office, without taking any fee, and he offered to do the same for the interior of the dome at the British Museum, but this suggestion was politely declined. During the next three decades, Goetze and his wife laboured tirelessly to provide sculptures and fountains of various kinds for the Park they loved so dearly. Their most spectacular benefaction, perhaps, was their gift of the great gilded wrought-iron gates at the entrance to Queen Mary's Garden. (They gave these gates in 1935 to celebrate the Silver Jubilee of King George V.) In 1937, the Triton Fountain, an elaborate sculpture in bronze by William Macmillan, was put up as a tribute to the memory of Sigismund Goetze, who had recently died.

In 1912, a million people visited the Zoo to gaze at the beasts that had been brought back from India by the Prince of Wales (by that time, King George V). In the following year, the outward appearance of the Zoo was radically changed by the construction of the Mappin Terraces, the gift of J. Newton Mappin, on which many of the larger animals could live more happily than they could in cages. Then came World War I, and further expansion of the Zoo had to be postponed until after the hostilities were over.

During the years between the two World Wars, the West End of London and Mayfair became increasingly commercialized, and, in many people's view, increasingly vulgar. These years saw the terrace houses round Regent's Park become highly desirable as homes for the wealthy, until, as a result of the economic crisis of the early 1930s, many of the houses were left standing empty, and began to deteriorate.

In 1932, some performances of William Shakespeare's *Twelfth Night* were given, under the inspired direction of Sidney Carroll, in a roped-off enclosure in the Inner Circle. This enterprise, in which Sir Nigel Playfair played Malvolio and Phyllis Neilson-Terry played Olivia, was remarkably successful. This was to lead to the foundation of the Open Air Theatre, an institution which now draws large audiences during the Summer months to its shows given in the most enchanting surroundings – bad weather, midges, and the sound of overhead aircraft being the worst of the hazards that the actors and actresses have to endure.

In 1937, St Dunstan's, the villa designed by Decimus Burton that had been the home of Lord Rothermere, fell empty and was promptly demolished. On its site, a plain brick residence was built for the immensely wealthy Countess Haugwitz-Reventlow. (Born plain 'Barbara Hutton', she was the daughter of the founder of Woolworth's 3d and 6d Stores.) After her marriage to the film star Cary Grant was dissolved, Miss Hutton gave up the lease of Winfield House, and her unhistorical dwelling, screened discreetly by high hedges and many trees, is at the time of writing the private residence of the United States Ambassador to the Court of St James.

World War II brought damage and dilapidation to Regent's Park – bombs destroyed Holford House (the grandest of all the villas built by Decimus Burton), the Master's House in the St Katharine Community, and part of the western curve of Park Crescent, and reduced many of the other buildings in the vicinity to a barely habitable state; damp and difficulties of maintenance hastened the process of ruin, with dry rot showing its ugly presence in many of the neglected buildings. By the time the war was over, the continued existence of Park Crescent and several of Nash's splendid terraces was seriously threatened. 'Pull them all down and put up working class flats in their place', counselled the St Marylebone Labour Party. This piece of advice was not acted upon; instead, some of the terraces were almost entirely rebuilt, the façades designed or approved by Nash being retained or reproduced for their scenic value. At the same time, the structures behind were completely re-designed to make them more suitable for our times.

In other respects, Regent's Park has been remarkably little altered since World War II, although the addition of some modern aviaries designed by Lord Snowdon has helped to change the external appearance of the Zoo, and the construction of the Post Office Tower a little way to the south-east of the Park has affected considerably some of the skylines planned with such care by John Nash. The slopes of Primrose Hill have been allowed to remain relatively undisturbed by any urge to develop or modernize, the few visible changes here being caused by the need to provide greater sporting and recreational facilities. The oak tree planted in 1864 near the foot of Primrose Hill by the actor Samuel Phelps, to commemorate the three hundredth anniversary of the birth of William Shakespeare, died in 1958. The dead tree was replaced by another oak planted on the great playwright's four hundredth birthday.

One of the most popular events to be held in London at Easter, the annual parade of van horses, brings large crowds of admiring spectators to the Regent's Park each year. Many people are drawn to the Park a little later in the summer by the magnificent floral displays now provided by the highly skilled gardeners connected with the Park who use, it has been recently estimated, over half a million bedding plants each year to achieve some extraordinarily colourful effects.

Despite the closeness of Regent's Park to some of the most crowded shopping streets in London – and Oxford Street, it has been said, is now one of the busiest streets in the whole world – its quieter corners support a surprising variety of wild birds; as many as a hundred different species are said to have been seen there in a single year, and of these at least thirty species are known to breed in the Park. (Two principal reasons have been separately advanced for this richness – the presence of the Zoo, which provides much welcome food for wild and half-wild intruders; and the number of very large gardens which are situated between the north side of the Park and Hampstead, providing a 'safety corridor' for birds between the Park and Hampstead Heath.) The biggest excitement of recent years has been the establishment of a heronry on one of the islands in the big lake. In a good season, as many as seven pairs are believed now to have their nests there.

Chapter 12

Envoi

There are, the reader of this book may have noticed, some other enclosed areas of London, besides those dealt with in these pages, that may have qualified at some time in history to be called a 'Royal Park' – Victoria Park in East London, for instance, which was laid out in the 1840s in an attempt to do for the poor what the Prince Regent's park was doing, to the west, for the better-off. Battersea Park, too, could at one time have been dignified with the same impressive title. But both of these parks, now controlled by the Greater London Council, have lost virtually all traces of their former majestic patronage and to have included them here would, the author feels, merely have laboured the point. The private gardens of Buckingham Palace, on the other hand, are quite inaccessible to the average member of the general public, unless he or she is fortunate or deserving enough to be invited to one of the Royal garden parties, and to have included them would have been equally pointless. But all these places, even though they may not have been described here, contribute their quota to the greenness and the openness of the vast sprawling conurbation we call London. Our debt to the royal enclosers of the past is so great that it can never be adequately acknowledged.

We owe a great debt of gratitude, too, to all the hundreds of men and women – associated with the Ministry of the Environment, so many of them – who work devotedly, day by day, to keep the Royal Parks of London in such an extraordinarily pleasant condition. These good people have no easy task – on a single day in high summer (to notice one of their main and quite unnecessary difficulties) half the staff of Regent's Park will be required to spend most of the day dealing with the problem of litter left by the public. And even the more thoughtful people who go to enjoy the Parks can take, in many other ways, a heavy toll of their lovely surroundings – at Hampton Court, for instance, $3\frac{1}{2}$ acres of grass have to be re-turfed every year, to make good the damage done by visitors' feet! The task of combating this steady process of deterioration is made no easier by certain unusual conditions that have to be observed – no weed-killers, for example, may be used on grass in the Parks that is accessible to the public, in case there should be any risk to children who run or play on that grass.

There is a nice story, possibly apocryphal, which tells how His Majesty King Charles II, to whom all Parks-lovers owe so much, met one day, when he was walking up Constitution Hill, his brother, His Royal Highness Prince James, Duke of York. The King was strolling there informally with a couple of his courtiers. The Duke of York was accompanied, according to his custom, by an escort of soldiers. The Duke chid the King for walking, in public, without a guard. The King is said to have replied, 'No danger, James, for I am sure no man in England will take away *my* life to make *you* king.' King Charles, historians point out, died safely in his bed, while James was deposed within three years of gaining the throne.

And this underlines, surely, another great advantage of London's Royal Parks – besides being so green and so open they are, still, so very safe. For this, much credit must go to the members of the Metropolitan Parks Police and to the general good sense of the public. All parties concerned – Royal owners, devoted Park servants and civilized Park users – are co-partners in the preservation and improvement of London's great pastoral masterpieces.

Notes

Abbreviations
RA=Royal Archives

Introduction
 1. *Walpoliana*, London, 1799. Volume 1

Chapter 1
Principal sources: A. D. Webster, *Greenwich Park: Its History and Associations*, Greenwich, 1902; Olive and Nigel Hamilton, *Royal Greenwich*, London, 1971; and Alan Glencross, *The Buildings of Greenwich*, Greenwich, 1974

Chapter 2
Principal Sources: Jacob Larwood, *The Story of the London Parks*, London, 1881; *London Old and New* (originally published as a part work); The Hon. Mrs E. Cecil, *London Parks and Gardens*, London, 1907; and Neville Braybrooke, *London Green: the story of Kensington Gardens, Hyde Park, Green Park and St Jame's Park*. London, 1959
 1. Christopher Hibbert, *London: the biography of a City*, London, 1969
 2. John Evelyn, *Diary*, 1 March 1671
 3. Conducted tours at 12.30, 1.30 and 3.30 from Monday to Friday from Easter Tuesday until the end of October. Also open on Saturdays, Sundays and Bank Holidays from 2 p.m. to 6 p.m.
 4. *Letters to Stella*
 5. *Spectator*, No. 324
 6. Christopher Hibbert, *London: the biography of a City*
 7. 12 January 1760
 8. John Brooke, *King George III*, London, 1972
 9. David Piper, *The Companion Guide to London*, London, 1964
 10. RA L23/45

11. RA L23/48
12. RA E2/4
13. RA A5/102
14. RA A6/32
15. Widow of the late King William IV
16. A body charged with, among other responsibilities, the punishment of offenders within the jurisdiction of the Royal Palaces
17. RA Add. PP/653 (1856)
18. RA Add. Q2/531
19. RA Add. Q2/546
20. RA Add. Q /741
21. RA Add. E/34
22. Eric Simms, *Wild Life in the Royal Parks*, London, Her Majesty's Stationery Office, 1974

Chapter 3
Principal sources: Jacob Larwood, *The Story of the London Parks*; *London Old and New*; The Hon. Mrs E. Cecil, *London's Parks and Gardens*; J. E. Hodgson, *The History of Aeronautics in Great Britain*, London, 1924; and Neville Braybrooke, *London Green*
1. Richard Church, *The Royal Parks of London*, London, Her Majesty's Stationery Office, 1965
2. Rugge's *Diurnal*, October 1660
3. RA Y54/84
4. RA C81/80
5. RA C81/80
6. RA PP Vic. 18368 (1865)
7. RA W62/26
8. Eric Simms, *Wild Life in the Royal Parks*

Chapter 4
Principal sources: Jacob Larwood, *The Story of the London Parks*; *London Old and New*; The Hon. Mrs E. Cecil, *London Parks and Gardens*; Mrs Alec (Ethel Brilliana) Tweedie, *Hyde Park: its History and Romance*, London, 1908; E. Dancy, *Hyde Park*, London, 1937; and Neville Braybrooke, *London Green*
1. Jacob Larwood, *The Story of the London Parks*
2. *London Old and New*
3. Jacob Larwood, *The Story of the London Parks*

Chapter 5
Principal sources: Jacob Larwood, *The Story of the London Parks*; *London Old and New*; The Hon. Mrs E. Cecil, *London Parks and Gardens*; Lloyd Sanders, *Old Kew, Chiswick and Kensington*, London,

1910; and Neville Braybrooke, *London Green*
1. Sir James Barrie, *Peter Pan in Kensington Gardens*, London, 1906
2. *The Times*, 23 May 1977
3. Sir James Barrie, *Peter Pan in Kensington Gardens*
4. *The Times*, 23 May 1977

Chapter 6
Principal sources: Jacob Larwood, *The Story of the London Parks*; *London
       Old and New*; The Hon. Mrs E. Cecil, *London Parks and Gardens*;
       Mrs Alec Tweedie, *Hyde Park: its History and Romance*; E. Dancy,
       Hyde Park; and Neville Braybrooke, *London Green*
1. 'Incident in Hyde Park, 1803'
2. Christopher Hibbert, *London: the biography of a City*
3. Christopher Hibbert, *London: the biography of a City*
4. Christopher Hibbert, *London: the biography of a City*
5. RA A25/75
6. RA A25/76
7. RA Add. Mss. Q 318
8. RA Add. Mss. Q 318
9. RA A25/83
10. RA A25/83
11. RA Add. Mss. Q 315
12. RA PP Vic. 4330 (1856)
13. RA Add. Mss. Q 3/766
14. RA Add. Mss. Q /777
15. RA Add. Q2/498
16. RA C81A/24
17. RA C81/25
18. RA C81A/37
19. RA C81A/38
20. RA C81A/39–41
21. RA C81A/44
22. RA C81A/45
23. RA E62/13

Chapter 7
1. RA W35/31 and 32
2. RA X32/291
3. Physician to the Royal Household
4. RA X33/366A
5. RA X33/366B
6. RA X33/366 C
7. RA X33/366 D
8. RA X33/366 E

8

9. For a fuller account of this extraordinary *cause célèbre*, see the Author's *The Hidden World of Scotland Yard*, London, 1972

10. Eric Simms, *Wild Life in the Royal Parks*

11. For information about the 'special' trees to be seen at the time of writing in Hyde Park and Kensington Gardens I am most grateful to the Superintendent of the Central Royal Parks and members of his staff.

Chapter 8

Principal sources: A. D. Webster, *Greenwich Park: Its History and Associations*; Olive and Nigel Hamilton, *Royal Greenwich*; Alan Glencross, *The Buildings of Greenwich*; and Joanna Richardson, *The Disastrous Marriage*, London, 1960

1. For information about the trees, animals and wild birds to be seen in Greenwich Park today I am most grateful to the Superintendent and members of his staff.

Chapter 9

Principal sources: E. B. Chancellor, *The History and Antiquities of Richmond, Kew, Petersham, Ham, &c.* Richmond, 1894; and C. L. Collenette, F.R.G.S., F.R.Ent.S., *A History of Richmond Park. With an Account of its Birds and Animals*, London, 1937

1. Brian Dunning, in *Country Life*, 11 December 1969

2. Eric Simms, *Wild Life in the Royal Parks*

Chapter 10

Principal sources: E. Law, *The History of Hampton Court Palace*, Vols. 1–3, London, 1885–91; P. Lindsay, *Hampton Court: a History*, London, 1948; and Peter Foster and Edward Pyatt, *Bushey House*, Teddington, 1976

1. *Mémoires de Martin et Guillaume du Bellay*, Vol. 2, Paris 1853 [i.e. 1753]; 1908–19

2. *Calendar of State Papers*, Henry VIII, Vol. 5, No. 308

3. Sebastiano Giustiniano, *Four Years at the Court of Henry VIII*, tr. R. Brown, 2 vols, London, 1854

4. *The Diary of H. Machyn, Citizen . . . of London*, London, Camden Society, 1848

5. From E. P. Shirley, *Some Account of English Deer Parks, with Notes on the Management of Deer*, London, 1867

6. John Nichols, *The Progresses and Public Processions of Queen Elizabeth*, 4 vols. London, 1788–1821

7. *Verney Papers*, Camden Society, *The Progresses, Processions and magnificent Festivities of King James the First*, 4 vols, London, 1828

8. *State Papers*, Vol. 203, 6 June 1659
9. Luttrell
10. Vernon's *Correspondence*
11. *Treasury Papers*, Vol. 126, No. 21
12. 31 July 1711
13. Eric Simms, *Wild Life in the Royal Parks*

Chapter 11
Principal sources: A. D. Webster, *The Regent's Park and Primrose Hill: History and Antiquities*, London, 1911; and Ann Saunders, *Regent's Park*, Newton Abbot, 1969
1. J. T. Smith, *A Book for a Rainy Day*, London, 1845
2. Sir John Summerson, *John Nash, Architect to King George IV*, London, 1935
3. *The Second Report of the Commissioners*, 1816
4. *The Times*, 26 March 1926
5. RA Y44/75

Index